Uniform Prejudice

This book examines the historical experiences of LGBTQ+ individuals facing discrimination in the early 20th-century military before same-sex acts were explicitly illegal. Centered on the court-martial of Private Laurence Edgar Moon in 1912, the book sheds light on the broader landscape of prejudice prior to the explicit criminalization of same-sex acts in 1916.

Through Moon's case, the narrative delves into the interplay of gender, sexuality, and power within the military and society. Army officers enforced a simplistic binary understanding of sexuality and masculinity, linking moral character to sexual behavior. Moon's experience challenges this narrow view, revealing the complexities surrounding turn-of-the-century notions of masculinity and sexual identity. Employing a microhistorical approach grounded in queer theory, the book uncovers often-overlooked stories of queer service members who faced discrimination yet remained dedicated to their duty. It also highlights the evolving language and legal definitions related to same-sex acts and the cultural anxieties surrounding them, illustrating the importance of queer theory and microhistory in understanding marginalized experiences.

Uniform Prejudice offers a compelling narrative of a century-long history of prejudice and persecution faced by LGBTQ+ individuals in the military. The engaging microhistorical approach captivates readers while addressing significant theoretical and historical themes. This accessible book is aimed at scholars, students, and general readers interested in LGBTQ+ history, military history, and the ongoing challenges and advancements of LGBTQ+ individuals in the U.S. military, urging a more inclusive and intersectional perspective.

Thomas C. Rust, a native Montanan, has been Professor of History at MSU Billings since 1999. He earned his B.A. from the University of Minnesota, an M.A. from the University of Denver, an M.Ed. from MSUB, and a Ph.D. from the University of Leicester. His research focuses on military history in the West, including the U.S. Army's role in Yellowstone National Park. He is currently studying the underrepresentation of Native Americans in Yellowstone's history and queer soldiers in the early 20th-century U.S. military. Dr. Rust also engages students in hands-on learning through archaeological research projects along the Lewis and Clark trail.

Microhistories

Series editors: Sigurður Gylfi Magnússon and István M. Szijártó

The *Microhistories* series is open to books employing different microhistorical approaches, including global microhistories aimed at grasping world-wide connections in local research, social history trying to find determining historical structures through a micro-analysis, and cultural history in the form of microhistories that relate directly to large or small scale historical contexts. They are interesting stories, that bring the everyday life and culture of common people of the past close to the readers, without the aspiration of finding answers to general "big questions" or relating them to the grand narratives of history. The series is open to publishing both theoretical and empirical works, but with a focus on empirical monographs which can communicate stories from the past and capture the imagination of our readers.

Published

A Criminal Hero
Justice, Politics and Media Culture in Eighteenth-Century Naples
Pasquale Palmieri

Deciphering Carlo Ginzburg
Form and Time
Deivy F. Carneiro and Daniel R. B. Dias

Factionalism and Dissent in an English City
Chichester, 1678–1685
Danae Tankard

Uniform Prejudice
Military Masculinity and the Queer Case of Private Laurence Moon, Troop F, First U.S. Cavalry, 1912
Thomas C. Rust

For more information about this series, please visit: https://www.routledge.com/Microhistories/book-series/MICRO

Uniform Prejudice

Military Masculinity and the Queer Case of Private Laurence Moon, Troop F, First U.S. Cavalry, 1912

Thomas C. Rust

Routledge
Taylor & Francis Group
LONDON AND NEW YORK

First published 2025
by Routledge
4 Park Square, Milton Park, Abingdon, Oxon OX14 4RN

and by Routledge
605 Third Avenue, New York, NY 10158

Routledge is an imprint of the Taylor & Francis Group, an informa business

British Library Cataloguing-in-Publication Data
A catalogue record for this book is available from the British Library

ISBN: 978-1-032-87063-2 (hbk)
ISBN: 978-1-032-87064-9 (pbk)
ISBN: 978-1-003-53075-6 (ebk)

DOI: 10.4324/9781003530756

Typeset in Times New Roman
by Apex CoVantage, LLC

Contents

Preface and Acknowledgments

Serendipity can be a wonderful and frustrating thing. I was introduced to Laurance Moon's case while researching another work on the U.S. Army's time in Yellowstone National Park. I first found a reference to the case in Private Joseph Bernard's court-martial. As luck would have it, it was late on my last day researching in the archives, thus preventing me from immediately following up on the case. However, I knew that there was some important historical information that needed to be explored. Fortunately, I knew people who were going to Washington, D.C., and were willing to help get copies of the documents I needed. A special thank you to my niece, Erin Kelly, who was attending graduate school at American University and photographed Laurance Moon's court-martial for me. Another thank you to Michael Herdina, who took over from me as the state coordinator for Montana National History Day and was able to go to the Archives when he brought students to the national competition and photographed Harvey Simpson's court-martial. Without them, I would not have been able to complete this study.

Laurance Moon's story was initially meant to be merely a chapter in the aforementioned work. However, the publisher (and two of the three blind reviewers) recognized the importance and the value of the information but nonetheless recommended that the chapter be removed. Their justification was that the rest of the work could be marketable in Yellowstone National Park gift shops, but including that chapter might upset some people and hurt sales. The editor of the press also discovered that the National Park Service has a policy forbidding the sale of books or merchandise with a sexual nature, meaning the book could not even be offered for sale in the park.

I engaged in what I still believe was an appropriate level of righteous indignation at the suggestion of removing the chapter and further discriminating against the LGBTQ+ community by erasing part of their history. I discussed my dilemma with my valued colleagues and gender history specialists at Montana State University Billings, Dr. Jennifer Lynn and Dr. Emily Arendt. Their input as I navigated my discussions was very valuable and much appreciated. In all fairness, during my conversation with the editor, I came to genuinely believe that she personally and professionally agreed with me but also had a competing professional interest in making the book marketable as well. I remained stubbornly intransigent and even contemplated finding another publisher. But serendipity intervened again.

During the summer when these discussions were happening, I presented a paper on Laurance Moon's case at the International Conference on Historicizing Masculinities at the University of Newcastle in the United Kingdom. On the day I presented my paper, I discussed my situation with some of the other attendees over drinks during the social hour. One of them, a former university press editor, talked me down off the ledge a bit by providing a broader perspective. University presses, while not designed to be significant money-making endeavors, have to keep the financial ledgers in balance. If my larger work had the potential to have above-average sales with eager tourists in Yellowstone Park, those profits would actually allow other scholars to get their important work published even though the press knew they might lose money on it. Besides, he offered, with additional work, Moon's case could be expanded and treated more completely on its own rather than losing it in the larger confines of another work.

With a fresh perspective and generously offered ideas of how to expand it offered by many at that happy hour, I relented and revised my other book, making only circumstantial and decidedly "PG-13" references to Moon's case. I then began to research and explore Moon's case in more detail and with greater complexity. Ironically, in my many trips to Yellowstone since, I have discovered that the original book has not been marketed within the park and the whole ordeal was for nothing.

Well, maybe not for nothing, as it did allow me to continue to mine Laurance Moon's story for greater nuance and experiment with a new methodology of computer-aided forensic linguistic analysis. My friend and colleague at Montana State University Billings, political scientist Dr. Paul Pope, is a certified forensic linguist and over several discussions, the idea of using the technique became a reality. To what end, scholars will have to decide after they read this work. I did find the journey intriguing and exciting, and I believe the methodology to be an interesting and useful tool for at least this particular study. It helped identify and clarify some interesting patterns and encouraged me to go back and ask some new questions, begging me to reengage with the sources and scholarship, bringing more depth and texture to the final product. I must thank Paul for helping me understand, craft, and implement the methodology and mentoring me through the interpretations of the results as well. Finally, he also diligently read and commented on the early drafts of sections that made their way into the following chapters. It is no small task to teach a "newbie" the intricacies of such a methodology. However, any errors or shortcomings are entirely my own and should not reflect on his tutelage. And finally, I want to sincerely thank Sigurður Gylfi Magnússon and István M. Szijártó, the series editors at Routledge, whose valuable commentary made the work significantly stronger.

If you have made it through this much of the preface, you've probably gathered by now that queer and LGBTQ+ history has not previously been my main area of research specialty. You'd be right. As a social historian, I do teach it in my classes and have a certain level of familiarity with the topic. This book, however, allowed me to re-engage with the scholarship on a much deeper level than I have before. At times, I felt as though I were in graduate school again. There are both detriments as well as positives to this. While I may be "new to the field," I feel confident this work does add to some small niche of the scholarship. The process has been a very rewarding professional experience that has added depth to my own thinking, future scholarship, and classroom teaching.

Another easily deduced conclusion is that I am not a member of the LGBTQ+ community, which this book is about. After all, I merely ran across this rich set of sources when researching another topic. This raised some interesting discussions with colleagues at a couple of conferences I've attended about whether someone other than a member of that community can or should conduct research on this topic. It is an interesting question and one that might be a topic of discussion in a graduate symposium somewhere. Again, I believe there are positives and negatives for an "outsider" to study a topic like this. Without experiencing the ordeal, inner struggle, or discrimination of the LGBTQ+ community, can I provide a fair and accurate representation? Without that familiarity, is this work inadequate from the start?

However, in my classes, I also tell my students not to lull themselves into a false sense of familiarity with any historical subject, especially one they already have an affinity with. While it is natural to gravitate to the familiar, by doing so, we often make the past what we want it to be rather than exploring it on its own terms. People in the past (even those with whom we have a common experience) act differently, have different morals than us, and even think differently. Common constructs that are taken for granted by later generations, labels that describe those constructs, and external and internal expectations are unique to place and time. Despite the false feeling of affinity, the past is a very different place, and the mindsets and pressures are not the same as they are today. The historian needs to keep that in mind, especially when researching people within a community to which we belong. Distance from a topic can sometimes add a different perspective. In the context of the vast scholarship on the subject, the diversity of scholars hopefully only adds to the discussion rather than limiting it.

In the end, it is a discussion worth having. Philosophically and practically, requiring membership in a group to study it makes historical scholarship difficult. Can only Egyptians study ancient Egypt? Can only people of faith study Reformation Europe? Can only Germans study the fall of the Weimar Republic and the rise of the Third Reich? The list could go on. Naturally, given that I've written this work, I believe that community membership is not necessarily required and that a diversity of scholars strengthens scholarly debates. So long as one is professional, ethical, and respectful to their subjects and the discipline, the diversity of scholars can add valuable insights to scholarship and contribute to the conversation.

I only hope that I have been fair to Laurance Moon's (and everyone else's) experiences, for this work has a strong personal component for me as well. I consider myself part of the "friend and ally" community for LGBTQ+ people and have for my adult life. However, I admit that in my early years, I may have done and said some things that I would be embarrassed about today. I grew up in Bozeman, Montana, in the 1970s and 1980s. While it was and is a land-grant college town, that probably only made it slightly more open-minded than the rest of the rural state, where the LGBTQ+ community was extremely underground and pretty openly scorned. While I don't remember anything explicitly, undoubtedly, in my wayward youth, I used derogatory, homophobic, and hurtful language, which was common at the time. I never targeted or harassed anyone, but to my embarrassment, I probably did not promote anything like tolerance and passively accepted and engaged with the hostile homophobic culture that surrounded me. As my fellow classmate, media personality, historian, and social commentator Sarah Vowell said in her book *Take the Cannloli*, "My high school was 1980s America in miniature – you either belonged or you didn't."[1] I am afraid I was someone who promoted that sense of isolation and passive or even open hostility for people of alternative lifestyles with the casual use of homophobic slurs. That is no excuse, and I refuse to normalize it as "common at the time." I simply should have been better.

There is a purpose for this unsolicited admission that goes beyond a simple *mea culpa*. Long after my soft, teenage brain finally developed and I recognized the ignorance and hurtfulness of my naively narrowminded adolescent predispositions, I found out that two of my very closest friends from that time were gay. One of them, I consider my oldest friend, predating even kindergarten. I had no idea. By the time I found out, some two decades after graduating high school, I already long considered myself a "friend and ally" and was teaching at Montana State University Billings, making a point to include elements of LGBTQ+ history in my classes and champion inclusivity. Nonetheless, I reflected with deep regret on how my youthful ignorance and callousness must have affected them. I see this work, then, as a demonstration of my personal growth as well as a sign of my genuine contrition. As for me, I promise not to judge anyone for the stupid things they did in high school, and I hope the majority will do the same in return. However, some readers may judge me for my past actions, and I have no choice but to accept it. I assure you that my views changed only a short time after high school. Yet, I cannot escape my past and denying it would be disingenuous. I only hope that it doesn't affect the judgment of this work.

I can never truly know nor fully understand their experience living in at least the passively, if not actively, hostile environment of an overly masculinized rural western town where prejudices were openly acknowledged and promoted at worst and passively embraced at best. While today, people in Montana consider Bozeman a liberal suburb of California, nicknaming it "Bozeangeles" because it has attracted a large number of wealthy out-of-state migrants, in the 1970s and 1980s, the mythical cowboy ethos ran deep in the town. There were many similarities (but also significant differences, to be sure) to the masculine ethos that enveloped Laurance Moon and his experience during his time in Yellowstone, which is incidentally only 90 miles (145 kilometers) from Bozeman. Through this work, I hope I gained and can convey at least a better understanding of the LGBTQ+ experience. I hope even more that I have been fair to Moon and everyone, including my friends, who have lived their own experiences. And finally, to my friends, whom I was so callously oblivious to, I heartfully dedicate this work to them.

Note

1 Sarah Vowell, *Take the Cannoli: Stories from the New World* (New York: Touchstone, 2000), 46.

Introduction

A Century of Prejudice

As unsuspecting tourists settled in for their lunch at the National Hotel in Yellowstone Park on July 8, 1912, 200 yards away in the gymnasium at the military post of Fort Yellowstone, the U.S. Army was undertaking the solemn duty of a general court-martial. Private Laurance Edgar Moon was by almost all accounts the ideal soldier: an excellent marksman, dutiful, intelligent, athletic, and well-liked by his comrades. His superiors had singled him out for promotion and considered him "the star of the troop." The 24-year-old native of Baltimore joined the army in 1910 and had been assigned to Troop F of the First U.S. Cavalry, finding himself stationed in the nation's first national park to protect it from poachers and careless tourists, a duty that the U.S. Army executed in Yellowstone and other national parks from 1886 until 1918. Despite his exemplary record, Moon faced four counts of "Conduct to the prejudice of good order and military discipline in violation of the 62nd Article of War" because he committed an "unnatural and immoral act," more specifically, performing oral sex on two other soldiers.[1] Same-sex acts were not yet explicitly enumerated as criminal in the military regulations and would not be for four more years. Until then, the generic 62nd Article of War would have to do.

Almost exactly 80 years later, on February 5, 1992, the Army Chief of Staff, General Colin Powell, was testifying before the House Budget Committee on what would seem to be a routine review of the Pentagon's operational budget. However, Representative Barney Frank (D-MA) unexpectedly changed the topic to the military's legal exclusion of gays in the military, a hot-button issue in that year's presidential campaign. After some preliminary posturing, Frank pointedly asked Powell, "Are we, to some extent, dealing here with a prejudice that a majority has against a group of people?" Frank then echoed the Democratic talking points on that year's campaign trail; maybe it was time to end the military's legal exclusion of gays. Perhaps he hoped using the word "prejudice" would conjure feelings of sympathy within the first Black man to be the nation's Chairman of Joint Chiefs of Staff.

Powell, nevertheless, saw the issue differently than Frank. In his mind, as he would later write, "skin color is a benign, nonbehavioral characteristic," while "sexual orientation is perhaps the most profound of human behavior characteristics." Powell thought that the implied comparison of the racial civil rights movement and the gay rights movement was a "convenient but invalid argument." Looking

DOI: 10.4324/9781003530756-1

for a reasonable and tempered response to Frank's question, Powell unknowingly responded with echoes of the charges against Private Moon decades earlier. "I think it would be prejudicial to good order and discipline to try to integrate that in the current military structure."[2] This would be the standard military response during the following debates in the coming year.

Eighty years, thousands of courts-martial and discharges, countless heartaches, and the same word kept coming up: prejudice. Of course, the army and General Powell used the term differently than Representative Frank, almost to complete opposite ends. But words and their meanings are important. According to the *Oxford English Dictionary*, the word "prejudice" has different meanings for its verb and noun forms.

Prejudice: verb, 1.a. *transitive*: To impair. To affect adversely or unfavorably as a consequence of some action; to impair the validity of (a right, claim, statement, etc.); 1.b. *transitive*. To injure materially, to damage.

Of course, this was the definition the army used when it charged Private Moon in 1912. It was also clearly the meaning General Powell used when he resisted lifting the ban against gays in the military in 1992. However, Representative Frank used the word's other definition, the noun form.

Prejudice. noun: 1.a. Preconceived opinion not based on reason or experience; bias, partiality; (now) *spec.* unreasoned dislike, hostility, or antagonism towards, or discrimination against, a race, sex, or other class of people; 1. b. An instance of this; a feeling, favorable or unfavorable, towards a person, thing, or class; an unreasoning preference or objection; a bias; 2.a. The action of judging an event beforehand; prognostication, presaging; 2.b. a prior judgment, esp. a judgment formed hastily or before due consideration.

For the century that the military actively and explicitly persecuted those who had same-sex attractions or engaged in same-sex acts, the word prejudice was impossible to escape. The military acted in accordance with the noun form of the word, with a "preconceived opinion" of "unreasoned dislike, hostility, or antagonism towards" them with a "judgment formed hastily or before due consideration." They assumed that the mere presence of people who had engaged in same-sex acts would result in the verb form of the word by "injuring materially" or "damaging" the U.S. Army's "good order and military discipline," as Powell and others put it. When Helen Hunt Jackson examined the double-dealing injustices inflicted upon Native Americans in 1881, she titled her book *A Century of Dishonor*.[3] For those who suffered under the U.S. military's increasing persecution from its officially criminalized sodomy in 1916 to its repeal of the prohibition on gay service members in 2011, it was nearly a "century of prejudice," using both definitions of the word.

Of course, even before the creation of Article 93 in the 1916 rewrite of the Articles of War made "assault with intent to commit sodomy" a criminal offense (and later generalized in 1920 to encompass all sodomy), queer servicemen were persecuted, as the case against Private Moon in 1912 demonstrates. The first recorded separation from service was Lieutenant Gotthold Frederick Enslin in 1778 after being found guilty of "abhorrence and detestation of such infamous crimes," meaning, of course, same-sex gratifications. Contemporary to Lt. Enslin, the man perhaps more responsible for creating the professional ethos of the Continental Army, Baron Friedrich Wilhelm von Steuben, was well known to have had same-sex relations both before and during his service to the Continental Army, perhaps even having relationships with two officers in George Washington's camp.[4] As is typical in U.S. military history, moral compunctions were often set aside to meet a greater military necessity, whether a skill set for training or, in later wars, the basic need for manpower.[5]

Most scholarship on gays in the U.S. military focuses on the periods between its explicit mention in the 1916 Articles of War and its repeal in 2011. Nevertheless, a thorough analysis of same-sex relationships in the army between Von Steuben and the criminalization of sodomy between 1916 and 1920 has yet to be written, and what has been done is primarily anecdotal.[6] Journalist Randy Silts briefly summarizes a few select cases, such as Lt. Frederick Enslin during the Revolution and naval Captains Richard Sommers and Stephen Decatur in the War of 1812.[7] Physician Thomas Lowry's book on general sexuality during the Civil War also detailed Confederate Major General Patrick Cleburne's intimate relations with some of his aides but explained most of his analysis through Walt Whitman's encounters with wounded soldiers. He could only find three cases in the entire war where soldiers were discharged for same-sex acts and concluded that contemporary gender roles and behaviors were not tied to a conventional heteronormative paradigm, thereby allowing different types of intimacy between men.[8]

Walt Whitman's prewar, war, and postwar experience has garnered significant attention in understanding the antebellum and early Gilded Age understanding of queer relationships. Scholars have offered diverse interpretations based on his poetry and personal relationships. The vivid homoerotic imagery found throughout his works, such as in the poems "Calamus" and "Children of Adam," hint at same-sex desire. Critics argue that Whitman's embrace of the male body and celebration of male companionship in his poetry reveals his queer sensibility. His personal letters contain expressions of affection and intimacy toward men, often characterized by passionate language and sentiment. Rather than confining himself to specific categories, he explores a spectrum of desire and connection, embracing the fluidity of human experience. Interestingly enough, Whitman had expressed his own concerns about masculinity before the war when he wrote a series of articles for the *New York Atlas* where he lamented "that dreary, sickening, unmanly lassitude, that, to so many men, fills up and curses what ought to be the best years of their lives."[9] In other words, in Whitman's mind, same-sex acts and masculinity need not be mutually exclusive.

The most examined case of same-sex relations in the postwar frontier army is the case of "Mrs. Nash" at Fort Abraham Lincoln in North Dakota. The "laundress" was biologically a man who passed as a woman for years and had married no less than three soldiers since beginning her employment with the army in 1866. Her first two husbands deserted her without revealing her biological sex. Her third marriage, to Corporal John Noonan of the U.S. Seventh Cavalry in 1873, was seemingly happy until her biological sex was discovered upon her death in 1878. Corporal Noonan claimed ignorance about her true sex and continued to express his undying love for her even when his comrades "gave him the cold shake." Ultimately, he committed suicide, according to the *Bismarck Tribune*.[10]

That is not to say that people in the antebellum and early Gilded Age periods were not concerned with the morality of people seeking same-sex gratification. From the moment Europeans stepped ashore, colonies and the later states all created sodomy laws heavily influenced by Judeo-Christian moral beliefs. The military, as seen with the dismissal of Lt. Enslin, merely mirrored society. However, the term "sodomy" remained ill-defined and generally meant any non-procreative sexual act, even if it was not exclusively a same-sex act.[11] Yet, the nation's relationship with queer individuals changed in the postwar era. Concurrent with the "scientific" quest to categorize and label sexual behavior in Victorian America, new anxieties arose regarding morals, gender roles, and the postwar Civil War American character.[12] Several intellectual and cultural forces, old and new, combined at that moment to develop typecasts of people with same-sex attractions, giving rise to labels and imposed stereotypes that went from condemning the act of sodomy to imposing an identity and condemning the entire character of people who engaged in such acts.[13]

The explosive growth of cities in the Gilded Age was the cause of much of the country's anxiety. Urbanization created a context where changing social structures, cultural mixing, the establishment of red-light districts, and communities of queer individuals were on open display. The growth of densely populated working-class neighborhoods with limited privacy created the opportunity for people with like-minded same-sex attractions to meet, gather, and form communities.[14] The potential for sexual encounters outside the confines of traditional norms led to anxieties among those who feared the erosion of established moral codes. The convergence of diverse communities and the destruction of conventional standards prompted concerns about moral decay, leading to the development of pseudoscientific theories and increased legal efforts to control and regulate sexuality. Activists and religious leaders sought to combat what they perceived as moral decay, including what they viewed as sexual deviance. Organizations and individuals within the social purity movement, such as the National Liberation League, aimed to suppress what they considered indecent and immoral sexual behavior through legal means.[15]

These cultural anxieties, combined with new "scientific" and medical thinking, gave rise to pseudoscientific theories attempting to create, label, explain, and categorize human sexuality, non-conforming sexual behaviors, and sexual "psychopathology." Austro-German sexologist Richard Krafft-Ebing first coined the term and concept "homosexual" in his 1866 book *Psychopathia Sexualis*, where he negatively classified it as "perverse" since it was not for procreation.[16] By the turn of the century, people who had engaged in same-sex activities were being slowly re-conceptualized by American academics and some physicians as having a definitive "identity" that would ultimately be known as "homosexuals" in the mid to late 20th century. Michel Foucault claimed that this process created a "species" out of people who engaged in same-sex acts, with assumed negative stereotypes, expectations, and limitations projected upon them with prejudice.[17] Borrowing from the medical field, people with same-sex orientation were categorized as almost diseased.[18] The labeled person thus had an identity imposed upon them as "sinners" rather than merely their "acts" being "sinful."[19]

As a result, sodomy laws were refined, strengthened, and systematized in the latter half of the 19th century as the country became increasingly anxious about this perceived sexual deviance. The definitions of sodomy expanded beyond mere sex that was "unnatural" or "against nature" to include a broader scope encompassing various sexual behaviors, including oral and anal intercourse, mutual masturbation, and other acts regardless of the participant's biological sex. The expanded definitions were driven partly by the desire to maintain a legal framework that could target any sexual activity considered deviant or immoral, regardless of the gender of the individuals. The expansion of sodomy laws mirrored the growth of new vocabulary regarding same-sex activity.[20] In the postwar period, an N-gram search revealed a marked increase in the words and concepts describing same-sex acts that correspond chronologically to the expanding definitions within the legal codes.

The change in vocabulary was significant. Sodomy was an act typically described as an "unnatural act" or an "act against nature." However, even the religious condemnation was focused on the act. The increasing use of words such

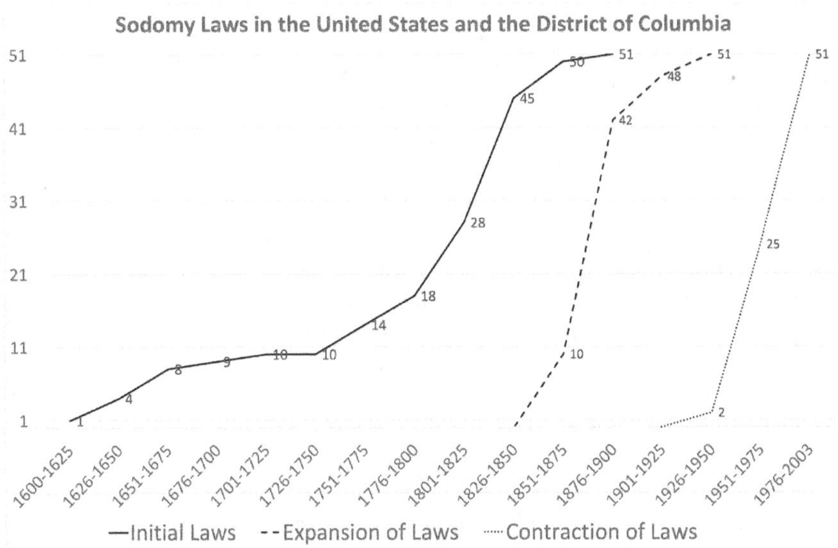

Figure I.1 Evolution of sodomy laws in the colonies, states, and territories that became the United States based on data from Eskridge (2008), pp. 388–407.

Source: Image created by the author.

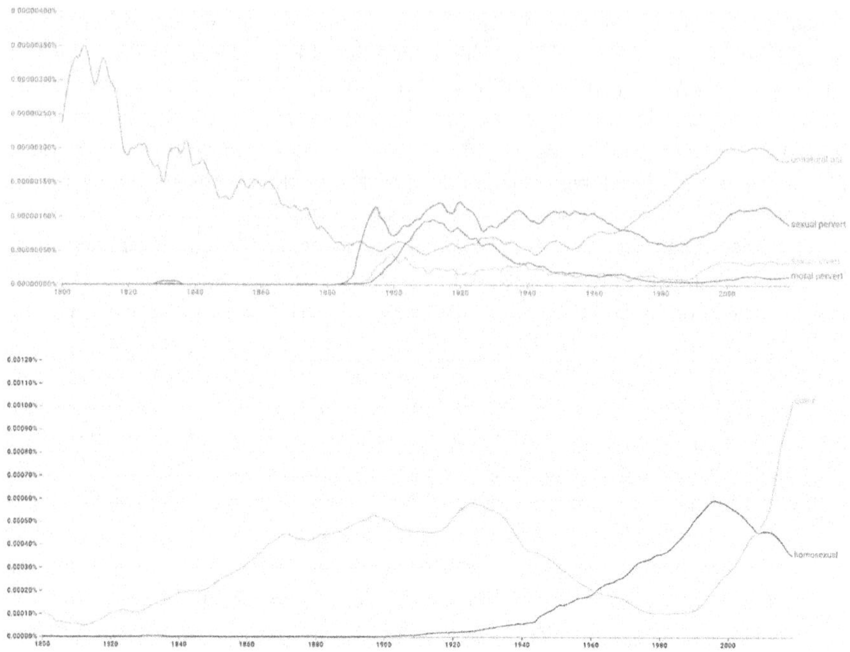

Figure I.2 N-gram search regarding changes in language regarding same-sex acts 1800–2003 (google.books.com).

as "sexual pervert," "moral pervert," and "sexual invert" indicated more broadly based character traits or states of being. One might *commit* an act of sodomy at some time in one's life or in certain contexts but maybe not others, but with the new paradigms, either one *was* or *was not* a pervert or an invert, transcendent of time, frequency, or action. The trend was toward a dichotomous view of sexuality where the act was no longer the end in itself. Instead, it became the determinator for a more prominent character trait or identity with a number of prejudiced conceptions that were mutually exclusive of one another. Someone could be either moral or perverted, either normal or inverted. There was little to no room for being both.[21]

The sexual invert was particularly concerning to many Gilded Age Americans since it was believed to eschew traditional masculine behaviors, something particularly prized in a world steeped with gender anxiety and Social Darwinism. In urban communities, many men purposely engage in effeminate behaviors as a coded signal of a preference for same-sex attractions. The idea of "inversion" assumed they were synonymous. If one were inverted in their sexual desires, they must, therefore, also be inverted in their masculinity and morality. It suggested that their sexual choices and gendered behavior patterns deviated from the accepted heteronormative relationships and traditional masculine virtues. As such, sexual inversion became both pathologized as a medical or psychological disorder and criminalized based on the belief that such people were against the natural and divine order and should be isolated from society, thus explaining the rise in the refinement and expansion of sodomy laws. In this dualistic way of thinking, same-sex acts and attractions seemed to directly attack American manhood and strength at a moment when Darwinistic thought emphasized that only the strongest would survive.[22]

The U.S. military was not immune to these broader cultural shifts and concerns about American masculinity at the turn of the twentieth century. The military's performance of masculinity, characterized by ideals of toughness, heroism, and physical strength, served as a façade that concealed the more complex and ambiguous motivations behind American military interventions. Some scholars have suggested that a crisis of masculinity, particularly among the American elites, was one factor in motivating the United States to engage in the Spanish-American War in 1898. This crisis stemmed from concerns over the perceived decline of traditional gender roles and fears of emasculation and that the war was seen as an opportunity to reaffirm and reassert American masculinity, strength, and dominance through imperial adventures.[23]

It is unsurprising, therefore, that the perceived crisis in masculinity was leading the U.S. military toward explicitly criminalizing sodomy in the early 20th century, like the rest of the country was doing. Official and unofficial behaviors attempted to maintain strict codes of masculinity and heteronormativity and intertwined them with nationalism, patriotism, and American values.[24] It was this interlinking of masculinity, morality, and heteronormativity that brought Private Laurance E. Moon before a general court-martial in 1912, and it was also the cornerstone of not only his prosecution but also the case for his defense.

The court-martial against Private Moon reveals something significantly more valuable than just the army's hostility toward those who committed same-sex acts. In fact, the case occurred before any same-sex act was explicitly illegal in the military, yet it was tried anyway. The way the case was presented and the words used by officers and enlisted men reveal the social construction of sexual orientation and masculinity across class lines in early 20th-century America. The officers, those with more political currency both in and outside the army, chose certain words to convey those concepts that differed markedly from the less-educated, working-class enlisted men and tried to use their social capital to impose their vision of morality on the latter. The intersection of class, language, and sexuality is well suited for analysis through queer theory, which examines how language plays a key role in constructing and regulating identities related to gender and sexuality. It focuses on how societal norms are communicated, enforced, and challenged through language, revealing how power dynamics shape the understanding of "normal" and "deviant" sexual behaviors.

Queer theory emerged in the late 20th century as an intellectual response to the rigid categorizations of gender and sexuality, drawing on post-structuralism and the works of scholars like Michel Foucault and Judith Butler to challenge conventional narratives and explore the complexities of sexual identity and desire. It strove to uncover how language reflects and reinforces social hierarchies, making it a central tool for studying the intersection of language, class, and sexuality. It draws heavily from poststructuralist and postmodernist theories, challenging fixed categories and highlighting the fluidity and performativity of gender and sexuality. Scholars challenge rigid categories of identity, gender, and sexuality, emphasizing fluidity and the instability of these concepts. The theory resists binary thinking (such as male/female or homo/hetero), instead embracing the complexities, contradictions, and nuances in how individuals experience and express their identities. By focusing on the ways that societal norms and power structures shape and regulate these identities, queer theory acknowledges and even celebrates the ambiguity inherent in human experience. This openness to ambiguity allows it to critically analyze categories that might otherwise be seen as fixed or popularly perceived as "natural."[25] At its core, queer theory aims to destabilize and disrupt normative assumptions about sexuality and gender, highlighting the fluidity, complexity, and diversity of human experiences. Private Moon's court-martial also provides opportunities to explore the queer theory's applicability to the historical study of the military on the cusp of its explicit criminalization of sodomy, which was in itself a cementing of binary thinking (legal/illegal, moral/immoral, or right/wrong) of sexual expression.

Queer theory also provides a critical framework that challenges essentialist and constructivist perspectives on identity and sexuality and offers an alternative approach to understanding and analyzing the complexities of gender and sexuality. The essentialism/constructivism debate emerged in the late 20th century within the fields of philosophy, humanities, social sciences, and cultural studies. It centers on whether identities and categories (such as gender and sexuality) are inherently essential to an individual or socially constructed and separate from biological sexual desire. Essentialism posits that inherent and fixed characteristics define individuals, including their sexual orientation and gender identity, and are biologically determined and exist as fundamental truths transcendent of cultural context. Conversely, constructivism argues that identities are socially constructed and shaped by cultural, historical, and discursive influences dependent upon a culture, place, and time. It emphasizes the role of language, societal norms, and power dynamics in establishing and shaping those identities.[26]

Queer theory challenges this dualistic opposition between essentialism and constructivism by questioning and deconstructing the very categories and assumptions that underlie these debates. It rejects the notion of fixed or stable identities and instead explores the fluidity, particularly the complexity of gender and sexuality. It is concerned with disrupting normative understandings of gender and sexuality and challenging the power structures perpetuating social hierarchies and marginalization. Rather than seeking to define or classify sexual identities, queer theory embraces a more inclusive and expansive understanding of gender and sexuality.[27] As Jacqueline Whitt charged in her article "Queering American Military History," historians should be "asking questions, interrogating sources, and taking seriously the questions, approaches, and theoretical perspective offered by scholars of the history sexuality; gay, lesbian, and bisexual history; and gender history."[28] The court-martial of Private Moon provides a perfect case to scrutinize sexuality and gender as central foundations of analysis.

Queer theorists argue that identities such as "man," "woman," "gay," or "straight" are not fixed, natural categories but are constructed through social, cultural, and historical contexts. By emphasizing the fluidity of gender and sexual identities, the theory suggests that they can change over time and are not bound by rigid, essential definitions. This opposes the essentialist view that identities are stable and biologically determined. By deconstructing the language around normative categories, such as "immoral" and "unnatural," as quoted in the charges against Private Moon, the theory demonstrates how they are imposed through power structures (such as a court-martial), not through any innate truth.

Since it focuses on breaking down essentialist views of sexuality and gender by emphasizing them as performances within a specific temporal and social milieus, queer theory examines the role of language and its representation in shaping the understanding of these concepts. It recognizes the unintended impacts of naming particular sexual behaviors and is rooted in the belief that identities and sexualities are fluid and shaped by society. Unlike earlier gay and lesbian studies, queer theory embraces a broader range of behaviors and experiences by avoiding rigid labels. It actively seeks out "constructed silences," bringing marginalized narratives to light and confronting institutional norms that shape social hierarchies. By using contemporary identity concepts, queer theory aims to understand how desires are culturally and historically expressed in specific contexts. The theory seeks to illustrate that people's experiences of these concepts are diverse and intricate while also considering how they intersect with other parts of identity, such as race and class.[29] This is particularly relevant to Private Moon's case where the officer class and the enlisted men use distinctly different language to describe him and the acts he was accused of performing.

Departing from the limitations of earlier gay and lesbian studies that predominantly centered on the experiences of white, middle-class gay men, queer theory encompasses a broader scope of identities and experiences. It actively seeks out "constructed silences," unearthing narratives and voices marginalized by dominant discourses. This theory critically confronts both discursive and institutional systems of normativity, recognizing their role in shaping social hierarchies. By employing contemporary identity concepts, queer theory strives to comprehend how desires are culturally and historically manifested within specific contexts. It acknowledges the unintended consequences of naming certain sexual orientations, like "homosexual," and is firmly rooted within the constructionist paradigm, emphasizing the fluid and socially constructed nature of identities and sexualities.

Queer theory offers a vital framework for understanding Private Moon's case, highlighting how soldiers, on the brink of the military's formal exclusion of queer individuals, "performed" masculinity and sexuality, with these performances interpreted differently by enlisted men and officers. Moon's case challenges the notion that sexuality must align with the hypermasculine ideal of the soldier. Rather than seeing gender as fixed, the case underscores its performative nature – shaped by societal and institutional norms, where sexual acts and preferences could be viewed separately from masculinity. The testimony during Moon's court-martial disrupts the binary understanding of gender and sexuality, allowing us to explore how gender roles were constructed, challenged, and resisted at a pivotal moment in the military's treatment of queer soldiers.[30]

Moon's trial demonstrates how the military shaped not only sexual and masculine identities but also the archetype of the hypermasculine soldier. Queer theory's "constructed silences" aligns with this analysis by showing how non-normative behaviors were pathologized. Labeling Moon as "immoral" and "unnatural" reduced his identity to a full character judgment based solely on sexual acts, overlooking his broader contributions as a soldier and person. Both officers and enlisted men could agree that Moon was a capable, if not exemplary, soldier. However, the trial reveals nuanced differences in how these groups viewed his masculinity. Enlisted men valued personal bonds, physical performance, and camaraderie, while officers, wielding socio-political power, imposed a moral judgment on his sexual behavior beyond his exemplary behavior, unable to separate his duties from his alleged sexual acts. This dynamic reflects queer theory's critique of institutional norms that reinforce social hierarchies. By labeling Moon's behavior as "unnatural," the military exposed the clash between fluid, socially constructed masculinities and rigid heteronormative standards, challenging institutional narratives and revealing the complexity of gender and sexual identities within the military.

That is not to say queer theory is not without its critics. Most notably, Lee Edelman, in his works *Bad Education: Why Queer Theory Teaches Us Nothing* and his earlier work *No Future: Queer Theory and the Death Drive*, views queerness as not having a fixed academic identity but rather as a concept representing emptiness or a gap that influences societal dynamics. Edelman argues that words like "queerness" can provoke tension and conflict by introducing a formless and undefined idea as something natural. He draws a connection between queerness and Jacques Lacan's psychoanalytic notion of "ab-sens," a term derived from the French words for "absence" and "sense." "Ab-sens" refers to things lacking meaning or sense, categorization, or labeling. Lacan used this idea to explore how language and meaning operate in the mind, suggesting that certain concepts elude complete expression through words and create gaps in comprehension. Edelman and others apply Lacan's "ab-sens" concept to queerness, describing how it actually complicates identity and disrupts academic analysis. Queerness, in this view, defies easy definition and common labels, creating a gap in our understanding of gender and sexuality while deceiving scholars to believe they are actually filling that same gap.[31]

Yet, scholars who embrace queer theory often use a framework to investigate the fundamental role of sexuality and other distinctions in the practice of rhetoric in establishing societal norms, establishing social hierarchies, and defining and then suppressing "deviant" identities. Moon's case demonstrates the intersectionality of class, power, and the mental constructions of gender and sexuality as the country shifted its understanding of same-sex acts and the people who performed them. Moon's case, however, demonstrates that the binary notions of masculinity and sexuality, a growing trend at that time, were not yet inextricably linked and, in fact, defy easy categorization. Certainly, Moon never identified, as far as we can tell, with any label such as "sodomite," "homosexual," "invert," or "pervert." By nearly all accounts, Moon was a paragon of the ideal masculine soldier, and he enjoyed sexual gratification from both men and women. He displayed none of the growing stereotypes nor demonstrated any "inversion," as it was understood at the time. The binary homo-hetero paradigm that came to dominate the 20th century, along with its stereotypes, did not apply to Moon, highlighting the value of using a queer lens. Examining Moon's case through this lens helps us understand the gender norms of the military and U.S. society as concepts and labels were emerging but not yet fully established.

To further explore the complexities of Moon's case, we can apply microhistory, a method that closely examines individual lives and events to infer larger meanings. Combined with queer theory, this approach reveals how larger societal forces shape personal identities in complex, often contradictory ways. Microhistory is a methodology that emphasizes analyzing small subjects and incidents to understand better those traditionally excluded from historical accounts. Microhistorical research focuses on specific individuals, events, or communities, aiming to shed light on broader historical contexts partially. It emerged as a distinct methodology in the 1970s, challenging traditional macrohistorical narratives that often overlooked the everyday experiences of ordinary people. Moon's case, therefore, is a valuable example of how a "microhistory" can reveal the broader differences between the upper classes and working classes, evolving concepts of masculinity, sexual orientation, and presumed attributions of people with same-sex attraction and moral judgments regarding them and the intersectionality of class and sexuality.

Microhistory's application to Private Moon's case can also enrich the queer theory lens by considering the "normal exception" idea, often explored through microhistory. Microhistory focuses on outliers – individuals whose lives drew the attention of authorities – using their experiences to examine broader societal norms and values, particularly those of average people, rather than the elite. This approach offers a unique lens to reconstruct marginalized or overlooked experiences, including how queer individuals navigated military environments. By delving into specific cases, microhistorians can ideally uncover rich and detailed accounts of social, cultural, and economic dynamics by disrupting dominant grand narratives and highlighting the contingency and complexity of historical processes. By zooming in on localized events or people, microhistorians reveal the diversity of historical outcomes and challenge deterministic interpretations.[32]

Moon's case fits this microhistorical methodology by offering an intimate look at a non-normative figure, whose behavior, deemed an exception by military standards, exposed the very mechanisms by which the military constructed normative sexualities and masculinities. The attention Moon received – being court-martialed, labeled, and judged – was a direct result of his deviation from the growing rigidity of standards about heteronormativity that governed military life. By focusing on such an outlier, we gain insight not just into Moon's personal struggle but also into how the military, as a powerful institution, enforced these norms and how soldiers navigated their identities within this structure.

The case, when viewed through the "normal exception" lens, not only reveals how non-normative behaviors were pathologized but also underscores how the very act of naming and categorizing identities can lead to their institutionalization, as queer theory critiques, which has consequences for both the individual and society's understanding of masculinity and sexuality. Moon's case, therefore, provides a deeper understanding of the socially constructed nature of these identities within the military, illustrating how institutional power shapes, categorizes, and enforces what is deemed "normal," "moral," and acceptable.

Microhistorical studies are not without their limitations. By their very nature, they focus on specific individuals or events, sometimes making it challenging to extrapolate broad conclusions or generalize findings to larger populations. The uniqueness and specificity of microhistorical cases can limit their applicability to broader historical contexts. Critics argue that emphasizing individual agency and local particularities may neglect larger structural factors and broader historical patterns.[33] Yet, with due diligence, Moon's story can transcend some of these critiques. The court-martial lasted for four days and accumulated almost two dozen testimonies in 186 pages of transcripts that can demonstrate the intersectionality of class and power as the military began to reflect the changes in society at large. Because of the diverse makeup of the army and its national institutional identity, the regional differences, overshadowed by the class and power dynamics within the military hierarchy, offer some insight into this previously overlooked aspect of society.

By interrogating the history of gender and sexuality, queer theory and microhistory expand the understanding of the past and help to shed light on the lives and contributions of individuals like Moon. Private Moon's case illustrates how the U.S. military reinforced and potentially shaped the heteronormative binary paradigm that underpinned its policies of exclusion for nearly a century. During the 1993 debate about lifting the ban on gays in the military, the Pentagon rested its argument on three pillars:

1. Homosexuals do not make good soldiers.
2. Integrating gay and lesbian personnel would damage unit morale.
3. Taking #1 and #2 together, lifting the ban would damage military efficiency.[34]

However, in 1912, on the eve of explicit criminalization, Private Moon's case struck at the heart of these arguments. Moon was undeniably a good soldier, perhaps the best in his company. Even after the charges came to light, his troop rallied around him. Summarily discharging a good soldier such as Moon would actually be what weakened military efficiency, not strengthen it. Gary Lehring's book *Officially Gay* contends that the military's exclusion in the early years of the 20th century was a broader and dynamic cultural force that extended beyond the armed services and helped cement homophobia and heteronormative ideals in both the military and civilian society at large by giving it official government sanctioning after criminalization in 1916.[35] Moon's case in 1912 demonstrates it need not have been that only path.

Moon's case highlights the diverse ways in which individuals can experience and express their sexual and gender identities while also recognizing the intersections of culture, class, and power and mainly how sexuality and various distinctions were constructed rhetorically. While the officers, who held the social and legal power in the army, attempted to force the developing binary construction and connection between sexual behaviors and masculine moral character, Moon's experience demonstrated that no such connection existed, and the categories of masculinity/femininity and natural/unnatural sexuality were significantly more nuanced, revealing why an intersectional understanding of sexual and gender diversity is needed. By embracing a more inclusive and intersectional approach, scholars can continue to push the boundaries of knowledge and challenge dominant narratives, ultimately contributing to a more comprehensive understanding of the queer history of the United States and the U.S. military.

Combining microhistorical methodology with queer theory in exploring Private Moon's case delivers a robust framework that is greater than the sum of its parts. Both microhistory and queer theory share a commitment to examining language and meaning, emphasizing how words shape identities and create, reinforce, or contest power dynamics. Microhistory looks at the specific language to reveal how individuals articulate their identities and experiences or exert social power and dominance. In contrast, queer theory critiques how language creates and enforces normative views of gender and sexuality, exposing the challenges to these norms. Together, they highlight the importance of context and the complexities of identity, providing a clearer picture of the historical landscape surrounding sexuality.

The connection of these methodologies in analyzing Private Moon's court-martial reveals the often-overlooked stories of queer service personnel, particularly before same-sex acts were officially criminalized in the military. This analysis highlights the evolution of social expectations and ideals within a system becoming increasingly designed to marginalize them. By placing Moon's experience within a broader socio-historical context, the emphasis on the evolving language of masculinity and legal definitions of same-sex acts uncovers the cultural fears and anxieties surrounding deviations from the evolving norms. This combined approach offers a more nuanced understanding of the forces at play, underscoring the need for inclusivity and intersectionality in historical narratives. Ultimately, this integration of microhistory and queer theory not only captures the intricate realities of LGBTQ+ lives in the military but also challenges prevailing narratives about identity, power, and discrimination in the early 20th century.

Both microhistory and queer theory's focus on the nuances of language makes them particularly amenable to the application of computer-aided forensic linguistic analysis, a powerful tool for dissecting the subtleties of historical texts and uncovering hidden meanings and conceptual models within individual narratives. Forensic linguistics leverages techniques like collocation, sentiment analysis, and hierarchical clustering of textual data-based modeling to identify abstract language patterns and associations. It plays a significant role in enhancing the understanding of language as a representation of conceptual understanding. This is valuable in both contemporary and historical cases, such as Private Moon's court-martial. Forensic linguistics becomes a powerful tool for exploring language's impact on articulating and revealing relationships, moral judgments, and conceptual understandings of the social phenomena.

Modern computer programs, offering robust data processing and visualization capabilities, contribute to a deeper historical analysis. The methodology for analyzing the court-martial testimony involved preprocessing with Orange Data Mining software, stop word removal, and tokenization. Orange's text mining capabilities extracted collocations and hierarchical clustering using Latent Semantic Analysis (LSA) and Non-Negative Matrix Factorization (NMF), creating concept models. These models, visualized with Orange's tools, enhance traditional forensic linguistic analysis by identifying key concepts and patterns within the text, contributing to a nuanced understanding of language patterns in the case. These can serve to augment, verify, or challenge traditional qualitative analysis, which together can deepen our understanding of Private Moon's case.

Private Laurance Edgar Moon, the recognized "star" of his troop, was an athletic, masculine, and well-liked soldier who just happened to enjoy sexual gratification with other men, at least occasionally. He would not have identified as a "Molly," "sissy," "fairy," or an "invert" since each had connotations of effeminacy, nor would his comrades have labeled him such since his performative gender identity was definitively masculine. He also would not have identified as a "homosexual" since that concept, becoming seemingly antiquated today, had yet to fully crystalize, at least in popular discourse, until further into the 20th century. Instead of labeling Moon with these imposed identities, his court-martial shows that he could be both a model of military masculinity and still someone who enjoyed sexual gratification with men, thus proving it would not interfere with his ability to be a good soldier nor damage his unit's morale. In addition, through the trial, his fellow enlisted men expressed a level of tolerance for same-sex gratification independent of their understanding of his masculinity.[36] To them, his actions were judged independently of his character or identity. However, the officers of his unit saw his actions as an indicator of his general moral and masculine character. While they may have wanted to find a way to acquit Moon of the charges brought against him and looked for every opportunity to do so as the trial progressed, in the end, when they were presented with the evidence of his action, they had to condemn him along two simultaneous lines, one "natural," and the other "moral" as stated in the charges that specified he committed an "unnatural and immoral act."

The trajectory of social and cultural forces was on display in his case, which would ultimately lead to the explicit criminalization of same-sex acts in just a few years. Moon's case highlights the complexity of sexual behavior and displayed forms of masculinity, emphasizing how multiple factors interacted and cautioning against oversimplifying different expressions of same-sex activity with a labeling identity. Allowing Laurance Moon "to be queer," at least in the more modern academic sense, will enable us to understand those nuances of his experiences in the army and for us to understand the culture of his fellow soldiers better, recovering and centering the history of queer soldiers at a critical moment when sexuality and gender identity were being molded in military environments.

Notes

1 General Court-Martial of Private Laurance E. Moon Court-Martial, 103. Records of the Judge Advocate General, Record Group 153, National Archives and Record Administration, Washington, D.C., 2–3.

2 Collin L. Powell with Joseph E. Persico, *My American Journey* (New York: Random House, 1995), 532–533.

3 Helen Hunt Jackson, *A Century of Dishonor: A Sketch of the United States Government's Dealings with Some of the Indian Tribes* (Boston: Roberts Brothers, 1881).
4 Randy Shilts, *Conduct Unbecoming: Lesbian and Gays in the U.S. Military, Vietnam to the Persian Gulf* (New York: St. Martin's Press, 1993), 6 7; William Benemann, *Male-Male Intimacy in Early America: Beyond Romantic Friendships* (New York: Routledge, 2006), 33, 57, 71–73, 93–97; Paul Lockhart, *The Drillmaster of Valley Forge* (Boston: Harper Perennial), 18, 203–204.
5 Shilts, *Conduct Unbecoming*, 294–295, 356, 419, 453; Gary L. Lehring, *Officially Gay: The Political Construction of Sexuality by the U.S. Military* (Philadelphia: Temple University Press, 2003), 4, 110–113; Colin J. Williams and Martin S. Weinberg, *Homosexuals and the Military: A Study of Less Than Honorable Discharge* (New York: Harper and Row, 1971), 47–48; Allan Berube, *Coming Out Under Fire: The History of Gay Men and Women in World War II* (Chapel Hill: University of North Carolina Press, 1990), 28, 262; Rick Harding, "Commanders Quietly Ignore Antigay Rule to Build Gulf Forces," *The Advocate*, February 26, 1991, 20.
6 The vast majority of valuable scholarship on same-sex relationships in the military focuses on the period after World War I. Even though G. Dean Sinclair, "Homosexuality and the Military: A Review of the Literature," *Journal of Homosexuality* 56, no. 6 (July 31, 2009), 703–704 claims that "[Randy] Shilts provides an exhaustive historical account of homosexuals In the military from 1778 through 1990," There are only a small number of studies on the subject in the period before World War I. Even Shilts can only examine a handful of anecdotal examples such as Lt. Enslin and Baron von Steuben from the Revolutionary War, naval officers Richard Sommers and Stephen Decatur in the early Republic, and Walt Whitman and Confederate General Patrick Cleburne in the Civil War era, and nothing from the frontier period. See Shilts, *Conduct Unbecoming*, 1–16. Benemann discusses von Steuben in greater detail but has only limited exposure to other military relationships. Thomas Lowry's *The Story the Soldiers Wouldn't Tell: Sex in the Civil War* (Mechanicsburg, PA: Stackpole Books, 2012) has an entire chapter entitled "Parallel Lives" devoted to same-sex relationships during the Civil War. He examined anecdotal evidence, primarily from Walt Whitman and General Cleburne, to suggest the presence of same-sex relations but found that no soldiers were discharged from the army and only two in the Navy. He did note that "conventional" gender roles and behaviors were not tied to a conventional heteronormative paradigm, and intimacy, in several forms, developed between men. The most examined case of same-sex relations is the case of Mrs. Nash at Fort Abraham Lincoln in North Dakota. See Peter Boarg, *Re-Dressing America's Frontier Past* (Berkeley: the University of California Press, 2011), 130–140, Nora Whiteley, "The Mysterious Mrs. Nash," *14th Annual Symposium Custer Battlefield Historical & Museum Association* (Hardin, MT: Custer Battlefield Historical & Museum Association, 2000), 29–31. Most literature regarding same-sex relationships in the military focuses on the period after "sodomy" was criminalized in 1916. See, for example, Lerhring, *Officially Gay*, who discusses how the criminalization within the military created an official identity of homosexuality outside of the military in America at large; George Chauncey, Jr., "Christian Brotherhood or Sexual Perversion? Homosexual Identities and the Construction of Sexual Boundaries in the World War One Era," *Journal of Social History* 19, no. 2 (Winter 1985), 189–211 examines the Newport Naval Scandal in terms of the changing conceptualization and discourse on same-sex relationships; during the Second World War and early Cold War era, Timothy Haggerty focuses on the legal and moral rationales and implications of the ban on homosexuals in the military after World War I "History Repeating Itself: A Historical Overview of Gay Men and Lesbians in the Military Before 'Don't Ask, Don't Tell,'' in *Don't Ask, Don't Tell: Debating the Gay Ban in the Military*, eds. Aaron Belkin and Geoffrey Bateman (Boulder, CO: Lynne Rienner, 2003), 9–49; Berube's, *Coming Out Under Fire* is the most comprehensive study of the World War II period. Berube found evidence of active discrimination but also how soldiers created and maintained

strong bonds in the face of official adversity; Mary Humphrey's *My Country, My Right to Serve: Experience of Gay Men and Women in the Military, World War II to the Present* (New York: Harper Collins, 1990) provides anecdotal stories of soldiers who served bravely in the country's armed forces since World War II but drew limited significance or conclusions. Even the RAND Corporation's *Sexual Orientation and U.S. Military Personnel Policy: Options and Assessment* (Santa Monica, CA: Rand Corp., 1993), which was commissioned to study homosexuality in the military by the Pentagon in 1993, began its historical summary after World War I.

7 Shilts, *Conduct Unbecoming*, 1–7, 9–16; Benemann, *Male-Male Intimacy in Early America*, 33, 57, 71–73, 93–97; Lockhart, *The Drillmaster of Valley Forge*.

8 Lowry's, *The Story the Soldiers Wouldn't Tell*, 109–123.

9 Walt Whitman, "Manly Health and Training," *The New York Atlas*, October 3, 1858, 1; Jonathan Ned Katz, *Love Stories: Sex Between Men Before Homosexuality* (Chicago: University of Chicago Press, 2001), 148–162, 166–175, 193, 223–224; William N. Eskridge, Jr., *Dishonorable Passions: Sodomy Laws in America, 1861–2003* (New York: Penguin Group, 2008), 13–16, 24–31, 73, 74; Michael Bronski, *A Queer History of the United States* (Boston: Beacon Press, 2011), 76–78, 83–85; Jay Grossman, "Whitman in Your Pocket: The History of the Book and the History of Sexuality," in *The New Walt Whitman Studies*, ed. Matt Cohen (New York: Cambridge University Press, 2020), 101–120; Fiona Anderson, "A Trail of Drift and Debris: Traces of Whitman in the Correspondence Art of Ray Johnson," *Journal of American Studies* 49 (2015), 55–75; Jay Grossman, "Sexuality," in *Walt Whitman in Context*, eds. Joanna Levin and Edward Whitley (New York: Cambridge University Press, 2018), 227–238; Christian Borch, *The Politics of Crowds: An Alternative History of Society* (New York: Cambridge University Press, 2012), 124–164; Juan Herrero Brasas, *Walt Whitman's Mystical Ethics of Comradeship: Homosexuality and the Marginality of Friendship at the Crossroads of Modernity* (Albany, NY: SUNY Press, 2010); John Campagne, "Walt Whitman, Our Great Gay Poet?" *Journal of Homosexuality* 55 (2008), 648–664.

10 "A Complicated Case," *Bismarck Tribune*, November 4, 1878, 1; "The Mystery of Mrs. Noonan," *Bismarck Tribune*, November 11, 1878, 6; "Straight Through the Heart, *Bismarck Tribune*," December 2, 1878, 1; See Boarg, *Re-Dressing America's Frontier Past*, 130–140, Nora Whitely, "The Mysterious Mrs. Nash," *14th Annual Symposium Custer Battlefield Historical & Museum Association* (Hardin, MT: Custer Battlefield Historical & Museum Association, 2000), 29–31.

11 Eskridge, *Dishonorable Passions*, 16–20, 49–58, 66–67, 75–77, 85–88, 123–125, 233; Katz, *Love Stories*, 402–406; Timothy J. Gilfoyle, *City of Eros: New York City, Prostitution, and the Commercialization of Sex, 1790–1920* (New York: Norton, 1992), 135–138; Robert F. Oaks, "'Things Fearful to Name': Sodomy and Buggery in Seventeenth-Century New England," *Journal of Social History* 12 (1978), 268–281; Caroline Bingham, "Seventeenth-Century Attitudes Toward Deviant Sex," *Journal of Interdisciplinary History* 1 (1971), 447–168; Jonathan Ned Katz, *Gay/Lesbian Almanac: A New Documentary* (New York: Harper and Row, 1983), 82–84, 104–131.

12 Bronski, *Queer History*, 84–85, 87, 95, 101; Edward J. Bristow, *Vice, and Vigilance: Purity Movements in Britain Since 1700* (Totowa, NJ: Rowman and Littlefield, 1977); Linda Gordon, *Woman's Body, Woman's Right: A Social History of Birth Control in America* (New York: Viking, 1976); David J. Pivar, *Purity Crusade: Sexual Morality and Social Control, 1868–1900* (Westport, CT: Holtzbrink, 1973).

13 Lerhring, *Officially Gay*, 31, 35, 37–41; Rictor Norton, "Essentialism and Queer History," in *The Myth of the Modern Homosexual: Queer History and the Search for Cultural Unity* (London: Cassell, 1997), 31–32, 95; Chauncey, "Christian Brotherhood," 203.

14 Chauncey, "Christian Brotherhood," 179–206.

15 Eskridge, *Dishonorable Passions*, 29–30, 36–40, 102, 369–371; Bronski, *Queer History*, 16–18, 137–143, 226; R. Danielle Egan and Gail Hawkes, "Producing the Prurient Through the Pedagogy of Purity: Childhood Sexuality and the Purity Movement,"

Journal of Historical Sociology 20, no. 4 (2008), 44–461; Sue Morgan, "'Wild Oats or Acorns?' Social Purity, Sexual Politics and the Response of the Late-Victorian Church," *Journal of Religious History* 30, no. 2 (2007), 151–168.

16 Richard von Krafft-Ebing, *Psychopathia Sexualis, with Especial Reference to Contrary Sexual Instinct: A Medico-Legal Study*, 7th edn. Trans. Charles Gilbert Chaddock (New York: F.A. Davis Co., 1894), 56, 79; J. C. Shaw and G. N. Ferris, "Perverted Sexual Instinct," *Journal of Nervous and Mental Disease* 10 (1883), 185–204; James G. Kiernan, "Perversion," *Detroit Lancet* 7 (1884), 483–484; [Author unknown], "Perverted Sexual Instinct," *Medical Record* 26 (1884), 70–71; G. Frank Lyndston, "Sexual Perversion, Satyriasis and Nymphomania," *Medical and Surgical Reporter* 61 (1889), 253–258; C. H. Hughes, "Erotopathia – Morbid Eroticism," *Alienist and Neurologist* 14 (1893), 531–578. Jonathan Katz, "The Invention of Heterosexuality," *Socialist Review* 20 (January–March 1990), 6–20.

17 Krafft-Ebing, *Psychopathia Sexualis*; Katz, "The Invention of Heterosexuality"; Norton, "Essentialism and Queer History," 8–15.

18 Jeffrey Weeks, "'Sins and Diseases': Some Notes on Homosexuality in the Nineteenth Century." *History Workshop* 1 (Spring 1976), 212; Bronski, *Queer History*, 95; Chauncey, "Christian Brotherhood," 189–211, 203. However, the medical implications of homosexuality were relatively short-lived since the works by Sigmund Freud were soon more interesting to physicians who considered it a psychological problem. See Hubert Kennedy, "Research and Commentaries on Richard von Krafft-Ebing and Karl Heinrich Ulrichs," *Journal of Homosexuality* 42, no. 1 (2001), 165–178 and Paolo Savola, "Sexual Science and Self-Narrative: Epistemology and Narrative Technologies of the Self between Krafft-Ebing and Freud," *History of Human Sciences* 23, no. 5 (2010), 18, 36.

19 Michael S. Kimmel, *Manhood in America: A Cultural History* (Oxford: Oxford University Press, 2006), 68; Chauncey, "Christian Brotherhood," 205; Weeks, "Sins and Diseases."

20 Eskridge, *Dishonorable Passions*, 39–73, 75–78, 87–94, 388–407.

21 Chauncey, "Christian Brotherhood," 205; Weeks, "Sins and Diseases"; Eskridge, *Dishonorable Passions*, 138–139; Katz, "The Invention of Heterosexuality," 13; Weeks, "Sins and Diseases."

22 Jonathan Ned Katz, *Gay American History: Lesbians and Gay Men in the U.S.A.* (New York: Penguin Group, 1992), 129–151; Bronski, *Queer History*, 95–96, 114, 129–130; Eskridge, *Dishonorable Passions*, 46–49, 60–62; Elizabeth Reis, "Impossible Hermaphrodites: Intersex America, 1620–1960," *Journal of America History* 92, no. 2 (2005), 436–438; Travis M. Foster, "Matthiessen's Public Privates: Homosexual Expression and the Aesthetics of Sexual Inversion," *American Literature* 78, no. 2 (2006), 236–239; Ivan Crozier, *Sexual Inversion* (London: Palgrave Macmillan, 2008), 1–2, 96–97, 115–116; Jennifer Terry, "Theorizing Deviant Historiography," *A Journal of Feminist Cultural Studies* 3, no. 2 (1991), 55–74.

23 See Kristin L. Hoganson, *Fighting for American Manhood: How Gender Politics Provoked the Spanish-American and Philippine-American Wars* (New Haven: Yale University Press, 2000); Amy Kaplan, *The Anarchy of Empire in the Making of U.S. Culture* (Boston: Harvard University Press, 2005); Aaron Belkin, *Bring Me Men: Military Masculinity and the Benign Façade of American Empire, 1898–2001* (New York: Oxford University Press, 2012).

24 Belkin, *Bring Me Men*, 30, 77, 236.

25 Judith Butler, *Gender Trouble: Feminism and the Subversion of Identity* (New York: Routledge, 1990), 3–4; Eve Kosofsky Sedgwick, *Epistemology of the Closet* (Berkeley: University of California Press, 1990), 22–23; David Halperin, *Saint Foucault: Towards a Gay Hagiography* (New York: Oxford University Press, 1995), 62–63; Annamarie Jagose, *Queer Theory: An Introduction* (New York: New York University Press, 1996), 1–2; Michael Warner, *Fear of a Queer Planet: Queer Politics and Social Theory* (Minneapolis: University of Minnesota Press, 1993), xviii–xix.

26 William S. Wilkerson, *Ambiguity and Sexuality* (London: Palgrave Macmillan, 2007), 135–155; Rictor Norton, *The Myth of the Modern Homosexual: Queer History and the Search for Cultural Unity* (London: Bloomsbury, 1997), 6–15; Raja Halwani, "Essentialism, Social Constructionism, and the History of Homosexuality," *Journal of Homosexuality* 35, no. 1 (1998), 25–51; Andrew Sayer, "Essentialism, Social Constructionism, and Beyond," *The Sociological Review* 45, no. 3 (1997), 453–487; John P. DeCecco and John P. Elia, "A Critique and Synthesis of Biological Essentialism and Social Constructionist Views of Sexuality and Gender," *Journal of Homosexuality* 24, no. 3 (1993), 1–26; Lehring, *Officially Gay*, 185–189.

27 Sean Brady, "All About Eve? Queer Theory and History," *Journal of Contemporary History* 41, no. 1 (2006), 185–195; Harry G. Cocks, "The Growing Pains of the History of Sexuality," *Journal of Contemporary History* 39, no. 4 (October 2004), 657–666; Peter Finney, "Beyond the Postmodern Moment?" *Journal of Contemporary History* 40, no. 1 (January 2005), 149–165; Daniel R. Ortiz, "Creating Controversy: Essentialism and Constructivism and the Politics of Gay Identity," *Virginia Law Review* 79, no. 7 (October 1993), 1833–1857; Steven Seidman, "Deconstructing Queer Theory or the Under-Theorization of the Social and the Ethical," in *Social Postmodernism: Beyond Identity Politics*, eds. Linda Nicholson and Steven Seidman (New York: Cambridge University Press, 1995), 116–141.

28 Jacqueline E. Whitt, "Queering American Military History," *International Journal of Military History and Historiography* 42 (2022), 108.

29 See David Halperin, "The Normalization of Queer Theory," *Journal of Homosexuality* 45, nos. 2–4 (2003), 339–343; David Halperin, *How to Do the History of Homosexuality*. (Chicago: University of Chicago Press, 2002); Sharon Marcus, "Queer Theory for Everyone: A Review Essay," *Signs* 31, no. 1 (Autumn 2005), 191–218; Michael Hames-Garcia, "Queer Theory Revisited," in *Gay Latin Studies: A Critical Reader*, eds. M. Hames-Garcia and E. J. Martinez (Durham: Duke University Press, 2010), 19–45; Katz, "The Invention of Heterosexuality," 7–34; John D'Emilio, "Capitalism and Gay Identity," in *The Gender/Sexuality Reader: Culture, History, Political Economy*, eds. Roger N. Lancaster and Micaela di Leonardo (New York: Routledge, 1997), 169–178; Eve Kosofsky Sedgwick, *Epistemology of the Closet*, 2nd edn (Berkeley: University of California Press, 1997); Teresa de Lauretis, "Queer Theory: Lesbian and Gay Sexualities," *Journal of Feminist Cultural Studies* 3, no. 2 (1991), iii–xvii.

30 See Judith Butler, "Performative Acts and Gender Constitution: An Essay in Phenomenology and Feminist Theory," *Theater Journal* 40, no. 4 (1988), 519–531 and Judith Butler, *Undoing Gender* (Boston: Routledge, 2004).

31 Lee Edelman, *Bad Education: Why Queer Theory Teaches Us Nothing* (Durham: Duke University Press, 2023); Lee Edelman, *No Future: Queer Theory and the Death Drive* (Durham: Duke University Press, 2004); see also Adam Isaiah Green, "Gay But Not Queer: Toward a Post-Queer Study of Sexuality," *Theory and Society* 31, no. 4 (2002), 521–545; for criticisms of how language is used by queer theorists, see R. Anthony Slagle, "Queer Criticism and Sexual Normativity: The Case of Pee-wee Herman," *Journal of Homosexuality* 45, nos. 2–4 (2003), 129–146.

32 Fabrice Langrognet, *Neighbours of Passage: A Microhistory of Migrants in a Paris Tenement, 1882–1932* (London: Routledge, 2022); Sigurður Gylfi Magnússon, *Emotional Experience and Microhistory: A Life Story of a Destitute Pauper Poet in the 19th Century* (London: Routledge, 2020); Thomas C. Cohen, *A Roman Tale: A Reader's Guide to the Art of Microhistory* (London: Routledge, 2019); Sigurður Gylfi Magnússon and István M. Szijártó, *Microhistory? Theory and Practice* (London: Routledge, 2013); Laurel T. Ulrich, *A Midwife's Tale: The Life of Martha Ballard Based on Her Diary, 1785–1812* (New York: Knopf, 1990); See John-Paul Ghobrial, "Seeing the World Like a Microhistorian," *Past & Present* 242, Supplement 14 (November 2019), 1–22; Georg G. Iggers, *Historiography in the Twentieth Century: From Scientific Objectivity to the Postmodern Challenge* (Hanover: NH, 1997), 108; Sigurdur Gylfi Magnusson, "The Singularization

of History: Social History and Microhistory Within the Postmodern State of Knowledge," *Journal of Social History* 36 (Spring 2003), 701–735; Edward Muir and Guido Ruggiero, eds., *Microhistory and the Lost People of Europe*, translated by Eren Branch (Baltimore, 1991); For examples of microhistory, see Natalie Zemon Davis, *The Return of Martin Guerre* (Cambridge, MA: Harvard, 1893); Carlo Ginzburg, "Just One Witness," in *Probing the Limits of Representation: Nazism and the "Final Solution"* (Cambridge, MA: Harvard University Press, 1992); Gene Brucker, *Giovanni and Lusanna: Love and Marriage Renaissance Florence* (Berkeley: University of California, 2004); Carlo Ginzburg, *The Cheese and the Worms: The Cosmos of a Sixteenth-Century Miller*, translated by John Tedeschi and Anne Tedeschi (Baltimore: The Johns Hopkins University Press, 1980); Thomas V. Cohen, *Love and Death in Renaissance Italy* (Chicago: University of Chicago, 2004); Carlo Ginzburg, "The Philosopher and the Witches: An Experiment in Cultural History," *Acta-Ethnographica-Academiae-Scientiarum-Hungaricae* 37 (1991–92), 283–292; Fernand Braudel, "History and the Social Sciences: The Longue Durée," in *On History*, translated by Sarah Matthews (Chicago: The University of Chicago Press, 1980), 27–38.

33 See Richard D. Brown, "Microhistory and the Postmodern Challenge," *Journal of the Early Republic* 23, no. 1 (2003), 1–20; Jill Lepore, "Historians Who Love Too Much: Reflections on Microhistory and Biography," *The Journal of American History* 88, no. 1 (2001), 129–144; Naomi R. Lamoreaux, "Rethinking Microhistory: A Comment," *Journal of the Early Republic* 26, no. 4 (Winter 2006), 555–561.

34 U.S. Code 654. Pub. L. 103–160 571, 107 Stat. 1547 (Washington, D.C.: GPO, 1993); RAND Corporation, *Sexual Orientation*, xxi–xxiv, 1–2; General Account Office, *DoD's Policy on Homosexuality* (Washington, D.C.: GPO, 1992), 11; Laura Miller and John Williams, "Do Military Policies on Gender and Sexuality Undermine Combat Effectiveness?," in *Soldiers and Civilians: The Civilian-Military Gap and American National Security*, eds. Peter D. Feaver, Richard H. Kohn, and Lindsay P. Cohn (Cambridge, MA: MIT Press, 2001), 361–402; Lehring, *Officially Gay*, 179, 271.

35 Lehring, *Officially Gay*, 1–9, 72–100, 149–179, 180–185.

36 This is reinforced in George Chauncy, Jr.'s examination of the Newport Naval Training Station scandal in 1919, which explores the social organization and dynamics within a community of individuals identified as "queers" during the early 20th century. It highlights the complexity of sexual identities and practices within this community, challenging simplistic categorizations. The term "queer" was used to describe individuals who defied traditional gender roles and engaged in same-sex relations. Effeminacy played a significant role in distinguishing these individuals from others, but there was diversity within the community, with some engaging in more overtly same-sex acts while others maintained heteronormative identities, including even marriages. Medical discourse did not play a significant role in shaping perceptions of "homosexuality" by the service members themselves, noting that working-class identities were influenced more by underground culture than by medical models. Additionally, Chauncy emphasized the fluidity and complexity of sexual behavior and identity, cautioning against conflating different forms of homosexual activity and identity. He highlights the societal tensions and struggles over defining and policing boundaries between homosociality and "homosexuality," shedding light on the historical complexities of sexual identity and community formation. See Gorge Chauncey, "Christian Brotherhood," 189–211.

1 The Moon Family

Laurance Moon was the seventh child of eight in a working-class family in Baltimore, Maryland. His childhood experiences undoubtedly impacted his later life, particularly his conceptions of masculinity. Moon grew up in a masculine ecosystem that promoted an active, risk-taking, assertive, if not heroic, male ideal that would later serve him well in the army. This idealized version of what it meant "to be a man" would likely affect how he performed his gender role later in life. Still, the lessons from his youth would not have affected his sexual orientation since "biologically based theories have been favored by experts" and "the available evidence indicates that the vast majority of lesbian and gay adults were raised by heterosexual parents and the vast majority of children raised by lesbian and gay parents eventually grow up to be heterosexual."[1] However, Moon's case demonstrates that while environmental factors can shape expressions of masculinity, one can effectively embrace strong masculine ideas independently of sexual desires.

Laurance Moon's father, Thomas Orlando Moon, was nearly larger than life, with many events of his career dramatic enough to be recounted in newspapers in at least three states on two coasts, providing a glimpse into the masculine ideals of the Moon household. Thomas O. Moon was born in 1849 to immigrant parents living in Virginia. He was studying for the ministry when, at age 14, he decided to commit himself to the Confederate cause during the Civil War. Being too young, he told friends and family that "he had eaten enough bananas to get his height to a point where he could pass the enlistment requirements." To get around the age requirements, he "told a sad story of being an orphan and was finally accepted and assigned to the cruiser *[C.S.S.] Nansemond*."[2] Joining the Confederate military while young, and often without parental consent, was a common way Southern youth would demonstrate their unique brand of Southern hegemonic masculinity.[3] The choice of the navy adds the element of heroic service by facing not only the dangers of combat against the enemy but also the threat from a ruthless and unpredictable sea.[4]

The *Nansemond* was a twin-screw gunboat commissioned by the U.S. Navy and christened just before the war. It was confiscated by the Confederate States in 1862 and put into service the following year. The 166-ton ship patrolled the Chesapeake Bay and James River, taking part in several engagements before being scuttled on April 3, 1865, when the Confederate government evacuated Richmond. Young

DOI: 10.4324/9781003530756-2

Thomas Moon would serve on the boat for most of its service.[5] When the war was over, Thomas briefly returned to his ministerial studies, but the sirens of the sea were too strong. After only a few months, he abandoned his studies and took his younger brother Robert with him to work for the Old Bay Line Steamship Company in the West Indian fruit trade.[6]

The choice of a life at sea had long been considered a "manly" occupation that provided opportunities for heroic tests of manhood where sailors faced extreme, if not mortal, risks, hardships, and natural hazards. The ever-present dangers of volatile weather, a vast and unforgiving ocean, and the need to ply one's specialized skills to survive and thrive were only part of the lifestyle. Dancing, drinking, fighting, and traveling to distant and sometimes exotic locations strongly appealed to many. Sea life could be nearly as romanticized, perhaps even mythologized, as much as the American cowboy, as both occupations faced the inherent dangers and displays of "reckless masculinity" in places where the confines of civilization were tenuous at best and men were predominant.[7] Life on the ship would also provide opportunities for homosocial relationships and bonding during dangers and hardships, while allowing the sailors to establish and reinforce hierarchies of power and command.[8]

The mythic sailor and cowboy paradigms resonated in the late 19th and early 20th centuries when many Gilded Age Americans felt that the country had begun to drift away from its seeming masculine ideals in the prewar years, which was exacerbated by the closing of the "frontier."[9] Urbanization and the increasingly dominant industrial economy brought diverse groups of people together in a context where impersonal economic and social forces stripped away elements of traditional masculinity while also allowing the exploration of alternatives to conventional forms and displays of manliness. Urban subcultures, particularly those in same-sex subcultures, often openly flaunted traditional masculine behaviors in favor of effeminate ones as cues for membership. A backlash against these changing times emerged, promoting an emphasis on an active lifestyle. Sports, self-control, and Roosevelt's much-celebrated "strenuous life" attempted to revitalize American masculinity and reestablish a level of pseudo-frontier morality.[10] Thomas Moon's choice of a career at sea allowed him to embrace these active and strenuous displays of manliness, and by all accounts, he excelled to a degree of gaining some distinction.

Three years after the end of the Civil War, Thomas Moon married Ellen Shafer, the daughter of a German father and French mother, and moved to the bustling seaport of Baltimore. It was five years before they began having children, and it would be 20 years before Laurance would be born. Their oldest child, Effie, was born in 1873, followed by George in 1875, Annie in 1878, Roland in 1880, William in 1882, and Mary in 1885. By the time Laurance was born in 1888, his three sisters and three brothers spanned a range of 16 years. Ellen was the youngest of the Moon family, born three years later in 1891.[11] The Moon household must have been a very crowded and busy place.

In 1889, the year after Laurance was born, his father Thomas took a position as the first mate on the 171 foot (52 meter) three-masted schooner *Carrie A. Lane*, which became famous for a mutiny on its maiden voyage under Captain Fred S.

Dyer. This single voyage demonstrated the potential human and natural perils of sea life but also the opportunities to display heroic or arguably toxic masculinity. Almost immediately after leaving Baltimore with 1,400 tons of cargo bound for San Francisco, Captain Dyer "noticed insubordination and an indisposition among the men to perform their work properly." He had "used them well and did not know what cause to assign for their action." He investigated, and a few crewmembers claimed that the First Mate, Thomas Moon, had begun to "abuse the men, calling them vile names and trying to get them to fight." Dyer promised that he would speak to Moon and have the abuses stop.[12]

Regardless of Dyer's actions, the tensions continued. Crewmember William Corbett later said that

> as we neared the Amazon River, the steward came to us with a proposition to capture the vessel. His idea was to steal the captain's weapons, and then we were to iron him. The mate (Moon), whom all of us hated, was to be thrown over the side. The fate of the captain was to be determined later on. Once we had captured the schooner, we were to put to Bahia, Brazil, and after reporting the loss of the captain and mate, were to escape. The boys refused to go into the job, and no more real trouble occurred until after rounding the horn.[13]

The heated emotions came to a head as the ship rounded Cape Horn. A gale struck, and Corbett recalled, "We lost nearly all the canvas we had standing." Capt. Dyer claimed the crew "refused to work" and wanted to reverse course and take shelter in Montevideo. The captain refused to turn back, and then "One of the men declared that the vessel would never get around the cape, and proposed setting fire to it with kerosene, and they all could all go to hell together."[14] Later in life, Thomas Moon recounted that he "had to fight the mutiny with a capstan bar as a club and, in the middle of a terrific gale, forced his men to work to save the ship."[15] A group of sailors then refused to work, and Captain Dyer "locked us up in the forecastle to starve until they would come to terms," recounted Corbett. The confinement was undermined, however, when the troublesome steward "cut a hole from the galley into the forecastle and passed the best of the food to the men. They were kept in captivity for forty-eight hours, but as they were getting plenty to eat unknown to the officers, the starvation plan would not work."[16] Ultimately, Corbet admitted the crew "finally consented to go back to their duty if the captain promised not to prosecute them upon arrival here [San Francisco]." They were released, and with good weather, they proceeded to San Francisco, but the mutineers were nonetheless arrested and stood trial.[17]

Moon's possible role as the catalyst for the mutiny demonstrates the seafaring opportunities for sailors to establish masculine hierarchies through displays of strength, authority, and ruthlessness. The mutiny, famous enough not only to be reported in both San Francisco and Baltimore at the time but also recounted in a Portland, Maine newspaper 38 years later, was perhaps not dramatic enough for Moon's personal tastes. His retelling of his role in fighting the mutiny "with a capstan bar as a club and in the middle of a terrific gale" is conspicuously missing from both Captain Dyer's retelling and the mutineer's account during the trial. Sea tales are typically rife with exaggeration, and Thomas Moon's colorful version of the story should not be surprising. Yet, his retelling emphasized his heroic role, showing masculine bravado in the face of hostile adversaries, both natural and human, to "save the ship." Even when the truth was probably sufficiently dramatic, Moon needed to shape and exaggerate the narrative to further establish his manliness and retold the story enough to be detailed in his obituary 46 years later.

Thomas Moon's adventures at sea continued. He became the captain of his own ship, the steamboat *Sampson,* in 1890 and later the *Hercules* (see Figure 1.1), both for the Standard Oil Shipping Company. When the Spanish-American War broke out in 1898, Moon again had the opportunity for heroic adventures at sea. The U.S. Navy purchased the *Hercules* and used it to take members of the press to Cuba to report on the war. Moon stayed with the ship.[18] Later in life, he bragged that he personally "located the Spanish fleet" off Cuba and "reported their whereabouts to Admiral Schley." And then, as the Battle of Santiago Bay was underway, Moon claimed he took the *Hercules* behind the *U.S.S. Merrimac* into the channel as it sunk, blocking the Spanish fleet's escape.[19] These seem to be another of Moon's exaggerated sea tales to theatrically inflate his heroic role. None of the official accounts or reports mention either Moon or the *Hercules* to corroborate his recollections. No newspaper accounts confirm it either, which is significant since the correspondents on board would hardly resist reporting how they would have been so close to the action or even be an actual part of it. Yet, in private company, presumably around a young Laurance, Thomas Moon added to his lore as the heroic maritime seaman.

Figure 1.1 The tug *Hercules* breaking ice on the Hudson River, date unknown but likely before the Spanish-American War. *Hercules*, an iron tug, was built at Camden, N.J., by J. H. Dialogue & Son in 1888. It was purchased from the Standard Oil Co. by the U.S. government on April 26, 1898 for use in the Spanish-American War and became YT-13 *Hercules*, commanded by Capt. Thomas O. Moon. After the war, she was employed by the U.S. Revenue Marine Cutter Service in various capacities from 1898 to 1913.

Source: Photographer unknown. Hudson River Maritime Museum, public domain.

The elder Moon's exaggerations should not overshadow his real dangers and exploits at sea, particularly after the war when the *Hercules* (and Moon) remained in the service of the U.S. government. The *Hercules* and Captain Moon were transferred to the U.S. Life-Saving Service, a precursor to the U.S. Coast Guard. In 1901, Captain Moon rescued 14 people from a sinking barge during a sleet and snowstorm off Diamond Shoals, North Carolina, and another damaged steamship named *Gladiator*, towing it to Hampton Roads.[20] The following year, the U.S. Light House Service had Moon take *Lightship No. 76* from Baltimore to San Francisco around Cape Horn, retracing his route with the *Carrie A. Lane* 13 years earlier. *Lightship No. 76* was basically a floating lighthouse that had been built in Norfolk, VA. This trip was significantly less dramatic, though the voyage was of enough interest to the *Baltimore Sun*, who reported it on Capt. Moon's dispatches periodically arrived in their offices as the journey progressed.

Captain Moon was also assigned local lightship duty off the Diamond Shoals near Cape Hatteras, North Carolina, in 1904. Moon oversaw *Lightship No. 72*, named "Diamond Shoals" for its station near that place, a common practice (see Figure 1.2). Lightships would anchor with their crews at their station for weeks or months at a time, regardless of weather. The duty was thankless and seemingly mundane. However, as the *Boston Globe* described it in 1905, few people "have any idea of the dangers faced by the brave men who make up the crew of that floating beacon and the hardships they endure." In fact, the duty was "so hazardous . . . that the government recognizes it by making a different and higher wage schedule for officers and men." Even still, the crews

> receive a small compensation for their daring and voluntary imprisonment . . . where storms rage with the tremendous fury known in any ocean, and the mountainous waves sweep from the broad Atlantic rolling and plunging. Every threatening to engulf the ship. . . . There are often winters when there is hardly a pleasant day on the dangerous spot and where the ship is momentarily in peril, not only of the waves but of collision during fogs and from the fact that it is impossible for the lighthouse tender to get close enough alongside to send aboard even necessary supplies. . . . In the wild storms that come in never-ending succession some seasons, there is very little chance for recreation of any kind; all hands are alert repairing here and there. . . . The engine room is, however, a busy place at all times, especially when a storm is in progress, for steam must be kept up and everything ready to start the ship's propeller should she go adrift or to ease ahead and relieve the strain on the chain cables.[21]

In 1907, Capt. Moon once again headed south, reassigned to the *Hercules,* towing the barge *Jack Towhy* to Brazil, "a trip of 10,000 miles" (16,093 km) which "required two months to complete." According to the newspaper *Virginia Citizen,* which recounted the journey, "There were many close calls with death or disaster that the men of the *Towhy* had. . . . For several days at a time, the sea literally swept over the highest part of the tug . . . the crew was locked-in, and the water was pouring in by the tons and tons."[22]

Figure 1.2 LS-72 "Diamond Shoal," c. 1912. Built in 1900 as a floating lighthouse, the boat was named after its stationed location of Diamond Shoals eight miles off the coast of Cape Hatteras, North Carolina. The ship was retired in 1937

Source: Photographer unknown U.S. Lighthouse Society Photograph NA RG 26 LS-72, public domain.

Even though Captain Moon was often gone for weeks or months at a time, that does not mean young Laurance and his family were not without some adventures at home. After Captain Moon was pressed into the government service, the family moved to 328 South Patterson Park Ave, described on the Sanborn Insurance Map as a two-story brick townhouse with wood cornice in a desirable neighborhood directly across the street from Patterson Park.[23] On Saturday night, October 20, 1902, a violent assault drew the family into the local press once again. Laurance's mother, Ellen, told *The Baltimore Sun* that she "was sitting in the second-floor window" after she "just put the children to bed . . . when I saw young Mr. [Edward] Williams . . . walking slowly and whistling." Two well-dressed men approached him from the opposite direction. They demanded money, and a scuffle ensued. Mr. Williams was struck in the head, ran across the street to the Moon household, and screamed, "Police!" and "Murder!" She opened the door, and Laurance's older brother William came down to help. It turned out that Mr. Williams was shot in the arm. "In the meantime, my son had called his attention to the fact that his shoulder was bleeding, and upon examination, we found the bullet had struck him." An off-duty fireman showed up, and 15 minutes later, a policeman. "I am sure it was fully 15 minutes after the robbery before a policeman came," Ellen Moon remembered. The wounded Mr. Williams berated the policeman for taking so long that the police chastised him until the fireman intervened and calmed the situation down.[24] As dramatic as the incident was for the Moon family, it is worth wondering if *The Sun* would have reported it if "Mrs. Thomas O. Moon, wife of Captain Moon," was not the primary witness.

Laurance's father, Captain Thomas O. Moon, clearly had set a high standard of heroic, almost hyper-heroic, masculinity, even if some of it had a flavor of self-aggrandizement. Facing both natural and human peril, Captain Moon and his exploits were well known, at least regionally. Shortly before World War I, the *Virginia Pilot* described him "a sea-rover of note, and during the 55 of his life has sought adventure in all climes and seas of the world . . . the old call of the sea wonder-lust which has impelled him through his younger days, still has its thrill."[25] Naturally, the newspapers did not report on all his adventures at sea. However, enough were reported that it is clear the "sea-rover" captain was at least locally celebrated in a seaport town that would have embraced the ideal that Moon typified. Young Laurance Moon and his siblings would learn from the examples of what was expected and celebrated in turn of the century masculinity.

Captain Moon's celebrated status undoubtedly shaped the Moon household, even if he was not always physically present. The mariner lifestyle required lengthy periods away from home and family, and Captain Moon was reported on long voyages that would take weeks or months to San Francisco in 1889 and 1902, Cuba in 1898, extended duty on Lightship No. 72 in 1904, and Brazil in 1907. Certainly, there were other long absences that were not reported in the papers. What that meant for the Moon children, not to mention his wife, Ellen, is hard to say, but clues arise in the scant evidence that his absences may have impacted the family even if the shadow of his reputation loomed large.

In many ways, the family appears to have been relatively tight-knit. The 1900 census had seven of the eight children living at home even though Effie, George, Roland, and William were over 18 years old. Only Annie did not reside in the Moon house, having married Harry E. Barnett in 1895 and had a son of her own, five-year-old William. However, the eldest daughter, 27-year-old Effie, had already been married and was almost divorced. She married Thomas D. Roberts, a printer and Democratic labor organizer, in 1890. They had a son, Clifton, in 1895, but the couple separated in December of 1897, and the divorce was finally granted in March of 1901.[26] Effie and Clifton moved back in with the extended Moon family, though she worked outside the home as a saleslady.

The family brothers also seem to have their own struggles but found the extended home a safe place to return. According to the Baltimore city directories, George and Roland seemed to have set out together in 1896, living together first on South Ann Street and then East Cross Street the following year. Both initially appeared to be following in their father's footsteps as their occupations were listed as "mariners."[27] In 1898, George married Dollie Kennard, but his marital bliss was even shorter than his older sister's. It lasted only one day before he abandoned her, though they would not actually divorce until 1906.[28] George and Roland would return to their parent's home, and both seem to have explored other career options. The 1900 census listed both brothers as clerks, but George experimented further. From 1900 to 1902, the city directories list him as an actor, still living at his parents' home. Roland moved out in 1901 and became a core maker. However, he, too, moved back home in 1904 and returned to sea as a mariner, a profession he would keep for the rest of his life. George briefly left his parent's house in 1902 and became a barkeep, perhaps to make ends meet while struggling to act, or perhaps he gave up on his stage dreams. He, too, returned home to South Patterson Park Ave in 1904, where he would stay until 1907. When he moved out, he was still listed as a barkeeper, but by 1908, he, too, had followed the family tradition of being a mariner.[29]

William was listed as a laborer on the 1900 census, but the city directory of 1906 indicates he, too, became a mariner and, like Roland, kept that profession for the rest of his life. In May of that same year, he married Marie K. Hackman, and they lived at the Patterson Park Avenue house until 1908. Laurance, now 18, also married Annie Bullock in May of 1906. However, like George and Effie, marital bliss was not forthcoming. The couple separated after only two weeks, Annie later claiming Laurance abandoned her. They would remain married but lived separately for nearly ten years before finally divorcing. During that time, Annie lived her own colorful life, being convicted of disorderly conduct in April 1909 and was non-fatally stabbed by barkeep Joseph Brozowski in 1915.[30]

Three of the eight Moon siblings had short marriages ending in divorce between 1890 and 1906. At a time when the national divorce average was 7.3% in 1900 and 8.2% in 1905, the Moon siblings' 42.8% was nearly four times that average.[31] Both George and Laurance's effective relationships were counted in days. It is entirely possible their father's long absences prevent the siblings from seeing and learning from constant, healthy marital interactions. However, that does not suggest that the home was not warm and welcoming. All the siblings were welcome there in adulthood until they found their way. Effie, George, and Roland left and returned. William lived there even after he was married. Laurance would remain with his parents until he joined the army. How much their mother, Ellen, who managed the home during Thomas Moon's long absences, played a role in that atmosphere is, regrettably, invisible in the record. However, it is logical to assume she had a significant role in keeping the family together, and Thomas Moon was at least silently complicit in her efforts.

After his brief attempt at married life, Laurance drifted between jobs while remaining at home. The Baltimore City directory listed him as a confectioner in 1907 and a driver in 1908. Living with his parents had its limitations, however. In 1909, Thomas Moon was transferred to Norfolk, VA, and sold the house on South Patterson Park Ave. Laurance, his older brother Roland, and his younger sister Ellen moved to Virginia with their parents. The 1910 census and Norfolk, Virginia city directory listed Roland as a steamship captain and Laurance as an "upholsterer." Of all the Moon brothers, only Laurance seemed immune to the sirens of the sea. George, Roland, William, and even Clifton, their nephew by Effie, followed in their father and grandfather's footsteps to the mariner's life – not Laurance. The 1910 census was taken in April, but by September 15, Laurance was back in Baltimore, turning as far as he could from the ocean and enlisting in the U.S. Army. Registered as a clerk, the 5'4" (162.56 cm), green-eyed, flaxen-haired 22-year-old would travel west, far into the land-locked heart of the continent, as a member of Troop F, First U.S. Cavalry.

Laurence Moon's height made him an ideal candidate for the cavalry. In the late 1800s and early 1900s, cavalrymen were often selected for their ability to ride and manage horses effectively, and soldiers of shorter stature had an advantage in maintaining balance and control during mounted maneuvers. Height requirements for cavalrymen in the U.S. military required them to be between 5 feet 4 inches and 5 feet 10 inches (approximately 162 to 178 cm) and weigh no more than 140 pounds (63.5 kg). These regulations were intended to ensure that cavalry soldiers were well suited to horseback riding, where extreme height could be a disadvantage due to the balance and strain of the horses. A more compact build placed less strain on the horse, allowing for greater endurance on long rides and during combat situations. Moon's height, within the preferred range for cavalry service, likely contributed to his being assigned to the cavalry, ensuring that he met the physical demands of the role while enhancing the mobility and agility required for mounted soldiers. While on the shorter end of the requirements, the men in his unit would all have been relatively smaller in stature. However, the Army Surgeon General also noted that the median height of all recruits for the year Moon enlisted was only 5'9" (175 cm).[32]

As he started his journey into the continent's heart, Laurance would have taken few personal belongings. However, he brought with him an understanding of what it meant to "be a man," which he learned from the masculine ecosystem of his youth. These experiences in gender socialization were, however, only part of how Laurance would understand masculine ideals and behaviors.[33] The individual and family's context within a set of diverse and dynamic groups and the influences of general social and cultural forces in which they are embedded create an environment or ecosystem where gender ideals, definitions, and norms socialize children.[34]

In Laurance's immediate microsystem, his father was such the embodiment of hyper-heroic masculinity that his exploits, exaggerated as they might be, made local and regional newspapers. The possibility that his father did exaggerate his exploits demonstrates how important his manly endeavors at sea were to his understanding of being a man and unquestionably created a basic operational definition of what a man was and how he should act. Laurance's brothers would emulate their father and choose a life at sea. Yet, it seems clear that they were allowed to explore other options, George was briefly an actor and a bartender, Roland would be a core-maker, and William a laborer, before all settled in as mariners. They were also allowed to leave but return home, just as their oldest sister Effie had with her child after her divorce. In other words, the Moon household provided a particular model of extreme masculinity and a supportive environment where the children could find their own way.

Unfortunately, the Moon family's social circles are unknown, as are Laurance's immediate peer groups, which would make up his mesosystems of masculinity. Presumably, the Moon family would have friends and neighbors who were similarly part of Baltimore's thriving port community, which would reinforce and glorify his father's exploits. Even Laurance's exosystem and macrosystem of indirect and societal environmental forces, such as the newspaper's accounts of the seafaring culture in the Chesapeake and general stereotypes of sailors in literature and the culture at large, would have reinforced an ideal of the hyper-heroic seafaring masculinity of his father. Without delving too deep into the Freudian Oedipal claptrap, Laurance's father nonetheless would provide a lens through which he would understand what being a man was, even if he did not completely or wholeheartedly embrace it.

But it was not just the hyper-heroic mariner masculinity that was a part of Laurance's masculine ecosystem. It is possible the family and Laurance had social peers outside Baltimore's port community. While the port was an essential facet of the city's dynamic, the railroads had made the city an important crux of connecting the nation's interior resources with the sea since the mid-19th century. By the turn of the 20th century, the city had over 200 national and international corporations that produced fertilizer (of which Baltimore had 27 different factories), canned seafood as well as fruits and vegetables, and was home to the Pennsylvania Steel Company's Sparrows Point Mill which brought Maryland coal and Cuban iron ore together in a massive 30,000 employee complex.[35] In other words, Baltimore had a solid working-class industrial character with all its conceptions and anxieties of masculinity and strong seaport ideals. This working-class orientation toward manhood was part of the "crisis" of masculinity after the Civil War as the antebellum notions of the heroic artisan and the genteel yeoman farmer gave way to the industrial marketplace's new realities. Gone were the traditional ways men could prove themselves by demonstrating mastery of their craft or producing a living from working the earth. As a result, the "crisis" resulted in the need, as Teddy Roosevelt put it, to live "a strenuous life." The cowboy and the sailor embodied this ideal.

Laurence Moon, living in the aura of a glorified ideal of his father, understood the hegemonic masculine role model in the context of family, friends, and a city that embraced them, understood an operational definition of manhood that he would take with him across the continent as he traveled to his new posting in the army, itself a unique social organization that also glorified extreme masculine ideals nearly as much as sailors.[36] Even if Laurance had not embraced the masculinity of his father beloved by others, and even if he chose to join Baltimore's queer urban subcommunities that often purposefully eschewed those ideals (something for which we have no evidence), Laurance would nonetheless understand what the masculine ideals were, the social capital that accompanied them, and could presumably emulate them. Regardless of his sexual inclination, his manliness could be a defining characteristic of his time in the military. While others wanted to conflate sexual desire with displays of traditional hegemonic masculinity, it would become evident that they were clearly two separate things.

Notes

1 American Psychiatric Association, *Application for Leave to File Brief Amici Curiae in Support of the Parties Challenging the Marriage Exclusion, Case No. S1477999 In the Supreme Court of the State of California* (2012), 33; B. L. Frankowski and the American Academy of Pediatrics Committee on Adolescence, "Sexual Orientation and Adolescents," *Pediatrics* 113, no. 6 (June 2004), 1827–1832.

2 "Capt. Moon, 86, Dies at Home in Lansdowne, Md.," *The Times Dispatch* (Richmond, VA), January 5, 1935, 15.

3 James M. McPherson, *For Cause and Comrades: Why Men Fought in the Civil War* (New York: Oxford University Press, 1997), 25–26; Anya Jabor, "Male Friendships and Masculinity in Early National South: William Wirt and His Friends," *Journal of the*

Early Republic 20 (Spring 2000), 83–111; LeeAnne Whites, *The Civil War as a Crisis in Gender: Augusta, Georgia, 1860–1890* (Athens, GA: University of Georgia Press, 1995), 39, 44–45, 53, 63.

4 Karen Downing, Johnathan Thayer, and Joanne Begiato, "A Sailor's Progress," in *Negotiating Masculinities and Modernity in the Maritime World, 1815–1940*, eds. Karen Downing, Jonathan Thayer, and Joanne Begiate (New York: Palmgrave-Macmillan, 2021), 15.

5 "NH 73908 CSS Nansemond (1863–1865)," *Naval History and Heritage Command*. Accessed November 17, 2022, https://www.history.navy.mil/content/history/nhhc/our-collections/photography/numerical-list-of-images/nhhc-series/nh-series/NH-73000/NH-73908.html.

6 "Capt. Moon, 86, Dies at Home in Lansdowne, Md.," *The Times Dispatch* (Richmond, VA), January 5, 1935, 15; "Veteran Skipper Dies After 43 Years' Service," *The Baltimore Sun* (Baltimore, MD), July 25, 1922, 3.

7 Downing, Thayer, and Begiato, "A Sailor's Progress," 15–16; Susan Lee Johnson, "'A Memory Sweet to Soldiers': The Significance of Gender in the History of the West," *The Western Historical Quarterly* 24, no. 4 (November 1993), 497, 498; Dee Garceau, "Nomads, Bunkies, Cross-Dressers, and Family Men: Cowboy Identity and the Gendering of Ranch Work," in *Across the Great Divide: Cultures of Manhood in the American West*, eds. Matthew Basso, Laura McCall, and Dee Garceau-Hagen (New York: Routledge, 2001), 149–168; Peter Boag, *Re-Dressing America's Frontier Past* (Berkley: University of California Press, 2011), 2; Jacqueline Moore, *Cow Boys and Cattle Men: Class and Masculinities on the Texas Frontier, 1865–1900* (New York: New York University Press, 2010), 8; William W. Savage, ed., *Cowboy Life: Reconstructing the American Myth* (Norman: University of Oklahoma Press, 1975), 3.

8 Downing, Thayer, and Begiato, "A Sailor's Progress," 16.

9 Kristin Hoganson, *Fighting for American Manhood*, 90–92, 105; John Whiteclay Chambers II, *The Tyranny of Change: America in the Progressive Era, 1890–1920* (New York: St. Martin's Press, 1992), 49; William W. Savage, Jr., *The Cowboy Hero: His Image in American History and Culture* (Norman: University of Oklahoma Press, 1979), 20; Savage, *Cowboy Life*; Joe Dubbert, "Progressivism and the Masculinity Crisis," *Psychoanalytic Review* 61 (Fall 1974), 433–455; Johnson, "A Memory Sweet to Soldiers," 497.

10 Kimmel, *Manhood in America*, 6, 167–171; Anthony Rotundo, *American Manhood: Transformations in Masculinity from the Revolution to the Modern Era* (New York: Basic Books, 1993), 19, 222, 227–228, 258–283; George Chauncey, *Gay New York: Gender, Urban Culture, and the Making of the Gay Male World, 1890–1940* (New York: Basic Books, 1995), 21; James Eli Adams, *Dandies and Desert Saints: Styles of Victorian Masculinity* (Ithaca: Cornell University Press, 1995), 7; Gregory L. Kaster, "Labor's True Man: Organized Workingmen and the Language of Manliness in the U.S.A., 1827–1877," *Gender & History* 13, no. 1 (April 2001), 24–64; Arnaldo Testi, "Theodore Roosevelt and the Culture of Masculinity," *Journal of American History* (March 1995), 1509–1533; Frank Tobias Higbie, *Indispensable Outcasts: Hobo Workers and Community in the American Midwest, 1880–1930* (Urbana: University of Illinois Press, 2003), 66–94; Clifford Putney, *Muscular Christianity: Manhood and Sports in Protestant America, 1880–1920* (Cambridge, MA: Harvard University Press, 2001), 2–11; Gail Bederman, *Manliness and Civilization: A Cultural History of Gender and Race in the United States, 1880–1917* (Chicago: University of Chicago Press, 1995), 16–17; Clyde Griffen, "Reconstructing Masculinity From the Evangelical Revival to the Waning of Progressivism: A Speculative Synthesis," in *Meanings for Manhood: Constructions of Masculinity in Victorian America*, eds. Mark C. Carnes and Clyde Griffen (New Haven: Yale University Press, 1989), 191–203.

11 1900 United States Census, Baltimore City, Maryland, https://www.ancestryheritagequest.com/.

12 "A Plot to Kill the Mate," *San Francisco Examiner*, May 2, 1889, 2.
13 "A Plot to Kill the Mate."
14 "A Plot to Kill the Mate."
15 "A Plot to Kill the Mate."
16 "A Plot to Kill the Mate."; "The Carrie A. Lane to Go to Sea," *San Francisco Chronicle*, May 15, 1889, 3; "Real Wonder Ship Was the Old Carrie A. Lane Built at Sewall Yard," *Portland Press Herald* (Portland, Maine), October 30, 1927, 3.
17 "A Plot to Kill the Mate."
18 "U.S.S. Hercules II (YT-13)," Accessed February 5, 2021, https://www.history.navy.mil/research/histories/ship-histories/danfs/h/hercules-ii.html
19 "Capt. Moon, 86, Dies at Home in Lansdown, Md." *The Times-Dispatch* (Richmond, VA), January 5, 1935, 15.
20 "Broken Down at Sea," *Virginian-Pilot* (Norfolk, VA), October 8, 1901, 9.
21 "Hardship in Floating Beacons," *Boston Globe*, December 17, 1905, 44.
22 Untitled, *Virginia Citizen* (Irvington, VA), July 12, 1907, 3.
23 1900 United States Census, Baltimore City, Maryland, https://www.ancestryheritagequest.com/; *The Baltimore City Directory for 1900*. Accessed February 15, 2022, https://lib.guides.umd.edu/c.php?g=327119&p=2197762 (hereafter, "*Baltimore City Directory*"); Sanborn Fire Insurance Map from Baltimore, Baltimore County, Maryland. Sanborn Map Company, 4, 1902 Library of Congress Geography and Map Division Washington, D.C. 20540–4650 USA. Accessed October 30, 2022, http://hdl.loc.gov/loc.gmd/g3844bm.g3844bm_g03573190204.
24 "Held Up by Two Men," *Baltimore Sun*, October 21, 1902, 12.
25 Untitled, *Virginia-Pilot* (Norfolk, VA), September 4, 1916, 7.
26 "Divorce Proceedings," *The Baltimore Sun*, September 30, 1898, 7; "Notes from the Courts," *The Baltimore Sun*, November 3, 1901, 7.
27 *The Baltimore City Directory for 1896*.
28 "Four Divorces Granted," *Baltimore Sun*, August 12, 1906, 20.
29 *Baltimore City Directory for 1908*.
30 "Deserted Bride, She Says," *The Baltimore Sun*, May 3, 1917, 5; "Ran Screaming into Street," *Evening Sun* (Baltimore, MD), February 18, 1915, 14.
31 Joseph Hill, "Statistics of Divorces," *Publication of the American Statistical Association* 11, no. 6 (June 1909), 489.
32 Douglas C. McChristian, *Regular Army O!: Soldier on the Western Frontier, 1865–1891* (Norman, OK: University of Oklahoma Press, 2017), 32–33; Brigadier General George H. Torney, *Report of the Surgeon General, 1910* (Washington, D.C.: Government Printing Office, 1910), 363.
33 Susan M. McHale, Ann C. Crouter, and Shawn D. Whiteman, "The Family Contexts of Gender Development in Childhood and Adolescence," *Social Development* 12, no. 1 (February 2003), 125, 127–130, 133.
34 Urie Bronfenbrenner and Ann C. Crouter, "The Environmental Models in Development Research," in *Handbook of Child Psychology: History, Theory, and Methods*, eds. P. H. Mussen and W. Kessen, Vol. 1 (New York: Wiley, 1983), 357–414; Urie Bronfenbrenner, "Environments in Developmental Perspective: Theoretical and Operational Models," in *Measuring Environment Across the Life Span: Emerging Methods and Concepts*, eds. S. L. Friedman and T. D. Wachs (New York: American Psychological Association, 1999), 3–28; Nancy Darling, "Ecological Systems Theory: The Person in the Center of the Circles," *Research in Human Development* 4, no. 3 (2007), 203–217.
35 Matthew A. Crenson, *Baltimore: A Political History* (Baltimore: Johns Hopkins University Press, 2007), 115–124, 316–328; "The Rise and Fall of a Steel Mill Town," *The Baltimore Sun*, October 19, 2001, 46.
36 L. Michael Allsep, Jr., "The Myth of the Warrior: Martial Masculinity and the End of Don't Ask, Don't Tell," *Journal of Homosexuality* 60, no. 3 (2016), 381–383, 385–387.

2 In the Army

Initially, Laurance Moon probably spent a few weeks at a recruit depot such as Jefferson Barracks, Missouri. There, he would be outfitted and learn some basics of military discipline before joining his unit. Unlike the modern army, much of his "basic training" would be conducted with his unit in the field. But as he transitioned into military life, Moon would learn what was expected of him and be indoctrinated into the army's ideal of manliness using the lens of his early life in Baltimore. Even before he enlisted, he might have been aware of the culture he was joining since the military also perpetuated strong masculine ideals through its recruitment campaigns, encouraging men to join the army by stressing the virtues of strong, aggressive masculinity. That ideal was carefully cultivated through both promotion and practice, where physical prowess and endurance were highly valued, and soldiers were expected to demonstrate bravery and feats of strength.[1]

The emphasis on strength and extreme masculinity was explicitly reflected in the physical training regimens designed to prepare men for war. In his 1914 book *Manual of Physical Training for Use in the United States*, Major General Leonard Wood outlined the physical expectations of soldiers in the early 1900s, noting that recruits must develop "strength, endurance – activity, agility, gracefulness, and accuracy."[2] This emphasis on masculinity was reinforced by the military's focus on physical prowess and emotional stability, creating an environment in which men were expected to live up to a set of ideals and values and be the epitome of masculine strength and courage to eschew the feminine.[3]

The military also imposed several restrictions on the behavior of its personnel in order to maintain the masculine ideal. For example, soldiers were expected to adhere to a strict dress code. They were prohibited from engaging in activities viewed as feminine or unmanly, such as wearing makeup or growing their hair long. Furthermore, there were also severe punishments, both official and unofficial, for any behavior that was deemed to be un-masculine. This further reinforced the idea that traditional masculine ideals were necessary for a successful military career.[4]

Within a month of enlisting, Moon was assigned to the First U.S. Cavalry, which, like Moon, was itself in transition. In August, the unit returned from a multi-year tour of duty in the Philippine Islands. The United States went to war in the Philippines during the Spanish-American War of 1898. When the war concluded, the

DOI: 10.4324/9781003530756-3

United States acquired the islands against the will of the Filipinos, who protested against merely shifting colonial rule from one master to another. The United States waged a particularly bloody war of pacification against the Filipinos from 1899 to 1902, resulting in the deaths of over 4,000 American troops and as many as 20,000 Filipino soldiers and civilians.[5] After the organized Filipino forces had been defeated, the American military continued to face a strong guerilla insurgency in many areas, led by the Katipunan, a group of Filipino revolutionaries, for another 11 years. The Katipunan and its supporters were ultimately defeated in 1913, though their legacy is remembered as a powerful symbol of Filipino pride and nationalism.[6] War in the Philippines was brutality executed by both American and Filipino forces, and the First Cavalry was no exception. At least one officer, Captain Edwin S. Hickman, Troop F's commander, had been publicly accused of using extreme interrogation techniques to gain intelligence for pacifying the guerillas in his province.[7]

Troops A, B, C, and D, half the First Cavalry's companies, were temporarily stationed at the Presidio in San Francisco when they returned to the United States. The other half, Troops E, F, G, and H, were temporarily sent to Fort Walla Walla, Idaho, before moving to Yellowstone National Park. The U.S. Army had been protecting national parks since 1886. In fact, the First Cavalry had started military administration of the national parks when General Philip Sheridan had ordered Company M to assume administrative control of Yellowstone after the park's first 14 years of underfunded and ineffective civilian management (Figure 2.1). The army created a

Figure 2.1 Soldiers by one of the park's thermal features, date unknown but probably after 1902.

Source: Photographer unknown, Yellowstone National Park Museum Collection (YNPMC), YELL 185160.

temporary camp at Mammoth Hot Springs that was later replaced by the permanent Fort Yellowstone in 1891. The soldiers patrolled the park for poachers, enforced protective regulations on the increasing number of tourists, and fought forest fires.[8] The commanding officers of the post usually had a dual duty of leading the troops and thus reporting to the Secretary of War and also that of the Acting Superintendent of the Park, who reported to the civilian Secretary of the Interior. The dual role that commanders faced was the same as the dual responsibilities of ordinary soldiers.

The duty was reminiscent of a bygone era. In 1901, the Inspector General for the Department of Dakota noted that

> conditions at Fort Yellowstone, resemble those existing thirty-odd years ago when the commands at military posts were split up by such detached service as guarding stage stations, escorting mail coaches, protecting surveying and construction parties, etc., along proposed transcontinental lines of railroad.

After the closure of the frontier, the army transitioned its mission to that of global imperial power. The soldiers in Yellowstone were "struggling to perform the varied and unusual duties" in the park while maintaining military readiness. This was especially true at the park's remote outposts spread throughout the park where soldiers were "permanently absent from the eye and supervision of a commissioned officer," and discipline could be somewhat haphazard.[9]

The remote soldier stations were a staple of the military's ability to enforce the rules of the two-million-acre park (Figure 2.2). They were occupied by a small contingent of three to five soldiers under the command of a non-commissioned officer who regularly patrolled the main roads and tourist areas. They also had responsibilities to prevent poaching and other violations in the backcountry as well. Given that enlisted men often lacked the necessary skills to stalk poachers in the rugged mountains, civilian scouts were hired to lead them on patrols in the park's remote areas. The unique duties of the army in Yellowstone were neither what soldiers expected when they enlisted nor were easily implemented, which made the isolated Fort Yellowstone an "undesirable post" for many soldiers.[10]

Various troops came into and out of all the parks on a regular basis and Yellowstone in particular. Units would work for a year or two and then go to the Philippines or come to the park after being in the Philippines for a couple of years. Some units sandwich their time in the park with tours in the Pacific. The contrast in duties could not be more pronounced. Working as a constabulary in a high, alpine national park like Yellowstone was a far cry from guerilla warfare in the hot jungles of the South Pacific. Over the years, it was becoming clear to the military brass that using soldiers to patrol the park was not always compatible with the new expectations of the United States as a global power. As early as 1889, the first military Acting Superintendent wrote to his commanders stating that patrolling the park risked "impairment of military efficiency," and he deemed "it a suitable time to urgently invite your attention to the importance of this subject."[11]

The soldiers themselves often disliked the duty. Tourist G.L. Henderson noted, "The soldiers do not like the new function of persevering a national park . . . because

Figure 2.2 West Thumb Soldier Station in Yellowstone National Park, circa 1904. Soldiers at isolated stations, such as this one, patrolled the park for poachers and monitored tourist activities. In the winter, the soldiers would remain in these structures, isolated from each other often by over 30 miles

Source: Photographer F. Jay Haynes, NPS Photo, YELL 10644.

it is not soldiers work."[12] In 1907 and 1908, the troops stationed in Yellowstone Park had one of the highest desertion rates of any post in the country. An investigation found that the soldiers needed a sense of common mission and skills to patrol the increasingly popular park effectively. Soldiers faced significant challenges enforcing a mission for which they had little enthusiasm or training in a physically and socially isolated environment. In addition, they struggled with externally imposed expectations regarding their social standing from the class-conscious tourists of late Victorian society. They encountered strains of a social class system that marginalized them. At the same time, they were legally put into the contradictory position of enforcing the park's regulations upon their perceived social superiors. Their mission, the social tensions, and the nature of their unique duties in a remote location neither lent itself to the best military discipline nor fit the expected duties of people who signed up for military service. These dynamics made the enforcement of park regulations inefficient at best and problematic at worst. This was the world Private Laurance Moon now found himself in.

Moon and other new recruits for the First Cavalry traveled to their post by train and disembarked in Gardiner, Montana, a small village on the northern border of the park and the only settlement for nearly 60 miles (96 kilometers). Little did Moon and the recruits know, but Gardiner was the best entertainment for the soldiers at Fort Yellowstone despite the fact most soldiers felt it was "not a desirable place to visit on the pass."[13] Only six miles (9.5 kilometers) from the post, it had the unique atmosphere of both a tourist town and a rough, isolated military town (Figure 2.3). A person known only by the pseudonym "Inquirer" even critiqued the town in its own newspaper, *Wonderland:*

> The people of Gardiner would like to enquire why the disorderly element is permitted. It disturbs the peace of the town, which is free from molestations. Nights are made hideous by drunken riots. Monday night, there was almost continuous yelling and shooting from midnight to daylight. Women of ill-fame live in the central part of town and exhibit themselves daily on the streets in bedroom wrappers and make a show of themselves at doors and windows on the arrival of the train, their housing being only a few yards from and facing the station.[14]

Another individual, only listed as "L.S.T.," asserted that something should be done about the "drunks that stagger along the streets day and night, using vulgar and profane language in every way imaginable," causing numerous fights "which are often seen and heard in Gardiner. Respectable women of this town will not stir upon the street in the evenings for fear of being insulted by some of these characters."[15] Undoubtedly, as the only place off the military reservation to recreate, the soldiers contributed to that atmosphere, particularly in the "off-season" when tourists did not frequent the park. Just like "Inquirer," "L.S.T." also lamented the prevalence of prostitutes. "The town is well represented with . . . women that are occupying houses of ill fame."[16] While the prostitutes catered to wealthy, transient tourists in the summer months, they could build relationships with their more regular clients of soldiers, particularly in the off-tourist season.

Figure 2.3 Park Street in Gardiner, MT c. 1902. Gardiner was the closest settlement to Fort Yellowstone and provided services to tourists during the summer months and soldiers year-round.

Source: Photographer unknown, Yellowstone National Park (YNP) Archives, YELL 9130.

The 100 recruits were met at the train station on October 27 and escorted into the park and their new post, Fort Yellowstone. The post held four companies of approximately 100 men each when at full strength, which was rare. The number of troops steadily expanded in the army's years of administering the park. Located at an elevation of approximately 6,700 feet (2042 meters) above sea level, the fort consisted of over 30 buildings. The most recent additions were built only the year before Moon arrived when Scottish stonemasons constructed seven large sandstone buildings using standard military plans in the Colonial Revival style. As the new recruits arrived, they were distributed equally among the four companies on the station, all of which had been grossly undermanned since their movement into the park the month before (Figure 2.4).[17] Moon was assigned to Troop F, commanded by Captain Edwin A. Hickman, First Lieutenant Edward M. Offley, Second Lieutenant Jonathan M. Wainwright, and First Sergeant Henry W. Bauder.

Being late in the fall, the tourist season had been over for months, and the weather at the high alpine fort would have been cool if not cold. The men lived in one-room barracks that held the entire company with precious little privacy. For the next couple of months, Moon and the other new recruits would engage in a mix of regular company duties as well as the basic training of a soldier. Their day would start at 6:15

Figure 2.4 Fort Yellowstone, c. 1910. The three-story stone building on the far left is the barracks built in 1909 and housed Private Moon's Troop F, First U.S. Cavalry in 1912. The smaller building adjacent to it is the Post Exchange, which also had a gymnasium, the likely place for Moon's court-martial. Today, the old fort houses the park administration

Source: Photographer unknown. NPS Photograph YELL 09191.

a.m. with Reveille followed by Mess Call and breakfast at 6:45. At 7:15, the troops would convene at the stable and care for their horses, followed by fatigue, where each troop would do their assigned duties. Some troops would engage in military drills (see Figure 2.5); others would take regular garrison duties to keep the post clean and functional, and the rest would do the park duties of patrolling the Mammoth Hot Springs Terrace, frequenting the tourist roads into the park, or patrolling the back-country for poachers.

The recruits would be excused from the company's duties to engage in mounted and dismounted drills and the basics from the basic military texts, *School of the Trooper*, *Manual of Saber*, or *Manual of the Pistol*. Mess Call for lunch was at 12:00 noon, followed by afternoon Fatigue or drill at 1:00 p.m., which would continue until 3:30 p.m. New recruits would undergo their afternoon training at this time, focusing on dismounted drills, target practice, and instruction on the basics from the texts *Instruction and Discipline*, the *Articles of War*, and *Personal Hygiene*. For soldiers who did not know how to read and write, a post-school, which served the officer's children in the early part of the day, was available after 3:30 p.m. until 5:00 p.m. At 4:15 p.m., all troopers not enrolled in the school groomed their horses and cleaned the stables until Retreat at 5:30 p.m., followed immediately by evening Mess. The evening provided some downtime until Tattoo (a bugle call ending activities for the day) at 9:00 p.m. and Taps (lights out) at 11:00 p.m.[18]

Even with 100 new recruits, the companies of the First Cavalry were still under-strength. When a man in the Commissary Department finished his term of service,

Figure 2.5 Machine gun platoon at drill on the parade ground between Fort Yellowstone and the National Hotel (in the background), circa 1910.

Source: "Petrarch" is listed as the photographer, YNPMC YELL 9741.

the commanders needed to find someone to take his place. With the entire command understaffed, they would need to entice someone to do "extra duty" in the Commissary for supplemental pay in addition to their regular duties. Still, the job required someone who they believed could handle their regular job as well as the additional responsibilities, often in the evening. Captain Hickman offered the job to the promising new recruit, Private Laurance E. Moon. It was unusual for someone still undergoing recruit training to be offered extra duty. Hickman later recalled that Moon "undoubtedly received considerable recognition being placed on extra duty in the Commissary Department, giving him practically a sergeant's pay."[19]

Moon took his additional duties well. The job involved significant paperwork and handling of goods and money. Sergeant Charles Swanson, the non-commissioned officer in charge of the Commissary, said Moon "performed his duties in an excellent manner." Swanson added that Moon was "one of the best men I have known in the service in my entire service, which is about twenty-two years. He is efficient, sober, and always attentive to his duties and performed them cheerfully."[20]

Moon's basic training ended as the New Year approached, and the high-altitude winter began to set in on the command. Maintaining military readiness became difficult. Only a few months removed from the jungles of the South Pacific, the command needed to adjust to uncompromising mountain winter. Surprisingly, the commander scheduled war games for late December. Not surprisingly, to anyone who has experienced a Yellowstone winter, they had to be postponed.[21] Winters could start early and be particularly harsh, especially for soldiers accustomed to warmer climates (Figure 2.6). First Lieutenant Edward Offley was on his second tour in Yellowstone. On his first posting in 1907, he wrote his brother, stating that "it seems ages since I left Old Virginia for this bleak and dreary land," adding, "I never was so tired of winter and cold and snow in my life before. It seems endless out there in this county."[22]

To keep the men physically fit and manage morale during the short winter days, the command organized an athletic competition to be held on January 12 and 13, 1911. The event was an individual competition but also a unit competition where the companies competed against each other. There were 21 events, and 5 points were given for first place, 3 for second place, and 1 for third place. The athlete who received the most points from all the events they entered received the title "Best All-Round Athlete" and a $5 prize. The company with the most accumulated points received the title "Champion Athletic Organization of the Post."

Emphasis on athletics had grown significantly in the late 19th century as schools, colleges, and the military promoted sports to demonstrate manly qualities and provided models of ideal masculine paradigms. In the heavily masculine society of the army, sports were highly encouraged. Soldiers competed against each other in fencing, boxing, gymnastics, sprinting, and weightlifting, among other things. These competitions were used to measure one's masculinity and, in Moon's case, were explicitly stated as such.[23] Of the 21 competitions for the January meet, most were typical gymnastic events, Olympic field events that could be adapted to a gymnasium, and a few feats of strength such as pull-ups, dips, "Indian clubs" as well as more martial events like boxing, saber, and the team event of tug-of-war.

Figure 2.6 Figure 10: Soldier escorting captured poacher Edward Howell (far right with his dog curled up by his feet) in 1894. Winters in the high altitude of Yellowstone Park could be very difficult, forcing cavalrymen to trade their horses for skis.

Source: Photographer unknown, YNPMC, YELL 1659.

In addition to the points for the individual and team competition, individuals could earn $2 for winning most events. Pull-ups were only worth $1, and the team event of tug-of-war offered a box of cigars as the prize. However, the more martial events of boxing, saber, and wrestling had a prize of $3 for first place, indicating how these manly events were more highly valued.[24]

The competition was taken seriously, with officers and sergeants taking a direct interest in training up their companies.[25] Hickman thought Moon was an excellent all-around athlete and encouraged him to participate. Regular company duties were put on hold as the competition neared so the troops could train. Ten days before the match, a memorandum was posted stating, "To enable contestants in the indoor meet to practice for it, afternoon stables will be discontinued" until after the match.[26] Some events like boxing, saber, tug-of-war, and wrestling needed preliminary matches and competitions, which began a week before the main meet. The right to challenge the advancement in these rounds also needed clarification since some troop commanders wanted to ensure they could get to the final bouts.[27]

According to Hickman, Moon entered several events and "earned as many points as any man in the troop."[28] The official record noted that he was first in the flying rings and first in pull-ups, for a total of 10 points and $3. Troop F also won the tug-of-war for a box of cigars and earned the title "Champion Athletic Organization of the Post" with a total of 74 points. Troop G was a distant second with 40 points.[29] Captain Hickman and his troopers must have been proud of themselves, but they could not rest on their laurels long. The event was so popular, and with much of the long winter still ahead, another competition was announced a week later to be held on March 16 and 17.[30] The gymnasium was exclusively reserved for each troop on a given day to ensure equity in training.[31]

For the second event, Moon also entered the lightweight division of boxing in addition to other events. His preliminary bout was on March 12 again Private Trout from the Machine Gun Platoon and announced for the whole command.[32] Moon advanced, and Hickman was very impressed by his new private, who "had done some good work in the lightweight division of boxing" and was "an excellent all-around gymnast."[33] In the second meet, Private Moon won first in flying rings and pull-ups again and first place in rope climbing for 15 points and $5. However, Troop F did not do as well as a group. They bettered their previous total with 75 points, but Troop G surpassed them with 100 points and took the best organization prize.[34]

As winter started to wane after the March meet, regular military and park duties returned to the forefront of the soldiers' minds (Figure 2.7). That is not to say sports were not still important. The post also had organized and competitive baseball and football teams. Only a week after the March meeting, the post commander had to remind soldiers that when practicing baseball, they "may leave off the blouse provided they wear a neat, uniform olive drab woolen shirt."[35] The teams competed against nearby communities and even against the employees of the hotel at Mammoth. Jack Haynes remembered that the rivalry with the hotel employees could be particularly sharp. One-Fourth of July game "went along without violence until the fourth inning when an altercation developed in the vicinity of second base." The hotel's second baseman, a drummer in the band, was also a prize boxer from Chicago named Jesse "Kid" Liponati. They exchanged words, and "three soldier players in succession set upon him with dire results. The commandant stopped the game promptly, but small group battles continued the rest of the afternoon and evening." The commander ate at the Haynes house that evening and "remarked that the guardhouse wasn't big enough to hold a fraction of the civilians – to say nothing of the soldiers – who should have been arrested."[36]

Ironically, the football games could be gentler, at least when the fort's team played the high school from Billings, Montana. The Billings team played a game against the Livingston high school and then traveled south to play the fort's team. When the team left Billings, some people were concerned "that the soldiers would treat them roughly and brutally, if necessary, to win . . . reminded of the great differences in their own weights and sizes compared to those of the troops." Once the game started, "the game was too one-sided to be interesting." However, "it took only a few minutes . . . to cause them to overcome all fears and misgivings, for the soldiers were gentleness itself and several times ceased playing when they believed one the visitors had been hurt." The gentlemanly sportsmanship did not end when the soldiers won 22–0.

> After the game, the soldiers allowed themselves to be jolly good fellows and entertainers. They took the Billings men into their quarters at Fort Yellowstone and fairly swamped them with attention and courtesies. The visitors were arrayed in uniforms . . . and given a ride of about 15 miles (24 kilometeres) into the park and shown the sights.

Figure 2.7 This 1910 real photo postcard shows the soldier in Yellowstone playing baseball at Old Faithful geyser, which is erupting in the background. The military highly prized athletic events as displays of masculine physical prowess. Recreational games like this were complemented by the more competitive team that practiced regularly, had uniforms, and played other teams from towns across the region. However, notice that one of the players in the middle of the photo did bring his baseball uniform deep into the park, far from Fort Yellowstone, where they played more frequently.

Source: Photographer unknown, Montana Historical Society, Lot 048 YENP-mi 10, used by permission.

The revelry continued into the evening as the players were "again entertained in the barracks and spent a hilariously happy night with their hosts." When they returned to Billings, "all wore yellow cords, crossed sabers and other emblems and devices indicative of the cavalry branch of the army." When they disembarked from the train, "they looked more like a detachment of cavalrymen returning from campaign than schoolboys coming home from a visit."[37]

Moon continued to impress his company commanders. First Sergeant Bauder

> found Moon to be an excellent man in every respect. He is a model young man, as much as I had to do with him. In fact, I never saw a better man in my service. Always done his duty right up to the handle, clean and neat in dress, and never to my knowledge was reprimanded in the troop.[38]

Captain Hickman considered his service as "most satisfactory" and "always regarded him as a man of excellent character."[39] In fact, he did both his regular and extra duties so well that by the end of summer, Hickman moved him to extra duty as a clerk in the Orderly Room with high expectations. "I expected, if he made good as a troop clerk, to have him a corporal in the near future."[40] Despite not even being in the army a whole year, Hickman felt that even the other soldiers in the troop, many of whom had been in much longer than Moon, also recognized his talents as a soldier. "I think pretty well abroad in the troop that he was to be made a non-commissioned officer in the near future," Hickman said.[41] First Sergeant Bauder said the other soldiers considered him "the star of the troop" and agreed it was generally known among the men that "there was some prospect of his being made and non-commissioned officer."[42]

Laurance Moon was an exemplary soldier, but he was also known to drink heartily and aggressively recreate in the small town of Gardiner, the only source of recreation in isolated mountains unless one took a 60-mile train ride to Livingston, Montana. During the summer tourist season, the town of Gardiner catered to the wealthy tourists who could afford to take the time to travel to and through the park. The other nine months of the year, the hotelkeepers, restaurateurs, saloonkeepers, and "sporting women" were more than willing to cater to the recreation-starved soldiers.

Soldiers on pass would come down individually or in groups to partake in Gardiner's limited entertainments. Heavy drinking and womanizing were common. Despite still being married to his estranged wife Annie in Baltimore, Moon was known on a first-name basis with many of the "sporting women" in town. "Moony" was known as a well-mannered and "a perfect little gentleman."[43] Meeting with the prostitutes in Gardiner did create health problems for the soldiers at the fort, though there is no evidence that Moon was one of them. Outbreaks of venereal disease were extremely common for soldiers at the post. It was such a problem that an official order explicitly stated that

> men who expose themselves to the danger of contracting venereal disease shall at once upon their return to the camp or garrison report to the hospital or dispensary of the application of such cleaning and prophylaxis as may be prescribed by the Surgeon.

The order added that "anyone who fails to comply with such instructions, if found to be suffering from venereal affection, shall be brought to trial."[44] At times, the post-surgeon also warned soldiers to avoid certain areas in Gardiner. In 1910, Captain Wallace DeWitt suggested to the post commander that "enlisted men of the command be warned that one of the inmates (name unknown) of the brothel in Gardiner, known as the 'Big Four,' is infected with venereal disease," and they should act accordingly. The post surgeon later ordered that in "each troop lavatory, one shower bath, and one water closet" be "set aside for the use of men with venereal disease, and plainly marked to show the purposes for which intended."[45]

After a enjoying the town, soldiers could either spend the night in one of the many hotels at low occupancy during the off-season or head back to Fort Yellowstone. Soldiers would frequently share a room to save money their money. If they choose to return to the fort, groups of rowdy, intoxicated soldiers would stumble up the narrow canyon road to the fort, where they would have to check in at the guard post. Soldiers might return as individuals, but that could be dangerous.[46] The cemetery records show that at least two soldiers died alone because of alcohol-related causes on the road between Gardiner and the fort.[47]

In the fall of 1911, as Moon approached the first anniversary of joining the army, things really seemed like they could not be going better for him. Immediately from the start of his service, he had distinguished himself as a diligent, dependable, and exemplary soldier who was well-liked within his unit. As a recruit, he earned the attention of his commanders for extra duty over his more seasoned comrades, and everyone seemed to understand that he was likely marked for promotion to corporal in the near future. As the troop began to prepare for the next indoor meet in winter, Private Moon's extra duty in the orderly room kept him from being able to train as regularly as before, but Captain Hickman could not hold that against him.[48] It seemed like the beginning of a promising military career.

The following spring, everything began to change. In April and May 1912, titillating rumors started to circulate among the men in the troop. When the stories reached the platoon sergeants, they began to endanger Moon's bright future. First, Sergeant George Ringer heard the rumors and told Sergeant Chadwell. On May 28, Sergeant Chadwell talked about the rumors with Sergeant William Hinshaw at the morning Reveille. Hinshaw could hardly believe what he heard. Private Moon, the clean-cut model soldier, was a "cocksucker," according to the rumors. Hinshaw tried to find out more. He approached Private Joseph Bernard, whose name was also mentioned as someone who knew about the actions, but Bernard claimed he did not know anything about it. Another man's name kept arising: Private Harvey Simpson, the company cook and a well-known drunkard. He would be someone Hinshaw would need to talk to since cooks were frequently the heart of troop gossip.[49]

At about the same time, Moon had become involved in a disturbance in the barracks (Figure 2.8). Moon had asked Private Bass to move bunks because Private Simpson kept coming up and inviting him to drink despite repeated refusals. Were the rumors and the incident related? The morning after the disturbance in quarters, Hinshaw went down to breakfast and ate in the kitchen. He casually asked Simpson about the rumors regarding Moon. Simpson said they were true.

"I don't believe it," Sergeant Hinshaw replied.

"It is true; you can ask [Private Joseph] Bernard or [Private George] Ross," Simpson retorted. "Even [Private Hughey] Hollins knows something about it."

Sergeant Hinshaw was unsure what to do. He later said, "I thought then that there was so much talk about it, I had better lay the matter before the First Sergeant, and he could talk to these men."[50] The next day, he conferred with First Sergeant Henry W. Bauder. It was not until the next day, May 30, that Hinshaw or Bauder acted in any way on the matter. As the troop prepared to go to the rifle range for target practice, Hinshaw pulled Private Irvin Harris aside and told him he "wasn't to be around with him [Moon] like he was the day before." Harris asked why, but Hinshaw would not say. "I didn't like to give any reason," Hinshaw later said, "for I didn't know and didn't know what to do in the matter."[51] Moon and Harris had been inseparable the day before because Harris "was rather green" but "wanted to be a sharpshooter" and Moon was helping.[52]

The confused Harris went to the rifle range, and Moon began to work with him. Harris told Moon that Sergeant Hinshaw told him to stay away from him. Moon was shocked. He asked the reason why, but Harris said he did not know. Moon

Figure 2.8 The interior of the barracks at Fort Yellowstone, date unknown.

Source: Photographer unknown, NPS photo YELL 14309.

pressed on and wondered if Hinshaw was worried he was "interfering with his shooting." Harris said he did not think the sergeant meant that but honestly did not know the real reason. Moon told Harris he would bring it up with Lieutenant Keller who had replaced Lieutenant Offley and was the acting troop commander while Captain Hickman was on leave. Harris became worried. "No," he told Moon. "You may be getting me into trouble, as Sergeant Hinshaw may not like me in the future."

Moon replied, "I would favor you by not saying anything, but I must report it as I consider it arousing suspicion on me in the troop."[53] After the morning's target practice, Moon kept true to his word. When he returned to the post, he went to Sergeant Hinshaw's room, knocked on the door, and Hinshaw let him in. Moon demanded to know why he told Harris to stay away from him at target practice. "I have nothing to say," retorted the sergeant. "But if I can, I'm going to stick it to you!"

The shocked and confused Moon could merely reply, "All right."[54]

Moon decided the next move would be up the chain of command to First Sergeant Bauder. He and Bauder had a close working relationship since Moon worked with him in Orderly Room. Moon did not know that Hinshaw had already informed Bauder of the rumors. Moon explained the situation, and the poker-faced Bauder only listened. The sergeant asked why Hinshaw would tell Harris that. "I have no idea why Sergeant Hinshaw doesn't want me to associate with Harris or that Harris has to keep away from me," answered Moon.[55]

Bauder believed Moon. He later recalled that "I don't believe Private Moon knew the reason why Sergeant Hinshaw gave Harris that order."[56] Bauder kept his information close to his chest for the rest of the day. Frustrated, Moon asked if he could go to Lieutenant Keller and have him deal with the matter. The First Sergeant gave his permission.[57]

The day was getting late when Moon found Lieutenant Keller in the Officer's Mess around 7 p.m. Moon explained the day's happenings and concluded that "certain remarks that were derogatory to his character were being made in the troop" and asked for Keller to investigate. Keller agreed and dismissed Moon. "I did not, at the time, learn the nature of the remarks," Keller later recollected, "but I judged they were of a scandalous nature."[58]

Given the late hour, Moon had to return to the Orderly Room for his extra duty as troop clerk with First Sergeant Bauder, who began to ask probing questions. He finally admitted to Moon that he had already started investigating the matter and disclosed the substance of the rumors. Bauder said he had questioned Privates Ross and Hollins, who claimed to have seen Moon "going down" on another man in the boiler room, but they would not say who the other man was.

Bauder and Keller's investigations merged the next day as Keller started to question the men, beginning with the sergeants. Bauder related everything he had already gleaned about the case, and together, they collected more statements. With Keller asking questions of the men, everything became more official. Ross and Hollins began to walk back parts of their accounts. They had not actually seen Moon and another man engaged in the act, nor was it in the boiler room. The incident had been with the troop's cook, Private Simpson, in his room just off the kitchen, and they only had circumstantial evidence that anything actually happened.[59] Keller nevertheless determined there was still enough evidence to put Moon under guard, confining him to the guardhouse by the end of the first day of his official investigation. However, Moon was still allowed to perform his duties in the troop and the orderly room so long as he was under the supervision of a sergeant.[60]

Ironically, while Keller was becoming convinced something "immoral" had happened, Sergeant Hinshaw had second thoughts despite his harsh words to Moon the day before. "I didn't believe it hardly at first," Hinshaw recollected later, "I never did believe it at any time very strongly." He added, "I changed my mind immediately the day following [the confrontation with Moon]." When asked the reason, he said, "I don't know what really did cause me to change my mind, except Moon has been in the troop quite a while, since the fall of 1910, and during the time I have known him, he has never been any such kind of man. . . . I couldn't believe it; in fact, I made up my mind then that it wasn't so."[61]

As Keller and Bauder's investigation entered its second day, things took a turn. It was becoming clear who all was involved and what the rumored actions were. Cook Simpson and Private Bernard were the other parties directly involved. More distressing, new rumors surfaced that Simpson had encouraged Moon to "go over the hill" or desert after the investigations began so as to prevent prosecution. When Keller asked Moon about that new rumor, he confirmed that Simpson had indeed encouraged him to desert. With more concrete details and concerns about Moon deserting, Keller thought it prudent to keep Moon in the guardhouse under sentry full-time to prevent that from happening.[62]

The next day, Captain Hickman, the permanent commander of Troop F, returned from his ten-day pass and fell right into the middle of the scandalous rumors and investigation. He could hardly believe it himself as he had always had a high opinion of Moon and saw his promotion as imminent. As acting troop commander, Lt. Keller had already drawn-up and signed charges against Moon for committing "unnatural and immoral acts" on Bernard and Simpson. He wrote separate charges against Simpson and Bernard for "allowing immoral acts to be committed upon them." The shocked Hickman asked a few questions of members of the troop as well but did not take his queries very far as he "did not want to form an opinion" on the matter since he knew he would likely be on the court during the court-martial. His prudence was well placed. After three days, Simpson was also separately charged with encouraging Moon to desert. The wheels of military justice were set in motion.[63]

Notes

1 Allsep, "The Myth of the Warrior," 384, 386–387; Belkin, *Bring Me Men*, 14–17, 27–28.
2 Leonard Wood, *Manual for Physical Training in the United States Army* (Washington, D.C.: Government Printing Office, 1914), 13.
3 Myameka Mankayi, "Masculinity, Sexuality and the Body of Male Soldiers," *Psychology in Society* 36 (2008), 24–44; Gregory Blackburn, "Army Men: Military Masculinity in Call of Duty," in *Masculinities in Play*, eds. Nicholas Taylor and Gerald Voorhees (London: Palgrave Macmillan, 2018), 37–53; William Arkin and Lynne R. Dobrofsky, "Military Socialization and Masculinity," *Social Issues* 34, no. 1 (1978), 151–168; Belkin, *Bring Me Men*, 25–28, 40.
4 Belkin, *Bring Me Men*, 25–28; Allan Bérubé, *Coming Out Under Fire: The History of Gay Men and Women in World War II* (Chapel Hill: University of North Carolina Press, 1990), 35–37.
5 Spencer C. Tuker, *The Encyclopedia of the Spanish-Americana and Philippine-American Wars: A Political, Social, and Military History* (Santa Barbara, CA: ABC-CLIO, 2009), 478.
6 Stanely Karnow, *In Our Image: America's Empire in the Philippines* (New York: Random House, 1989), 73–74.
7 "Believed to Have Been Acquitted," *The San Francisco Examiner*, July 25, 1902, 7; "Hickman Trial Ended," *The Los Angeles Times*, July 25, 1902, 6; "The Court-Martial of Hickman," *San Bernardino Times* (Calf.), July 25, 1902, 1; Allan W. Vestal, "The First Wartime Water Torture by Americans," *Maine Law Review* 69, no. 1 (2017), 36, 54–55; Christopher J. Einolf, "The Fall and Rise of Torture: A Comparative and Historical Analysis," *Sociological Theory* 25, no. 2 (2007), 161.
8 H. Duane Hampton, *How the U.S. Cavalry Saved Our National Parks* (Bloomington: Indiana University Press, 1971), 32–52; Aubrey L. Haines, *The Yellowstone Story*, Vol. 2 (Boulder: Yellowstone Library and Colorado Associate University Press, 1977), 4–6.
9 Lieutenant Colonel Philip Reade, Inspector General Department of Dakota, to Adjutant General, Department of Dakota, June 10, 1901. "Annual Inspection of Fort Yellowstone, WY." Annual Inspection Report, Record Group 93, Records of the Adjutant General United States Army, National Archives and Record Administration, Washington, D.C., 24.
10 Thomas C. Rust, "'An Undesirable Station': U.S. Army Soldiers at Fort Yellowstone and the Creation of the National Park Service Ranger Program," *Montana: The Magazine of Western History* 67, no. 4 (2017), 17–38.
11 Captain Moses Harris, *Report of the Acting Superintendent of the Yellowstone National Park to the Secretary of the Interior, 1889* (Washington, D.C.: G.P.O., 1889), 11–12.

12 Quoted in Elizabeth A. Watry and Lee H. Whittlesey, *Images of America: Fort Yellowstone* (Charleston, SC: Arcadia Publishing, 2012), 43.
13 Fredrick C. Ainsworth to Samuel W. Miller, October 2, 1908, Letters Sent (hereafter L.S.), R.G. 93, Records of the Adjutant General's Office, NARA, Washington, D.C., 10–12.
14 Inquirer, "Wants to Know," *Wonderland* (Gardiner, Mont.); June 18, 1903, 2.
15 L.S.T., "Wants Some Law and Order," *Wonderland* (Gardiner, Mont.), October 11, 1902, 4.
16 L.S.T., "Wants Some Law and Order."
17 Memorandum, October 27, 1910. Record Group 393, Records of Continental Commands, Fort Yellowstone, General Orders and Memoranda, National Archives and Records Administration, Washington, D.C. (hereafter Records Fort Yellowstone, RG 393, NARA); Post Returns September 1910, October 1910, Adjutant Generals Office, Record Group 94, U.S. Army, U.S. Military Post Returns, 1800–1916, Fort Yellowstone, WY. National Archives and Records Administration, Washington, D.C. (hereafter post Returns, Fort Yellowstone, R.G. 94, NARA).
18 General Order No. 7, December 12, 1910, Memorandum November 7, 1910, General Order No. 29, November 19, 1910, Memorandum December 4, 1910, RG 393, Fort Yellowstone, NARA.
19 Testimony of Captain Edwin A. Hickman (hereafter Hickman), General Court-Martial of Private Laurance E. Moon, Martial, Records of the Judge Advocate General, Record Group 153, National Archives and Records Administration. Washington, D.C. (hereafter Moon Court-Martial, RG 153, NARA), 139.
20 Testimony of Sergeant Charles Swanson (hereafter Swanson), Moon Court-Martial, RG 153, NARA, 126.
21 Memorandum, December 23, 1910, RG 393, Fort Yellowstone, General Orders and Memoranda, NARA.
22 Diary of Edward M. Offley, 18. Yellowstone National Park Library (hereafter YNPL), Vertical File (hereafter V.F.).
23 Robert Nye, "Western Masculinities in War and Peace," *The American Historical Review* 112, no. 2 (April 2007), 428; Axel Bungaard, *Muscle and Manliness: The Rise of Sport in American Boarding Schools* (Syracuse, NY: Syracuse University Press, 2005), 109; Michael Oriard, *Reading Football: How the Popular Press Created an American Spectacle* (Chapel Hill: University of North Carolina Press, 1993), 189–276; Testimony of First Sergeant Henry Bauder (hereafter Bauder), Moon Court-Martial, RG 153, NARA, 135; Hickman, Moon Court-Martial, RG 153, NARA, 138–139, 142.
24 General Order No. 43, December 19, 1910. RG 393, Fort Yellowstone, General Orders and Memoranda, NARA.
25 Hickman, Moon Court-Martial, RG 153, NARA, 142.
26 Memorandum, January 4, 1911 RG 393, Fort Yellowstone, General Orders and Memoranda, NARA.
27 Memorandum, January 7, 1911; Memorandum, January 8, 1911.
28 Hickman, Moon Court-Martial, RG 153, NARA, 138.
29 Memorandum, January 15, 1911. RG 393, Fort Yellowstone, General Orders and Memoranda, NARA.
30 Memorandum, January 21, 1911. RG 393, Fort Yellowstone, General Orders and Memoranda, NARA.
31 Memorandum, January 25, 1911. RG 393, Fort Yellowstone, General Orders and Memoranda, NARA.
32 Memorandum March 12, 1911. RG 393, Fort Yellowstone, General Orders and Memoranda, NARA.
33 Hickman, Moon Court-Martial, RG 153, NARA, 138.
34 Memorandum, March 18, 1911. RG 393, Fort Yellowstone, General Orders and Memoranda, NARA.

35 Memorandum, March 25, 1911. RG 393, Fort Yellowstone, General Orders and Memoranda, NARA.
36 "Livingston Beats Fort Yellowstone," Gre*at Falls Tribune*, May 2, 1904, 4; "The Livingston Team Successful," *The Billings Gazette*, July 23, 1907, 8; Jack Ellis Haynes, *Yellowstone Stage Holdups* (Denver, CO: Brand Books, 1952), 6.
37 "Players had a Royal Time," *The Billings Gazette*, December 1, 1903, 1.
38 Bauder, Moon Court-Martial, RG 153, NARA, 135.
39 Hickman, Moon Court-Martial, RG 153, NARA, 137.
40 Hickman, Moon Court-Martial, RG 153, NARA, 137–138.
41 Hickman, Moon Court-Martial, RG 153, NARA, 139.
42 Bauder, Moon Court-Martial, RG 153, NARA, 132, 135.
43 Testimony of Myrtle Gregg (hereafter Gregg), Moon Court-Martial, RG 153, NARA, 82.
44 Special Order No. 13, Orders 1915–1917, RG 393, Fort Yellowstone, Special Orders, NARA; See, for example, Court-Martial Private Frances Smith, November 12, 1906, Summary Court-Martial Records, Fort Yellowstone, WY, RG 393, NARA, Washington, D.C.
45 Special Order No. 13, Orders 1915–1917, Fort Yellowstone, WY, RG 393, NARA; See for example, Court-Martial Private Frances Smith, November 12, 1906, Summary Court-Martial Records, Fort Yellowstone, WY, RG 393, NARA, Washington, D.C.; Major Wallace DeWitt, Medical Corps to Post Adjutant, March 21, 1910. Letters Received, Fort Yellowstone, WY. RG 393, NARA, Washington, D.C.; Summary Court-Martial Private James Severns, November 26, 1908, Summary Court-Martial Records, Fort Yellowstone, WY, RG 393, NARA.
46 Testimony of Private Laurance Moon (hereafter Moon), Moon Court-Martial, RG 153, NARA, 149–151.
47 Statement of Jerome Chapin, Esq. of Battle Creek, Michigan, July 23, 1907, Letter Box 15, "Letters Received 1906–1909." Yellowstone National Park Archives; The court-martial cases for drunkenness in Gardiner are very numerous, but see, for example, the summary courts-martial of Wagoneer James Lewis, October 8, 1912; Private Emil Hebing, May 18, 1911; Private James McBee, January 1, 1911; Private James Healey, September 3, 1911. Summary Court-Martial Records, Fort Yellowstone, WY. RG 393, NARA; Private Presley H. Vance, October 16, 1908; Private Frank F Monaghan, November 22, 1910. Fort Yellowstone Cemetery Records, Yellowstone National Park Library, V.F.
48 Hickman, Moon Court-Martial, RG 153, NARA, 142.
49 Testimony of Sergeant William Hinshaw (hereafter Hinshaw), Moon Court-Martial, RG 153, NARA, 113, 108.
50 Hinshaw, Moon Court-Martial, RG 153, NARA, 110.
51 Hinshaw, Moon Court-Martial, RG 153, NARA, 108, 114.
52 Bauder, Moon Court-Martial, RG 153, NARA, 129.
53 Moon, Moon Court-Martial, RG 153, NARA, 145.
54 Moon, Moon Court-Martial, RG 153, NARA, 145.
55 Bauder, Moon Court-Martial, RG 153, NARA, 128.
56 Bauder, Moon Court-Martial, RG 153, NARA, 128.
57 Moon, Moon Court-Martial, RG 153, NARA, 145.
58 Testimony of First Lieutenant Frank Keller (hereafter Keller), Moon Court-Martial, RG 153, NARA, 142.
59 Bauder, Moon Court-Martial, RG 153, NARA, 127–128.
60 Keller, Moon Court-Martial, RG 153, NARA, 143.
61 Hinshaw, Moon Court-Martial, RG 153, NARA, 111.
62 Keller, Moon Court-Martial, RG 153, NARA, 143.
63 Hickman, Moon Court-Martial, RG 153, NARA, 141.

3 The Court

Private Moon's court-martial began at 1:30 p.m. on July 8, 1912, in the gymnasium in the canteen building at Fort Yellowstone.[1] Moon wore his dress uniform according to the regulations outlined in the *Manual for Courts-Martial: Court of Inquiry, Retiring Boards, and of Other Procedure under Military Law*, published in 1908, which were still in effect.[2] Moon and his counsel, Captain Timothy Coughlan, sat at a table directly across from where the officers of the court would sit. The Judge Advocate, First Lieutenant Frank Keller, would either have his own table or would have sat at the end of the table with the other court officers. There would have been a chair for witnesses near the Judge Advocate, and the court reporter would have had their own table as well.[3]

Everyone stood at attention when the members of the court entered. According to regulations, the court should consist of between 5 and 13 commissioned officers who would act as both judge and jury in the case. Nobody in the room was explicitly trained in the law. Still, officers in uniform were believed to have a definitive understanding of military regulations and thus qualified to act as counsel or render judgment. The military justice in place for Private Moon's trial significantly differed from the civilian justice system or the more modern military system. The early American military justice system, put in place during the Revolutionary War, was modeled after the British system and changed very little up to 1912. The Continental Congress broke away from the British system by creating the American Articles of War, which were created by legislative enactment and not executive order. This showed that in the American system, the legislature would have control over the military and justice system, reinforcing the balance of powers rather than leaving it to the executive.[4]

In the early days of the U.S. Army, there were three types of courts-martial: general, for the most serious charges; regimental, for less serious offenses; and garrison, for the least serious. Different officers convened them, and the punishments they implemented had to be reviewed by the convening authority. The membership of regimental and garrison courts-martial consisted of three officers, and the jurisdiction was limited to officers and soldiers of the respective regiment or garrison and had limited procedures and protections for the accused. For the general court-martial, a Judge Advocate was appointed by the Military Department's commanding officer and chosen from the officers of the command who was assigned to

DOI: 10.4324/9781003530756-4

prosecute the case as well as make all the arrangements for the hearing and protect the accused's rights.[5]

In 1806, Congress amended the regulations regarding court-martial proceedings, changing who had the power to convene the court. The composition and jurisdiction of the courts remained the same. In 1874, additional changes were made to incorporate some minor due process considerations. Despite this, there was a reluctance to expand the accused's rights. Over time, regulations and orders slowly made court-martial proceedings more sensitive to individual rights and fairer. Private Moon's general court-martial was governed by the 1908 revisions to the manual for court-martial and Articles of War. While strides had been made to make military justice more responsive to the rights of the accused, it did not uphold some of the customary American legal traditions. Like all general courts-martial, Moon would be tried by a jury of officers who were anything but impartial, nor his enlisted peers. Officers at a given post would be selected based on convenience rather than impartiality. This group of officers acted as a jury and was known collectively as "the court."

Given the relatively small garrison of Fort Yellowstone, Private Moon knew most, if not all, of the officers, and they knew him, as well as the other principal parties involved. Major Edmund S. Wright was the ranking officer and would act as the court's president. The rest of the court sat to his left in descending order of rank: Captain Edwin A. Hickman, First Lieutenant Guy Kent, Second Lieutenant Jonathan M. Wainwright, Second Lieutenant Robert L. Lounsbury, and Second Lieutenant Herman Kobbe. Of all the First U.S. Cavalry officers on duty in Yellowstone, only Captain Robert Foy, 1st Lieutenant Alden Graham, and the Commanding Officer Colonel Lloyd M. Brett were not present.[6] Lieutenant Keller rose to commence the proceedings as the court members took their seats. The acting Judge Advocate would present the prosecution's case. It was aspirationally expected that he "should do his utmost to present the whole truth . . . and oppose every attempt to suppress facts to torture them into false shapes that evidence may so exhibit the case that the court may render impartial justice."[7]

Keller turned to Moon and read the allegations. They consisted of two parts. First was the "charge" or the specific violation of the Articles of War. The second was the "specification" that set forth the basic facts contributing to the charge.[8] The charges and specifications against Moon were:

Charge 1: Conduct prejudice of good Order and military discipline in violation of the 62nd Article of War.

Specification 1: In that Private Laurance E. Moon, Troop "F" 1st Cavalry, did commit an unnatural and immoral act on the person of Cook Harvey G. Simpson, Troop "F" 1st Cavalry. This is at Fort Yellowstone, Wyo, on or about May 10, 1912.

Charge 2: Conduct prejudice of good Order and military discipline in violation of the 62nd Article of War.

Specification 2: In that Private Laurance E. Moon, Troop "F" 1st Cavalry, did commit an unnatural and immoral act on the person of Cook Harvey G. Simpson,

Troop "F" 1st Cavalry. This was at Fort Yellowstone, WYO, on or about May 11, 1912.

Charge 3: Conduct prejudice of good Order and military discipline in violation of the 62nd Article of War.

Specification 3: In that Private Laurance E. Moon, Troop "F" 1st Cavalry, did commit an unnatural and immoral act on the person of Pvt. Joseph Bernard, Troop "F" 1st Cavalry. This was on the road between Gardiner, Mont., and Fort Yellowstone, Wyo., on or about March 2, 1912.

Charge 4: Conduct prejudice of good Order and military discipline in violation of the 62nd Article of War.

Specification 4: In that Private Laurance E. Moon, Troop "F" 1st Cavalry, did commit an unnatural and immoral act on the person of Pvt. Joseph Bernard, Troop "F" 1st Cavalry. This was at Gardiner, Mont., on or about April 20, 1912.[9]

The 62nd Article of War was a rather wide-ranging, generic charge for various unspecified offenses. According to the Articles of War, it could include

> all crimes not capital, and all disorders and neglects, which officers and soldiers may be guilty of to the prejudice of good order and military discipline though not mentioned in the foregoing Articles of War are to be taken cognizance of by a general, or a regimental, garrison, or field officers' court-martial, according to the nature of the degree of the offense and punished at the discretion of such court.[10]

The *Manual for Courts-Martial* did provide for maximum sentencing guidelines of certain offenses against the 62nd Article of War and listed several possible violations such as burglary, forgery, perjury, robbery, disobedience of an order, drunkenness on duty, disobeying a sentinel, lewd or indecent exposure of a person, committing nuances in or about quarters, among others. Noticeably absent were specific references to sodomy.[11] It would not be until the 1916 rewrite of the Articles of War that sodomy officially became a specified military crime. Until then, the 62nd Article of War would have to suffice.

After the charges and specifications were read to Moon, Keller asked how he pleaded. Captain Coughlan interjected as Moon's counsel. According to regulations and another striking contrast to the civilian legal system, the accused was "not of right entitled to counsel," but, admittedly, "the privilege is almost invariably conceded" and was usually appointed from the list of officers at the post by the commanding officer.[12] Again, like the court members, the defense counsel would not typically have special training in the law. Coughlan addressed the members of the court.

> Before replying, I would like a continuance in this case. I received these charges and specifications this morning at about eleven o'clock, while they have been in the hands of the judge-advocate for months, and I want a little time to prepare this case, at least twenty-four hours.

Major Wright responded, "You may name the time you want."

"I think twenty-four hours would give me sufficient time. By that, I mean also the cases of the other two men who are implicated," Coughlan replied, referring to Privates Simpson and Bernard, who Coughlan would also be defending at the conclusion of Moon's trial. The military system of justice at the time saw no ethical dilemma in having one counsel representing the three men.

Having investigated the case and decided there was seemingly clear evidence against Moon, Lieutenant Keller objected:

> I received these charges on the afternoon of July 6th. While I preferred them and am more or less familiar with the case, I am at present on duty in the park and came to the post for the purpose of trying the cases, and my duties require that I get back to my post in the park at as early a date as possible. I believe the case could go on this afternoon without injury to the accused and would be a saving in time, labor, and probably expense to the government.

Everybody rose and stood at attention as Major Wright took the court members out of the room to confer. With no single judge to determine procedural questions, this judicial ballet would happen with every question, objection, and request. They returned after 10 minutes and granted Coughlan a day to prepare his case. The court was adjourned until 1:45 p.m. the next day.[13] With that, everyone snapped to attention again as the six court members rose and left the room, leaving Moon and Coughlan time to consult with each other and formulate their defense.

Clearly, the military justice of a general courts martial in 1912 was very different from a civilian court. The lack of a single judge, the ability of all "the court" members to question witnesses, and the lack of professionally trained legal experts clearly stand out. In addition, it should be noted that "the court," acting collectively as both judge and jury, was neither randomly selected nor in any way a jury of Laurance Moon's peers. They could also be called as witnesses in the case, and several would be. All were career military officers chosen simply because they were at the duty station. The same was true for the Judge Advocate prosecuting the case and Moon's counsel. Together, these eight men, the six members of the court, the Judge Advocate, and the defense counsel, would determine Moon's fate. They all knew each other with absolutely no impartiality at play. As Coughlan formulated Moon's defense, he would clearly understand what might sway his fellow officers. Coughlan may not have been a trained lawyer, military or otherwise, but like a reasonable attorney in any courtroom drama, he knew that understanding the background of the jury would be important in shaping the narrative to gain an acquittal. Understanding the jury also helps the historian make sense of the eventual verdict vis-à-vis the cases of both the prosecution and defense.

All the court members were career military men, several from proud military families. Most attended West Point, and several recently served in the Philippines against a determined guerilla foe. The court's president, Major Edmund Sehon Wright, was born in Georgia in 1865. His father, Moses H. Wright, graduated from the U.S. Military Academy at West Point in 1859 but became a captain in the Confederate Army. Edmund also received an appointment to the Academy in 1882 and graduated in 1886. After graduation, the young officer traveled around the western plains until he returned to West Point as an instructor in 1892. When the Spanish-American War broke out, Wright fought in Cuba and was awarded two Silver Stars "for gallantry in action" at Las Guasimas and the Battle of Santiago. He served at least one tour in the Philippine Insurrection. Upon his return, he was part of the military contingent administering Sequoia and Grant National Parks in California before being posted to Yellowstone Park in 1911.[14]

Captain Edwin Albert Hickman was born in Independence, Missouri, on March 26, 1874. Unlike most of the rest of the court, he had not attended the U.S. Military Academy at West Point. Instead, Hickman entered the Virginia Military Institute in 1892 and played on their football team before graduating in 1895. He served as a brevet Major in the Spanish-American War and also served in the Philippines during the height of the insurrection in 1902. Hickman was subject to his own court-martial in the Philippines for abusing two locals. The charges asserted that Hickman dunked the two men in a stream, nearly drowning them, in order to obtain information. One of the men later died from the maltreatment. Hickman did not deny the allegations but instead claimed the actions were justified "given the condition prevailing in Tayabas Province," where he was stationed. The court agreed with his assessment, and he was acquitted. After his return, he was appointed to the Wentworth Military Academy in Lexington, Missouri in 1904 before being posted in Yellowstone Park.[15]

First Lieutenant Guy Kent was a native of Wyoming and was appointed to the USMA at West Point in 1897 and graduated in 1901. Upon graduation, he served four years in the Philippines from 1901 to 1905. After two years on the Texas border at Fort McIntosh, he married Ms. Sue Rich of Boston, the sister of one of his fellow officers. Kent returned to West Point as an Instructor of Tactics from 1907 to 1909, then acted as an assistant to the Quarter Master at the Academy until 1911, when he was stationed in Yellowstone.[16]

Second Lieutenant Jonathan Mayhew Wainwright was appointed to the USMA in 1902 and graduated in 1906 (Figure 3.1). He was stationed in the Philippines from 1908 to 1910 and saw combat on the Moros Island of Jolo. He showcased his ability to adapt to challenging environments and foster rapport with local communities. His expertise in coastal defense earned him accolades, and he played a vital role in fortifying American positions. Upon returning to the States in 1910, his unit was stationed at Yellowstone National Park. Wainwright's familiarity with the Philippines and his proven leadership skills set the stage for his later accomplishments during World War II, where he would earn further acclaim and demonstrate unwavering resilience in the early years of the war as the commander of the forces defending the Bataan Peninsula before ultimately succumbing to Japanese and then enduring the infamous "Bataan Death March."[17]

Second Lieutenant Robert L. Lounsbury was born in Cathcart, Ontario, in 1884 but was appointed to West Point in 1903 and graduating in 1907. He was described as "at all times active and earnest in any good or progressive cause; he embodied the spirit of the ideal soldier." After graduating, he saw combat in the Philippines from 1907 to 1910 alongside Wainwright and then stationed in Yellowstone

Figure 3.1 Troops of the First U.S. Cavalry, led by 2nd Lieutenant Johnathan Wainwright (future general of World War II fame), drilling on the parade ground of Fort Yellowstone, circa 1912. It is possible many of the principal individuals in the events around Moon's court martial are unnamed soldiers in this picture.

Source: YNPMC, YELL 36941.

in 1910. Sadly, only four months after Moon's trial, Lounsbury was thrown from his horse and killed while on duty in Yellowstone. He is buried at Mammoth Hot Springs in Fort Yellowstone's old cemetery.[18]

Second Lieutenant Herman Kobbe was from a long and distinguished military family. His father, William Kobbe, was a distinguished Union general in the Civil War. His maternal grandfather, William Hoffman, was a general in the Mexican War. His great-grandfather, also William Hoffman, was a colonel commanding a regiment in the War of 1812. In 1901, 16-year-old Herman and his younger brother Eric recklessly would shoot their .22 caliber rifle from the trees and bushes on their parents' property near the Presidio in San Francisco at seagulls, ships, and even passersby. "From the number of shots they fired daily, they were apparently conducting an exclusive Budesfest, with the difference being the whole bay of San Francisco was their target." After several days, their dangerous games came to a nearly tragic conclusion when one of the bullets hit Paul Wissing at the nearby Dolphin Boat Clubhouse, who was critically injured and almost died. As a prominent general's son, authorities let their father handle the matter rather than arrest them.[19]

Figure 3.2 1st Lieutenant Kobbe performing an equestrian stunt on his horse "Goblin," c. 1915.

Source: Photographer unknown. (San Francisco Historical Photograph Collection, San Francisco Public Library AAD-6924, public domain).

Herman entered the U.S. Military Academy in 1904, "but his stay was brief" for undisclosed reasons, and he never graduated. Nonetheless, his family connections paid dividends, as President Theodore Roosevelt commissioned him a second lieutenant in 1908. He served in the Philippines for two years before being stationed in Yellowstone. Kobbe was also a distinguished equestrian and, in 1920, would become a U.S. Olympic riding team member but was injured before he could compete (Figure 3.2).[20]

Five of the six court members attended the U.S. Military Academy, and four of them graduated. Throughout its history, the institution has been characterized by a strong masculine culture, where notions of ruggedness, toughness, and traditional masculinity were deeply ingrained. The socialization of cadets at the U.S. Military Academy was instrumental in reinforcing masculine ideals. Cadets were subjected to a rigorous system of discipline, hierarchy, physical training, and hazing designed to mold them into military leaders. The strict codes of conduct, adherence to traditional gender roles, and the expectation of stoicism and bravery created an environment where masculinity was celebrated and upheld as the ideal.[21]

The 19th and early 20th centuries witnessed significant societal shifts that influenced even the ultra-conservative West Point, including the urbanization during the industrial revolution and the rise of some urban subcultures that eschewed traditional manly behaviors and gave rise to the so-called "crisis of masculinity." These factors influenced the reactionary perception of military service as a patriotic duty, reinforcing traditional notions of the masculine warrior's virtue. The conventional idea of the masculine warrior myth ran deep in the Academy and the military at large. Despite lacking evidence, there was a widely held belief that men must embody ruggedness, toughness, and machismo to succeed in battle. These attitudes were closely tied to the idealized and highly valued image of the powerful, virile heteronormative male while simultaneously degrading and negatively portraying those who are perceived as weak, powerless, or effeminate.[22]

The masculine culture of the U.S. Military Academy profoundly impacted cadets and their subsequent military careers. The socialization processes, educational practices, and gender expectations shaped the mindset and behavior of cadets, influencing their understanding of leadership, valor, and patriotism. This influence extended beyond their academy years, as they carried these notions of masculinity into their roles as military officers. The unofficial cadet culture of hazing first-year students reinforced the masculine culture of West Point in the 19th century.

That hazing culture was most personified by the Judge Advocate in Moon's case, First Lieutenant Frank Keller. Keller was admitted to the Academy in 1897 and was at the center of arguably the most publically notorious case of hazing the cadet corps had seen (Figure 3.3). This spurred both a military and a congressional investigation that began a concerted effort to eradicate the practice.

In the fall of 1898, Cadet Oscar L. Booz was subject to the typical rounds of hazing. He was forced to drink "pepper or tropical sauces" similar to Tabasco sauce, sit in stress positions, and other "unmanly and disgraceful things," cadet Sigmund S. Albert confessed during the investigations.[23] Booz did not take the hazing with the usual stoicism expected by the corps. Cadet Birchey O. Mahassey claimed:

> He acted in the barracks as if he were scared. I happened to meet him alone one day and told him "brace up'" . . . Cadets would make insulting remarks as Booz passed, and he didn't seem to take any pride in defending himself or his rights where he should. It was a case where I thought he should show some resentment.[24]

Cadets "called him out" to bare-knuckle box Cadet Frank Keller on August 6, 1898, to toughen him up. Such fights were common, and Booz was ordered to meet at the remote area of West Point known as Fort Putnam (Figure 3.4). Two cadets were to act as sentinels in case any staff members came by. Another cadet served as the referee for the match. Keller recounted his version of the fight to the congressional committee investigating the incident.

> I was chosen by a committee of my class to "call out" Cadet Booz. . . . The referee was Cadet J.B. Wray. We stripped to the waist. . . . For the first thirty seconds, after the call of time, Booz showed a little fight as he struck me a couple of times about the shoulders. I struck him under the left eye, cutting

Figure 3.3 Cadet Frank Keller, U.S. Military Academy Class Album, 1900.
Source: Photographer unknown. USMA Library Special Collections.

it slightly. After this, I found great difficulty in getting to him, as he turned his back and kept running away. I frequently told him to face me, or I would hit him in the back. I did hit him with a couple of blows under the right arm. He kept running and did not want to stand up and fight. In the second round,

Figure 3.4 "Hazing at the West Point Military Academy" from *Harper's Weekly*, vol. 45 (1901), p. 120. Keller's fight with Cadet Oscar Booz resulted in nationally publicized investigations about the brutal hazing at the U.S. Military Academy.

> he came up all right and shaped for me. I thought then that he was going to put up a fight after all, but he immediately began running around again. I struck him in the right eye and then to the stomach. He went down altogether, although the blow was neither a knockdown nor a knockout blow. He lay on the ground and was counted out. He was not knocked out.[25]

Purposely laying down and being counted out seemed like an unmanly act of cowardice to the other cadets. Cadet Edmund K. Sterling said, "After the fight with Keller, Booz was very much left alone." Cadet Frederick Hinnich, Jr. claimed that there was extreme prejudice against cadets "who go out to fight and then won't" and Cadet Phil A Sheridan, son of the famed general, claimed, "Booz was ignored by his associates after the fight and considered a coward." If Booz wanted sympathy from those outside the corps, he did not find it. Mr. Charles Burnett of the West Point YMCA knew Booz and condemned him as well.

> [I]nstead of showing himself to be a man of spirit and courage, he was struck about but a few blows before he lay down and cried like a child and refused to get up. . . . After such a display of cowardice, he was severely let alone.[26]

The condemnation by those at West Point indicated a culture of extreme, if not toxic, masculinity, which Booz violated. The hazing was meant to strip one of masculinity by having them do "unmanly and disgraceful things" while simultaneously demonstrating one's masculinity through fighting. Booz's failure in the latter caused him to be stripped of his adult masculinity because "he cried like a child" and had displayed "cowardice," contrary to the masculine ethical code of the cadet corps, giving him a pariah status. The investigations brought light on the culture of hazing at West Point, but none of the cadets who testified claimed to have any problem with it. Sigmund Albert claimed, "he took the hazing because it was expected." Even Keller accepted his hazing; the worst, he claimed, was being forced to shave with a bayonet.[27]

Booz remained at the Academy for the remainder of the fall but wrote to his family complaining of health problems. "I have been suffering with my heart of late very much, the result of the blow I received in the fight," he wrote his brother.[28] Booz left the Academy in January and returned home, but his family claimed he was always sickly and never himself again. Oscar Booz died the following fall, and the family publicly blamed the USMA's hazing in general and the fight with Cadet Frank Keller specifically as the cause for his death, prompting the investigations.

Neither investigation found any culpability in Booz's death, but the open nature of the investigations drew national headlines to the cadet culture that had hitherto been kept from public view. While efforts were made to limit or end the hazing, they were of only limited effect. With the investigations closed, Frank Keller graduated in 1901 and was commissioned a Second Lieutenant in the Eighth U.S. Cavalry stationed at Guantanamo, Cuba, for two years and then served a tour in the Philippines from 1905 to 1906 and again in 1908. He attended the elite U.S. Cavalry school in 1910 and, upon completion in 1911, was stationed in Yellowstone Park with the First U.S. Cavalry.[29]

The connection to the U.S. Military Academy by the members of the court was an important perspective as Coughlan and Keller shaped their cases. The military was closely intertwined with the concept of hegemonic masculinity, as it embodied the pursuit of violence on a large scale. Military academies exerted influence by actively establishing and reinforcing norms and expectations related to masculinity by demanding individuals conform to the hegemonic ideal. Training and culture not only promote physical fitness and economic security but also authorize the use of violence and aggression to dominate others, as demonstrated by the Booz case. The goal was to create an idealized masculine norm, highlighting toughness, stoicism, and the willingness to employ violence to achieve objectives. The military and its academies have long been spaces where hegemonic representations of masculinity are constructed, perpetuated, and utilized. Despite evolving political, social, and technological landscapes, the masculine warrior archetype remained a central symbol of the army.[30]

As Private Moon and Captain Coughlan conferred on their strategy, they must have looked at the membership of the court, which seemed to embrace a collective sense of the ideal soldierly masculinity imparted at West Point. Even Captain Hickman's time at VMI would likely have cultivated a similar mindset. Most of the court had also been touched by combat in the Philippines or Cuba and were willing to stretch the line of even accepted military ethics such as Hickman's extreme interrogation tactics. Captain Coughlan could use their masculine biases to raise doubt about whether Moon could ever have committed the charges of which he was accused. For at least a generation, both popular and scientific culture propagated the idea that men who performed same-sex acts were "inverted," in other words, not masculine. Despite witnesses who would admit to the acts, Moon's demonstrated masculinity would be the best path to clearing him of the charges. While the prosecution's case was strong, including two witnesses, themselves about to be court-martialed for the same acts, Coughlan only needed to raise reasonable doubt. If it could be proven that Moon exhibited a highly masculine ethos, there should be skepticism in the court's mind about whether he could have committed the acts.

Captain Timothy Michael Coughlan, Moon's defense counsel, knew and understood his fellow officers and was very much a part of their culture, but also an outsider in a way that had a unique perspective. Born in Ireland in 1875, he migrated as a child to the United States and, like most of the other officers involved in the case, he briefly attended the USMA in 1895 but left for unknown reasons the following year. In 1898, he joined the 201st New York Infantry to fight in Cuba and was appointed a sergeant in Company M. By 1899, he received a commission as a second lieutenant and joined the regular army in 1901, serving in the Cavalry. He was deployed to the Philippines in 1903 and ultimately came to Yellowstone in 1910. From experience, Coughlan knew both the world of the enlisted man and the culture of the officers.[31]

Both Coughlan and Keller knew that the masculine warrior ideal was the key to their cases. However, the ideal they and the court embraced was little more than fiction. Their masculine warrior myth emphasized Victorian heteronormative masculinity as an essential characteristic of military strength and valor. However, the existence of same-sex relationships among soldiers in ancient and medieval times challenges these assumptions and presents alternative, inclusive, and diverse narratives of warriorhood. In ancient civilizations such as Greece and Rome, queerness was not only prevalent but also accepted and integrated into various aspects of society, including the military. In Greece, the sacred bond of "*erastes*" and "*eromenos*" existed between older and younger soldiers, fostering mentorship and camaraderie.[32] Accepting same-sex relationships did not diminish their warrior spirit but acknowledged the diversity of human relationships and connections.

In ancient Sparta, often considered the best army of the ancient world, homoerotic relationships held a unique place within the social and military structure of the city-state. Spartan society greatly emphasized physical fitness, military training, and the state's well-being. Sex between male soldiers, particularly between older warriors (*erastai*) and younger soldiers (*eromenoi*), was an integral part of the military and social fabric. They believed that the bond between an *erastes* and *eromenos* would inspire the younger soldiers to fight with greater dedication, knowing they were fighting not only for themselves but also for the honor and protection of their beloved companions. In Sparta, same-sex relationships were seen as a means to strengthen the military, reinforce social bonds, and instill a sense of unity and purpose among soldiers. It served as a way to foster resilience, discipline, and loyalty within the Spartan warrior culture.[33]

Another notable example from ancient times was the Sacred Band of Thebes, an elite military unit consisting of 150 pairs of male lovers. These soldiers fought side by side, believing that their bond and love for each other would enhance their dedication to the unit. The unit's formation, rooted in the concept of mutual love and devotion, challenges the notion that homoerotic behavior weakens military prowess, highlighting the strength that can arise from deep emotional connections and shared purpose among soldiers. The Sacred Band achieved numerous victories, including their pivotal role in the Battle of Leuctra in 371 BCE, where Thebes defeated the vaunted Spartan military machine. Their success challenges the notion that gay relationships between soldiers weaken military prowess or damage unit cohesiveness, instead demonstrating how love and emotional connections can strengthen soldiers' fighting spirit.[34]

The medieval period witnessed the rise of chivalry and the code of conduct among knights. Close relationships between knights, often referred to as "brotherhood," included emotional bonds that could include same-sex relations. The Knights Templar, a powerful religious medieval military order, was known for their fierce loyalty and brotherhood. Historical accounts suggest they engaged in rituals and practices promoting intimacy and love among the knights. These relationships did not undermine their military prowess but instead provided a sense of unity and shared purpose, reinforcing the commitment to their cause.[35]

The historical acceptance and integration of same-sex relationships within military contexts did not undermine the strength or effectiveness of these soldiers in their historical context. Instead, it highlights the possible importance of diversity, emotional bonds, and the redefinition of masculinity in shaping formidable and successful military units. Of course, Coughlan, Keller, and the members of the court did not embrace the idea that these sexual and emotional bonds and different redefinitions of masculinity could shape formidable and successful military units. They were a product of their time, and in their worldview, only the heteronormative, rugged, tough, and strong soldier could succeed in battle. Coughlan and Keller would likewise shape their cases through that lens.

During the 24-hour recess, Coughlan made an impressive list of witnesses to testify on Moon's behalf, though he likely did not interview them before they testified. Some would attest to Moon's exemplary skill as a soldier, others to masculine character, his well-known heteronormative proclivities, his demonstrated athletic ability, and lastly, many in his troop would testify to Moon's general character and their friendship which remained unchanged despite charges levied against him. There were some surprise witnesses, including officers who were sitting members of the court, again emphasizing the difference between a court-martial and a civilian trial, and even the Judge Advocate Lt. Keller, prosecuting the case, would be called as a defense witness. The "proof of masculinity" defense was designed to exploit the officer's biased understanding of soldierly masculinity and raise reasonable doubts about Moon's guilt despite the prosecution's key witnesses. But before Coughlan and Moon could present their defense, Lieutenant Keller would present the prosecution's case, which was very strong indeed.

Notes

1 General Court-Martial of Private Laurance E. Moon, Martial, Records of the Judge Advocate General, Record Group 153, NARA. Washington, D.C. (hereafter Moon Court-Martial, RG 153, NARA), 2–3.
2 United States Army, *Manual for Courts-Martial: Court of Inquiry, and Retiring Boards, and of Other Procedure Under Military Law* (Washington, D.C.: Government Printing Office, 1908), 21. Hereafter, *Manual for Courts-Martial.*
3 *Manual for Courts-Martial*, 21.
4 Military Justice Review Group (MJRG), *Report of the Military Justice Review Group.* (Washington, D.C.: U.S. Department of Defense, 2015), 41–58.
5 MJRG, *Report of the Military Justice Review Group*, 48–53.
6 Moon Court-Martial, RG 153, NARA, 1–2.
7 *Manual for Courts-Martial*, 25.
8 *Manual for Courts-Martial*, 16.
9 Moon Court-Martial, RG 153, NARA, 2–3.
10 *Manual for Courts-Martial*, 113–114.
11 *Manual for Courts-Martial*, 55–57.
12 *Manual for Courts-Martial*, 25–26.
13 Moon Court-Martial, RG 153, NARA, 3.
14 George W. Cullum, *Biographic Register of the Officers and Graduates of the U.S. Military Academy at West Point, New York Since Its Establishment in 1802. Vol. IV, 1890–1900* (West Point, NY: Association of Graduates U.S. Military Academy, 1901), Cadet #3140. Hereafter *Cullum's Register*; Cullum's *Register, Vol. V,* 1900–1910, 391; *Cullum's Register, Vol. VI*, 1910–1920, #3140; *Cullum's Register, Vol. VII*, 1920–1930, #3140; *Cullum's Register VIII*, 1930–1940, #3140.
15 "Edwin Albert Hickman, Roster #4161," Virginia Military Institute Roster Database. Accessed March 10, 2021, https://archivesweb.vmi.edu/rosters/record.php?ID=4161.
16 Cullum's *Register, Vol. V,* 1900–1910, #4064; *Cullum's Register, Vol. VI*, 1910–1920, #4064; *Cullum's Register, Vol. VII*, 1920–1930, #4064; *Cullum's Register VIII*, 1930–1940,#4064; "Society," *San Antonio Gazette*, March 10, 1906, 5.
17 *Cullum's Register Vol. IX, 1940–1950*, #4477.
18 *Cullum's Register, Vol. VI, 1910–1920,* #4618; "Robert Lee Lounsbury," *Annual Reports of the Association of Graduates* (West Point, New York: United States Military Academy Association of Graduates, 1913), 54–56.
19 "Boys' Reckless Shooting Makes Life Uncertain," *The San Francisco Examiner*, July 22, 1901, 1, 6.
20 "Fortunate Lads Who Will Enter West Point," *San Francisco Call*, June 4, 1904, 2; "Live in Pasadena," *Evening Express* (Los Angeles, CA), July 29, 1916, 1; "Eric Kobbe," *Pasadena Star News* (Pasadena, CA), May 9, 1942, 13; "Herman Kobbe, Ex-Cadet of 1908," *Assembly: United States Military Academy Alumni and Alumnae* 28, no. 1 (1968), 112–113.
21 Historian Elizabeth D. Leonard, in her book *Men of Color to Arms!: Soldiers, Indian Wars, and the Quest of Equality* (Lincoln, NE: Bison Books, 2012) explores the experiences of African American cadets during the Civil War era, highlighting how they had to navigate and challenge the dominant masculine culture within the Academy facing harassment and ostracism by white cadets.
22 Lance Betros, *Carved From Granite: West Point Since 1902* (College Station: Texas A&M University Press, 2012), 22–23; Robert L. Caslen, Cindy R. Jebb, Daniel Gade, and Hope C. Landsem, *Getting to the Left of Sharp: Lessons From West Point's Efforts to Combat Sexual Harassment and AssauLieutenant* (Carlisle, PA: Strategic Studies Institute, U.S. Army War College, 2015), v–vi, 3–5.
23 "Official Inquiry Proves Booz Was Ill-Treated," *Philadelphia Times*, December 18, 1900, 7.

24 "Booz's West Point Fight," *New York Times*, December 21, 1900, 2.
25 "Keller (and Everyone) Faced Hazing," *New York Times*, December 21, 1900, 6; "Cadets Describe Various Hazing at Booz Inquiry," *Philadelphia Inquirer*, December 20, 1900, 16; "Official Inquiry Proves Booz Was Ill-Treated," *Philadelphia Times*, December 18, 1900, 7; "He Would Have Strangled," *Buffalo (N.Y.) Weekly Express*, December 20, 1900, 6; Philip W. Leon, *Bullies and Cowards: The West Point Hazing Scandal, 1898–1901* (Westport, CT: Greenwood Press, 2000), 27–29, 125–133, 155.
26 "Official Inquiry Proves Booz Was Ill-Treated," 7.
27 "Keller (and Everyone) Faced Hazing."
28 "Booz Brother, Fainting, is Led From Stand," *Philadelphia Inquirer*, January 5, 1901, 16.
29 *Cullum's Register*, Vol. V, #4062; *Cullum's Register*, Vol. VI, #4062; *Cullum's Register*, Vol. VII, #4062; *Cullum's Register*, Vol. VIII, #4062.
30 R. W. Connell, *Masculinities*, 2nd edn. (Los Angeles: University of California Press, 2005), 213; Ramon Hinojosa, "Doing Hegemony: Military, Men, and Constructing a Military Hegemony," *Journal of Men's Studies* 18, no. 2 (2010), 179–194; Daniel Morgan, "Theater of War: Combat, the Military, and Masculinities," in *Theorizing Masculinities*, eds. Harry Brod and Michael Kaufman (London: Sage Publishers, 1994), 165–182; Leon, *Bullies and Cowards*, 125–133.
31 "Col. Timothy M. Coughlan," *New York Times*, November 24, 1937, 23; "Starlight March," *The Boston Globe*, January 25, 1900, 6; "Timothy Michael Coughlan," U.S. Army Form No. 84a-2; "Timothy Michael Coughlan," U.S. Army Form 4-5-27-5000; Reed Museum. *Reed Museum Gallery Guide, 2D Cavalry Regiment* (Vilsek, Germany: Reed Museum, 2019), 30. Accessed February 22, 2022, https://history.army.mil/museums/fieldMuseums/reedMuseum/docs/2CRGalleryGuide2019.pdf.
32 Victor Davis Hanson, *The Western Way of War: Infantry Battle in Classical Greece* (Berkeley: University of California Press, 2009), 122–124; David Leitao, "The Legend of the Theban Band," in *The Sleep of Reason: Erotic Experience in Sexual Ethics in Ancient Greece and Rome*, eds. Martha C. Nussbaum and Juha Shivola (Chicago: Chicago University Press, 2002), 149; Eva Canterella, *Bisexuality in the Ancient World* (New Haven: Yale University Press, 2002), 70–74; Donald G. Kyle, *Sport and Spectacle in the Ancient World* (Oxford: Blackwell, 2007), 88–90, 183, 196, 210–211, 275; David D. Leitao, "Sexuality in Greek and Roman Military Contexts," in *A Companion to Greek and Roman Sexualities*, ed. Thomas K. Hubbard (West Sussex: John Wiley & Sons, Ltd, 2013), 235–238.
33 Paul Cartledge, *The Spartans: The World of the Warrior-Heroes of Ancient Greece* (New York: Overlook Press, 2003), 69–70, 82, 93, 200–213; Paul Cartledge, "The Politics of Spartan Pederasty," *Proceedings of the Cambridge Philological Society* 27, no. 207 (1981), 17–36.
34 See Paul Sheridan, *The Sacred Band: Three Hundred Theban Lovers Fighting to Save Greek Freedom* (London: Routledge, 2008), *passim*; Leitao, "The Legend of the Theban Band," *passim*.
35 Anne Gilmour-Bryson, "Sodomy and the Knights Templar," *Journal of the History of Sexuality* 7, no. 2 (1996), 151–183; Michael D. Barbezat, "Bodies of Spirit and Bodies of Flesh: The Significance of the Sexual Practices Attributed to Heretics From the Eleventh to the Fourteenth Century," *Journal of the History of Sexuality* 25, no. 3 (2016), 387–419.

4 The Case for the Prosecution

The court reconvened the next day at 1:45 p.m. After the court had entered and taken their seats, Judge Advocate Keller re-read the charges and specifications to Private Moon and asked him how he pleaded.

The first specification is "Not Guilty."
The second specification is "Not Guilty."
The third specification is "Not Guilty."
The fourth specification is "Not Guilty."

With the preliminaries out of the way, Major Wright called upon Judge Advocate Keller to present his case. Lt. Keller planned to call witnesses who could testify with direct knowledge of the acts in question either by being participants or personally witnessing Moon and others immediately thereafter. Undoubtedly, Keller must have felt confident in his case. He had two men who would testify to being the individuals with whom Moon performed his "unnatural and immoral acts." That alone should have seemed sufficient evidence for a conviction. He first called Private Harvey J. Simpson, the Cook for Troop F, who had already admitted to being party to the act during the investigation.

Lieutenant Keller swore Simpson in and began questioning him, getting right to the heart of the matter with his first question. "Did you have any immoral dealings with the accused during May of this year?"

"Yes sir," Simpson replied. His admission under oath placed him in legal jeopardy since he was charged in his own court-martial for "allowing an immoral act" to happen to himself. Therefore, his admission was equivalent to pleading guilty for his court-martial. He would be committing perjury if he told one story in Moon's court-martial and another in his own. If Moon were acquitted in his court-martial, but Simpson maintained his assertation in his, there would be an interesting legal paradox, to say the least.

When Keller asked how this situation came about, Simpson stated that as early as January, there had been rumors that "Moon was a cocksucker." Still, he could not believe the accusations since Moon was such an exemplary soldier. Therefore, he decided he would "see if there was the truth about the fella." The rumors had been swirling around for several months. "We heard so much talk about it at

DOI: 10.4324/9781003530756-5

Figure 4.1 Troop F of the First U.S. Cavalry in front of the stone double barracks, October 1911. It is likely that most or all of the principal participants in Private Moon's court martial are shown in this picture.

Source: Photographer unknown, YNPMC, YELL 90106.

different times," Simpson said. "Just as the talk will go around among enlisted men, especially around the kitchen wherever there are different men every day, and it seems it is a regular hang-out for them to use that kind of talk."[1] Talk about men who engaged in same-sex activity appears to have been somewhat common as Simpson admitted that he heard rumors "about other men in the troop because last winter there was one occasion [Private Hollins] used to bring up and talk about when that man was over in the quarters. He was a civilian, and he came in with a quart of whiskey. He used to kid about that." Who the civilian was is not clear, perhaps a tourist passing through the park or a hotel employee, but the soldiers were aware of such talk and possibly acts. But he added, "A man gets sick and tired listening to that kind of talk – they were kidding about the men drinking out of the same bottle with him. He was down in the kitchen, the first place I saw him until they kicked him out of there."[2]

The vague references were peculiar, especially about the "drinking out of the same bottle with him." This would also reappear in an incident with Moon in Gardiner. The importance of drinking out of the same bottle was based on the popular idea that moral perversion of same-sex acts was a contagious disease resulting from ignorance and prejudice rather than science or facts. This belief can be seen in the works of many prominent figures of the time, such as the German psychiatrist Richard von Krafft-Ebing, who wrote that "homosexuality is a contagious disease, the contagion of which is spread by personal contacts."[3] It was slowly becoming a widely held view that moral perversion and same-sex gratification might be "an infectious disease, transmitted through physical contact" and further reinforced by the medicalization of "homosexuality" during the later part of the 19th century, which saw it classified as a "disease" and treated as such.[4] This attitude was further perpetuated by the belief that same-sex acts were a sign of moral depravity and a symptom of a "sick society" and was often used to justify the criminalization of same-sex acts and the growth of homophobic attitudes of the period.[5]

As Keller continued to press his witness, Simpson claimed that he enlisted Privates Hughey Hollins and George R. Ross to help him in a plot to verify the rumors about Moon.

> Of course, Hollins and I used to have these talks, and I said, "I don't know whether to believe it," and I said, "I'm going to find out whether it is the truth or make some of these people keep their mouth shut about it."[6]

Simpson claimed he would invite Moon, who worked in the clerk's office, to come for some paperwork and entice him. Hollins and Ross would then come in and catch Moon in the act if one occurred. "[W]e fixed it . . . to catch him. . . . It was a fixed affair to catch him after I came in the room with him."[7]

According to Simpson, the plan started well. Moon came to the kitchen a little after ten o'clock in the evening. Simpson offered Moon some whiskey, to which Moon only took a few sips because he was on duty in the orderly room with the First Sergeant. Then Simpson told Moon,

> "I believe I'll turn in," and knowing that if I went to sleep and if he was one of those kind of fellows, as much as I have heard about them, he would make some kind of an effort knowing I was pretty full [i.e., drunk] and if he wasn't one of those fellows, he would take his drink and leave, and when Ross and Hollins came in they wouldn't see anything.[8]

Simpson retired to the cook's sleeping room with the lights out. Moon followed. Simpson claimed that he was

> laying on my bunk and [Moon] sat down on the edge of my bunk after putting the lights out and started to play around with my penis. He then put my penis in his mouth. I was waiting for Hollins and Ross to come in on us. After he was there for a while, Hollins and Ross finally did come in.[9]

Then, the plan began to unravel. Ross reached for the light but could not turn it on. After that, Simpson did something quite curious. "I said to Hollins: 'Don't come in on a fellow that way, Old Trapper.'" "Old Trapper" was Hollins' nickname. Exactly why Simpson said that or what he meant by it was never established, even after the court questioned Simpson, Hollins, and Ross. But it foiled the "plan," if there was one, because "Hollins then pulled Ross out of the room through the door. . . . After they went out, Moon and I got up. We went out in the kitchen, and Moon had the bills of fares and then went out."

Moon passed by Ross and Hollins sitting casually in the next room. Simpson went to his supposed accomplices and bragged about what had just happened.

> Then I said to Ross and Hollins that that man went down on me; what do you think of that fellows? It is the truth, and we found out at last. They said they didn't believe me at first, practically kidding; they were. I showed [a wet spot] my shirt and said: "What the hell do you think of that." They said: "It must be the truth."[10]

Simpson claimed that "Ross said: 'If it was anyone else but you, you son of a bitch, I would report you right now,' and he commenced laughing. Those are the very words he used when he saw the shirt."[11]

To make sure it was clear what had happened, the Judge Advocate asked Simpson, "Did the accused cause you to have an emission at this time?"

Simpson replied, "Yes sir, and after he got up from me, I asked him, I said 'My God, what makes you do a thing like this?' He said he couldn't help it."[12]

"What was on your shirt?"

Simpson answered, "It was part of the discharge or slobber of some sort." The court was curious about why he called out to Hollins as it seemed to foil the supposed plan. "That would have been a warning to the other men, wouldn't it?" they asked.

"Yes sir," Simpson replied.

"Then, by your own words, you spoiled the little plan."

Simpson was corned in a tight spot. He tried to deny any blame and suggested he thought the plan had proceeded flawlessly. "It wasn't spoiled. I supposed they could see. I didn't think they couldn't see as well as I could on account of being in a dark room, and they just come out of the light."[13]

The next night, the second act on Simpson for which Moon was charged never reached the finish of the first. According to Simpson, Moon asked for a few drinks while both were in the post library. After a short period, Simpson went to bed.

> The next I knew, he was sitting on the edge of the bed and was playing with my penis and putting it in his mouth again. As soon as I realized fully what he was doing, I shoved him away with my arm, raised up in the bed first, then took my foot and shoved him away and said, "For Christ's sake, go upstairs and let me alone! I'm tired and want to sleep." That's about all there is to that, sir. He went upstairs then.[14]

Keller continued the questioning. "Was Moon drunk?"

"I didn't see the signs of liquor on him because I had so much myself. I don't think he was drunk because he was in the orderly room with the first sergeant," Simpson replied.

"Was he drunk the next night?" asked Keller.

"No sir," Simpson responded.[15] The question was an important one, at least for Simpson. While not an exonerating factor, drunkenness might be mitigating.[16] When pressed on cross-examination about how drunk he was, Simpson admitted,

> I was drinking pretty heavy, sir, was drinking all that day for when I drink, I drink, and when I don't drink, I let it alone. Up until that time, I hadn't a drink from the first of the year until the last part of April or the first of May.

While admitting that the act occurred, Simpson preferred to blame it on his drunkenness.

> If I hadn't been drinking, I wouldn't have gone into a thing of that kind. It is the first time in my life I ever had anything like that happen to me. There is no one who can say anything against me with the exception of drinking.[17]

After the judge advocate had finished his questions and Coughlan had completed his cross-examination, the court members could ask the witness questions directly. The names were not recorded, but one court member asked if Simpson bore any grudge against Moon before or after the alleged incidents. He claimed not to, even with all the trouble that had arisen after the instances.

> I had nothing against him, only this thing, and you couldn't beat a man up for that, thinking as much of him as I did. . . . I felt more sorry for him than any man in the place, knowing truthfully what [he] was because there is not a man in the troop thought more of him before this occasion.[18]

If Simpson was truthful, it is worth noting that Moon's actions did not drastically change Simpson's feelings toward him other than some additional empathy. Even though Simpson recognized that Moon now laid outside an acceptable social norm and pitied him, he nevertheless currently "had nothing against him." Still, as we will see, once the defense opened its case, there was more than enough to suggest that Simpson may have been less than truthful in a great many things.

The Judge Advocate next called the other person that Moon was accused of having performed an act upon, Private Joseph Bernard. If Simpson was brash but articulate about his encounters with Moon, Bernard seemed almost dazed. The Keller opened with a simple question: "What was the nature of this experience you had with the accused?"

Bernard replied, "How do you mean?"

"What was it that happened between you and the accused?" Keller clarified. It was not the last time he or the court would have to rephrase a question for him. Finally, Bernard responded with the simple and direct response, "Why, he sucked my cock." Again, the admission was equivalent to pleading "guilty" to the chargers in his court-martial to follow Moon's.

Keller then sought more details. "Where did this take place?"

"Halfway between the Post and Gardiner, on the way coming up," replied Bernhard.

"State for the court how it happened," requested Keller. Bernhard then explained the first encounter in detail.

> We were all in a bunch downtown, leaving Gardiner for the post. It was half-past one or two o'clock [in the morning] – somewheres around there, and we started up from Gardiner, and we were all in a bunch, and Moon was there, and he took me by the arm and asked me to run. I was drunk, and I said, "All right," and we started to run a ways, and I got tired, and we got to the first bridge or the second, I don't remember which bridge – I am sure it was either the first or second, and I told him I wanted to rest, and he said "Come up a little way," and we went off the road under a tree there, and I sat down, and laid there a bit, and it was like – you know – could hardly see or nothing, staggering all the ways coming up almost, and he had taken my cock out and then kind of leaned up and started sucking my cock and I didn't realize what he was doing until he was about done, and then I didn't care, I was that drunk, I didn't care anything about it. Then he shook me up and started up the road again, and my pants were unbuttoned, and my cock was out.[19]

The prosecution asked if Bernard had any other similar experiences with Moon. Bernard said he did, and Lt. Keller asked him to recount it. The story of the second experience was lengthier and more confusing. Bernard and a group of soldiers had gone to the town of Gardiner to perform in a minstrel show in February. Many of them frequented bars and brothels after the show, staying in the hotels after the revelry. To save money, several soldiers shared hotel rooms, often with just one bed. The practice of two soldiers sharing the same bed when visiting the town was not uncommon.[20] Bernard was sharing a room with a Private Rader at the *Shaw and Powell Hotel*, and after drinking, both were in the room already going to sleep (Figure 4.2).

Moon came to Bernard's room and said, " 'Push Cart Joe [Bernard's nickname], get up' or something like that." Bernard shook Rader awake, and he opened the door. Moon came in and asked Bernard to his room. "No, not now," he replied, but Moon insisted. Bernard got up and went to Moon's room, where there were several bottles of beer and liquor. Moon's roommate, Private Robert Allen, was not there, and Moon said he would not be back as he was "going to sleep with a whore all night. [Moon] told me I could go to sleep there if I wanted." Bernard added, "We were chewing the rag there a bit, and he got in bed first, and I got in with him, and no sooner I got in bed than he started to suck my cock again."[21] Later, the prosecution asked if he had "an emission," which confused Bernard. They rephrased the question, and Bernard admitted he had.[22] After the act was over, Bernard turned over and started to sleep in the same bed as Moon, only partially dressed. Private Allen unexpectedly entered a short time later and exclaimed, "Jesus Christ, Push Cart Joe." Then, he also partially undressed and got in bed alongside Bernard, sandwiching him between Moon and himself. Then another trooper, Private Collins, came in, and Bernard returned to his room and got in bed with Rader.[23]

Figure 4.2 Shaw and Powell Hotel in Gardiner, MT, c. 1913. The second incident between Moon and Bernard happened on the first floor of this hotel.

Source: Photograph by Bill Whithorn, from *Yellowstone Park by Camp*, a commercial brochure published by the Shaw and Powell Camping Company, printed by Mc Kee Printing, Butte, Montana, 1908, p. 5.

A striking element of Bernard's account was there seemed very little evidence of homophobia or the worry about being labeled morally perverted or suspect by sleeping in the same bed in various stages of undress with men of the same sex. This probably should not be surprising because the concept, stereotypes, and pariah status of a "homosexual" was not yet culturally established. It would stand to reason that without those, neither homophobia nor the fear of being wrongly conceived as one yet existed. Until that was firmly established, men apparently had greater freedom of action and expression in homosocial environments.[24] Also, the reaction of Private Allen, seemingly aware of what likely happened between Moon and Bernard, made an exclamation but then climbed into bed with them. Like Hollins' and Ross' reaction to Simpson's story, the exclamation of surprise was clearly evident, but little or no shaming or social exclusion.

Under cross-examination, Coughlan asked familiar questions. "On the first night, what was your condition as to sobriety?" The phrasing confused Bernard and had to be rephrased. "Had you been drinking?. . . Were you drunk?"

"Yes, sir," confirmed Bernard.

"Very drunk?"

Bernard admitted, "I was pretty full. I was staggering on the way up. I fell down a couple of times."

The defense tried to exploit Bernard's admission. "If you were as drunk as all that, how do you remember stopping on the road, going under a tree, and all the rest?"

Bernard replied, "I remember everything when I'm drunk." He also admitted he was "pretty full" on the night of the second incident as well.[25]

The defense then moved to a curious line of questioning about what happened the next day that had echoes of some testimony from Simpson. Eight or more soldiers congregated in Moon and Allen's room the next morning. Private Rader opened a pint of whiskey and passed it around. The defense counsel, Captain Coughlan, asked, "Who drank out of the bottle first?"

Bernard made sure to claim that he did not drink after Moon, again echoing back to the disease theory of those with queer tendencies. "I had my eye peeled, so I wouldn't drink after Moon."

"You didn't drink after Moon?" Coughlan pressed.

"No, sir."[26] The Captain not only continued to press Bernard on whether or not he drank from the bottle after Moon but, later in the trial, asked other soldiers in the room if they saw Bernard drink from the bottle after Moon. Later, Private Allen, who was also in the room, testified that Moon "took the first drink and Private Bernard took the second drink and I took the third."

Coughlan continued by asking, "Was there any hesitation on the part of Private Bernard taking a drink after Private Moon?"

Allen replied, "No, sir."[27] The sequence of the drinking from the bottle was significant enough that Lt. Keller challenged Allen under cross-examination about how he would know who drank from it when. Allen answered, "Because I was going to take the first myself, but [Moon] took it first, so Private Bernard was sitting right next to him and took the second."[28] Coughlan even mentioned it in his closing statement for the defense since the incident was significant enough.[29]

The court then had its turn to question Bernard. They focused on the relationship between Bernard and Moon after the encounters took place. "After this first occurrence, were you willing to go on living in the same troop with a man like that?"

"I wasn't eating at the same table. I didn't want anyone to know about it," Bernard said. He claimed that he kept his distance from Moon, trying to even self-deceived himself that the incident had ever occurred.

> I was figuring all the time that I didn't want Moon to know that I knew anything about it – I was trying to keep it quiet myself . . . about sucking my cock, but I didn't want to show that I knew anything about it, that I was so drunk that I didn't remember nothing.

They asked particularly about the "dance classes" in the fort's gymnasium under the instruction of the unnamed "dancing professor." Bernard admitted that he had danced with Moon "two times I think." Soldiers danced with each other in these classes, presumably because of a lack of women and in an atmosphere of more open homosocial affection before the development of homophobia that arose with the acceptance of the later negative homosexual stereotypes. Bernard could not keep away from him in the classes because people rotated partners,

> I happened to run into Moon twice one night and once another night, and we danced. Never had any conversation or anything after the dance, just walked right away from him. . . . I was showing off that I didn't know anything about it, didn't want to let anybody know that I knew anything about it.[30]

After a few more clarifying questions, Bernhard was dismissed.

To that point, Judge Advocate Keller had made a strong case against Moon. He called upon two witnesses who admitted that the incidents had happened and provided sufficient detail, even at their own legal peril. Captain Coughlan, for the defense, had only made limited inroads on their accounts. However, Keller then made a decision that began to unwittingly undermine his own case, namely calling on Simpson's supposed accomplices, Privates Ross and Hollins, to testify.

First was Private George R. Ross. His account started in concert with Simpson's. Private Hollins asked Ross to come downstairs and see something. They went into Simpson's room, where the lights were out, and Ross tried to turn on the lights but could not when Simpson yelled at Hollins, "Don't walk in like that, Old Trapper!" Hollins and Ross left, and a few minutes later, Simpson came out bragging and showing the wet spot on his shirt.[31] However, Ross' story had missed the motivation for entering the room. Keller asked about the "trap" to catch Moon, and Ross suddenly became a bit dodgy. "We said earlier in the evening, Simpson said, 'If that's so [about Moon], I'm going to find out.'" Keller asked, "What was the idea in setting the trap to begin with?" "Well, to convince our own minds, I guess."[32]

Under cross-examination, Coughlan first tried to sow doubt about whether the figure Ross saw in the room was really Moon. "What did you see when you went in [the cook's room]?"

"I couldn't see anything, sir."

"Nothing at all?"

"No."

Coughlan pressed the issue. "Did you see the accused in there?"

"No, sir," Ross had to admit.[33]

Coughlan then asked, "What do you suppose Simpson meant when he said: 'Don't come in on me like that, Old Fellow'?"

Ross replied, "I suppose he meant to stay out of there . . . I guess he must have backed down or something . . . he didn't want to be seen."

"You mean he didn't want you two men to disturb him?" asked Coughlan.

"Yes, sir," replied Ross.

Then Coughlan drove his point home. "How could you make up your mind about it if you saw nothing in that room?"

"I couldn't see why Simpson would lie about such a thing as that," answered Ross uneasily.[34]

After Coughlan's questioning, the court pressed the question of the supposed "trap." They asked about the origins of the plan. "When you were drinking with Hollins and Simpson in the evening, was the plan made there that Simpson was to get Moon in his room and you were to come in on him?"

Ross answered with an astonishingly straightforward reply that not only walked back his own testimony but also undermined Simpson's story and would help open the door to question Simpson's entire character. "Not with me."

The court jumped on the contradiction. "You weren't party then to Simpson's proposed scheme of proving this on the accused?"

"No sir," answered Ross. "He made this remark, though, that he was going to find out, but I didn't think anything about it."[35]

"Your going in there [the cook's room] unknown to Simpson, was it not?" asked the court.

"As far as I'm concerned, yes, sir."

Another court member made sure to clarify precisely what Ross knew or did not know in a way most sympathetic to the defense. "Your whole knowledge of the affair hangs on what Simpson told you and what Simpson showed you on his shirt, does it not?"

"Yes, sir," Ross had to admit.

After several additional questions about Simpson's sobriety level, the exact time of the incident, and whether Ross had heard any rumors about Moon before the incident, Ross was dismissed. The court adjourned for a short recess at 4:37 p.m. and relocated to the post Hospital and hear the testimony of Private Hughey Hollins, the second cook of Troop F. Hollins, who had taken ill and was "unable to appear before the court in the court-martial room."[36] If Ross's testimony had caused some fractures in Keller's case, it would only have gotten worse with Hollins' statement. Next to Moon, Simpson, and Bernard, Hollins was the most crucial figure in the trial. Had it not been for Hollins, the whole incident may have been avoided. His account started with how the rumors about Moon arose (see Figure 4.3).

> Well, sir, about along in January, thereover in the canteen one evening, and I was passing a group of men, and I heard someone making the statement somewhere about a cocksucker in the "F" troop. It struck me as funny. I didn't know anyone in the group. Sometime after that, I should judge about two weeks, this man Private Bernard was on kitchen police, and I got to telling him about what I heard in the canteen, and he told me, he said, "Yes, there is such a party in F Troop, such a man," and I asked him if he knew who it was and he said he would tell me if I wouldn't say anything, and he told me it was Private Moon, that Private Moon had gone down on him, and he didn't want me to say anything about it.[37]

Considering that Bernard had made significant efforts to pretend he knew nothing of the incident, his admission to Hollins is somewhat surprising. Bernard had

Figure 4.3 The interior of the old Fort Yellowstone Post Exchange at an unknown date. The Post Exchange was the best place for soldiers to relax off duty and served as the primary social center for the garrison. Rumors about Moon started to circulate here and led to his court martial.

Source: Photographer unknown, YNPMC, YELL 36921.

claimed in his testimony that he had been caught off guard when Hollins asked about it.

> I told him no. And he says, are you sure? And I say, I believe there is a cock-sucker in the troop or something like that, and I thought he knew something about it, so I told him. . . . . The way he asked me was sudden and all that; I thought he knew something about it, and I told him.[38]

The court later asked Hollins why he spoke to Bernard about it specifically. He stated there "seemed to be general talk about the troop that there was some kind of a person in the troop. . . . [Bernard] was a man who knocked around a good deal, and he was a man likely to know about such a person . . . he knew everything that was going around."[39]

Hollins told Simpson what Bernard said about three weeks later. Then, on the night of Simpson's first encounter, they discussed Moon. "Simpson said to me one night; we had been speaking about Moon, he said, 'The Party's coming down here tonight, and if he comes down, I wish you would step outside.'"[40] The supposed plan or trap was conspicuously missing from Hollins' account.

Already in damage control after Ross' testimony, Keller noticed the discrepancy and asked, "Did Simpson arrange with you on the first evening to set a trap to catch Moon?"

Hollins replied, "There was to be no trap set. He simply asked me if Private Moon had come down into the room, and he asked me to step outside. When I stepped outside, I got Private Ross and fetched him down."

Keller asked again, "This was on your own initiative and not at the suggestion of Simpson?"

"No sir, I simply got Private Ross."[41]

The rest of the account was similar to Simpson's. Ross and Hollins went into the room and fumbled with the light until Simpson called out, and they left. When pressed, he had to admit that "the only thing you could see was a dark outline where Simpson's bunk was, and a man was there from the light that was in the kitchen . . . just the outlines of two men." He could not even identify positively one of the men as Moon.[42] A few minutes later, Moon emerged and left the kitchen. According to Hollins, the only difference is that he and Ross went into Simpson's room and "started to joke with Simpson about his actions," where Simpson bragged about the experience and showed him the wet spot on his shirt.

On cross-examination, Coughlan re-asked the question and reinforced the lack of a plan. Hollins replied, "Simpson didn't fix no scheme with me to find out what was coming off. If he had any arrangement, he hadn't said anything to me about it."[43]

Still belaboring the point, Coughlan asked again about Simpson's supposed "plan" to entrap Moon, and Hollins again replied, "Simpson hadn't made a suggestion to go in and find out. It was my own suggestion to get [Ross] and find out what they were doing in the room."[44]

Coughlan then made sure that Hollins really could not identify Moon. "What did you see in that room when you were in there that night?"

"The only thing you could see was a dark outline where Simpson's bunk was, and a man was there from light in the kitchen," replied Hollins.

"Did you actually see anything?" pressed Coughlan.

"Didn't actually see anything," admitted Hollins. "Just the outlines of two men."

After some additional questions about his sobriety, Simpson's sobriety, and Ross' role in the affair, Coughlan finished his questioning. However, to mitigate the testimony's damage, Keller needed to redirect the witness.

"After you had gone into the room for the second time and had seen this spot on Simpson's shirt, did you form an opinion as to what had occurred in there?" asked Keller.

"Yes, sir, he told us what had occurred; he said Private Moon had gone down on him."

"And you believed it to be a fact at that time, did you?" pushed Keller.

"Yes, sir."

After a few inconclusive questions about the shape of the outlines of the silhouettes in the dark room, Keller turned questioning over the court, which seemed focused on determining who Hollins had overheard at the canteen. Other questions were asked about his nickname "Old Trapper" and some details of the investigation after the indicants came to light. After that, Hollins was then dismissed, and the court adjourned for the day at 5:45 p.m. and agreed to reconvene at 1:45 p.m. the next day, July 10.

Keller must have spent the evening reflecting on his case. It had seemed pretty straightforward, with two witnesses who admitted to participating in the acts and two who had witnessed at least one of them. Yet, it had probably not gone as well as he had hoped. Despite being witnesses for the prosecution, Ross' and Hollins' testimony did not support the case. Someone was lying, and that certainly did not help. Was Simpson lying about setting a "trap," or were Hollins and Ross lying? Hollins and Ross's testimony rang more truthfully since they had less to lose. They needed no excuse or justification for what happened as they had not been brought up on charges the way Simpson had. But more telling for the historian was what they agreed upon. The encounter witnessed by Ross and Hollins was something that even Simpson admitted was a joke more than a detrimental moral weakness or character flaw. Hollins had indications of what would happen when Simpson asked if he would leave "when the Party's coming down." Yet, there was nothing explicitly negative said. After the act, all accounts suggest that the three "joked" about it. While it certainly was outside the norm of accepted sexual behavior, there was no chastising, marginalizing, or ostracizing the participants. Still, Keller must have hoped the admissions would be sufficient to seal the case against Moon. He decided that the next morning, he would rest his case.

The language Lt. Keller used also reveals a specific conceptual model of Moon's supposed actions that can be illuminated by forensic linguistic analysis. Forensic linguistics, a field often used in legal settings, leverages linguistic techniques like collocation-based concept modeling, sentiment analysis, and pragmatics for valuable insights into language patterns and conceptual meanings behind words, aiding in identifying linguistic associations pertinent to a specific case. It often plays a significant role in enhancing the understanding of language in the context of legal disputes and investigations by revealing insights through examining language evidence, interpreting linguistic nuances, and providing models and patterns related to communication.

In historic court cases, such as Private Moon's, where written and spoken words serve as primary evidence, forensic linguistics has become a powerful tool for unraveling the intricacies of legal discourse. It provides a structured methodology for delving into the language-centric aspects of historic legal narratives, whether uncovering linguistic subtleties in legal arguments, exploring the impact of language on jury perceptions, or revealing a conceptual understanding of psychosocial concepts. Modern computer programs are powerful analytical tools, offering robust data processing and visualization capabilities. As a result, the proper use of forensic linguistics has the potential to contribute not only to a deeper understanding of the linguistic dimensions of the case but also to a more comprehensive historical analysis of how people conceptualized psychosocial phenomena, such as same-sex acts and those who performed them, through language articulation. These models can identify patterns that might be easily overlooked, and traditional qualitative methodologies help the research ask new questions and find meaning in the patterns they reveal.

Even though a historic court-martial lends itself to forensic linguistic analysis, the approach for analyzing the testimony of the participants requires several methodological steps.[45] In the context of the court-martial involving Private Moon, the Orange Data Mining program from the University of Ljubljana (Slovenia) was the primary program to process the text of the court-martial transcripts. The testimony was organized into distinct data sets based on the categories of the witnesses and participants. Adjutant General Lt. Keller's statements and questions formed one data set, while defense counsel Capt. Coughlan's statements and questions constituted another. Witnesses were further categorized based on their military status as enlisted men, non-commissioned officers, commissioned officers, or civilians, each forming their own corresponding data set. The questions asked by the members of the court formed the final set of data.

Prior to analysis, each data set underwent preprocessing using Orange Data Mining, involving the removal of stop words, punctuation, and extraneous information. Stop words, which encompass common grammatical elements like articles, prepositions, and conjunctions, are typically excluded during natural language processing tasks due to their limited meaningful contribution. Their removal allows a more focused analysis of terms that better represent the core content of the text.

Following preprocessing, the data sets underwent tokenization, breaking down the text into individual words. Tokenization, a critical step in text analysis, facilitates effective understanding and processing of textual information by reducing data dimensionality. Tokens representing the semantic meaning of words or sub-words contribute to a more structured interpretation of the text. Using the tokenized data sets, Orange's text mining capabilities extracted collocations or groupings of words often occurring together, revealing significant linguistic and conceptual patterns. Parameters for collocation extraction considered factors such as frequency, mutual information, and point-wise mutual information. The analysis focused on two key parameters: the conceptual understanding of sexual acts described in the case and the conceptual representation of Private Moon by the members of each data set (i.e., officers, enlisted men, non-commissioned officers, etc.).

Orange's data mining tools employing algorithms, like Latent Semantic Analysis (LSA)[46] and Non-Negative Matrix Factorization (NMF),[47] were utilized to create a concept model with hierarchical clustering in addition to collocation, which can identify linguistic patterns or structures within each data set. This model unveiled latent semantic structures within the data sets crucial for recognizing similarities or differences in language and concepts across the different groups of people in Moon's court-martial record. A visual representation of the psychosocial concept models, employing Orange's visualization tools, featured interactive graphs and word cloud visualizations that help identify and visualize key concepts, patterns, and linguistic associations within the text for more qualitative analysis. This comprehensive approach enhances the forensic linguistic analysis, providing a nuanced understanding of the language patterns relevant to the case.

While this method may appear excessively reductive, it should be remembered that linguistic analysis is only a tool and does not provide answers without further evaluation. As a tool, it does serve a valuable purpose in facilitating some additional analysis by identifying and illuminating certain abstractions and possible associations that beg additional qualitative explanation or evaluation. This initial reduction provides a foundational framework that must then be enriched through meticulous qualitative analysis with a re-engagement with the text. This qualitative phase is essential to ensure that the process prevents oversimplification and adequately captures the nuanced interplay of various contextual factors within the complexities of the social system where the concepts were used. Together, the computer-aided analysis helps the researcher see things they may not otherwise notice. Still, only the human researcher can contextualize analyzed data, combining qualitative and quantitative methods for a better understanding of the text.

Examining Lt. Keller's language in the presentation of his case, as well as the cross-examinations of defense witnesses and his closing arguments, are presented in Figure 4.4.

Lt. Keller's language revolved around two discernible paradigms concerning same-sex acts. Firstly, within the domain of more scientific speech, Lt. Keller

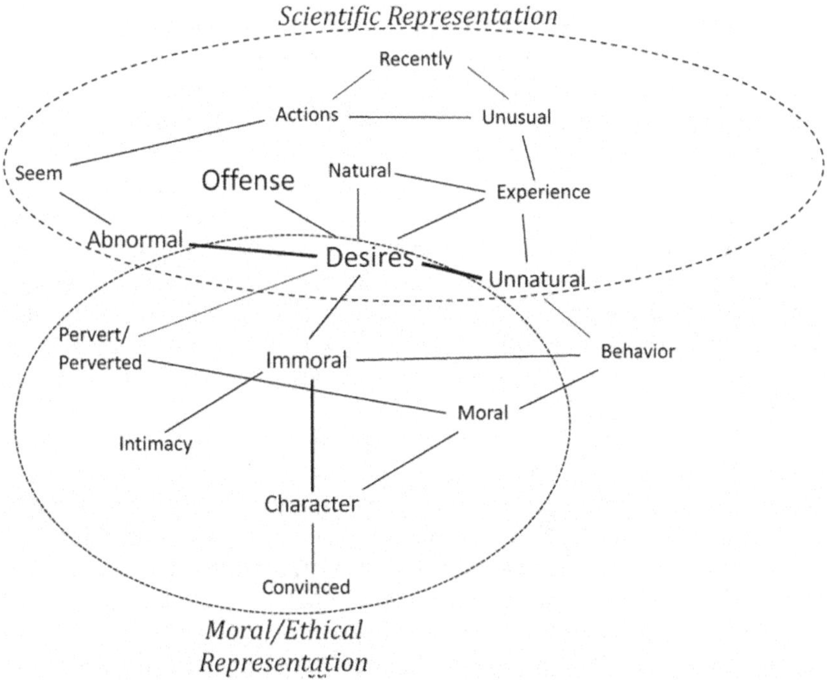

Figure 4.4 Conceptual word cloud of Judge Advocate Keller's presentation of the same-sex acts or "offense" for which Moon was accused. The core concept was presented as his "desires." The forensic analysis indicates that Lt. Keller used two primary paradigms, one "scientific" and the other "moral/ethical" to characterize the acts. The larger the word, the more it was used. The darker the line, the more the connecting words indicate a higher frequency of use together.

Source: Image created by the author.

characterized these acts as "unnatural" or "abnormal," framing his perspective based on observable actions and experiences inherent in the scientific understanding of the time. This scientific discourse categorized same-sex acts as deviations from established "natural" expectations. These "behaviors" indicate they were action-oriented, and he asked questions of his witnesses if they had noticed Moon's "recent" "actions" in this regard and if they "seemed" "abnormal." This reflected an assumed belief grounded in perceived evidence, positioning these acts as departures from what was considered the objective scientific reality at that time regarding what is deemed "natural," "unnatural," or "abnormal." However, it should be remembered that scientific knowledge often draws from contemporary cultural or societal norms that are not always absolute or objective, even if people believed them to be so at the time. What Keller was trying to demonstrate, however, was that Moon's assumed actions were contrary to the natural order, as the members of the court would have understood it in the early 20th century.

In contrast, Lt. Keller also engaged in morally laden speech, scrutinizing same-sex acts through an ethical lens and associating these behaviors with "immorality" and "perversion," thus implicating Private Moon's character traits. Here, the discourse transcended the realm of "nature" to encompass judgments about the inherent moral standing of Private Moon for engaging in such acts. This moral perspective delved into notions of "right" and "wrong," intertwining ethical considerations with personal character. It underscored the profound impact of societal values and norms on shaping moral judgments related to same-sex acts.

Of particular interest is the common thread linking these two distinct conceptual paradigms in Lt. Keller's discourse: the emphasis on "behavior." This served as a crucial bridge between the scientific and moral viewpoints, suggesting a complex interplay between empirical observations and moral judgments in the discourse surrounding same-sex acts. The linkages drawn through behavior highlight the intricate relationship between the perceived objectivity of scientific discourse and the subjective nature of moral judgments, showcasing the multifaceted nature of Lt. Keller's perspective.

Keller's presentation of same-sex acts was specifically directed to the members of the court, and his approach carried a strategy to persuade the officers that Moon's supposed offenses were, in fact, a detriment to military order. By framing same-sex acts as "unnatural" or "abnormal," they might have appealed to jurors who prioritized empirical evidence and dispassionate reasoning and established the premise of the argument through presumed scientific objectivity. Simultaneously, Lt. Keller engaged in morally laden speech, associating same-sex acts with terms like "immorality" and "perversion." This might have resonated emotionally with jurors who held strong moral, religious, or cultural beliefs, aiming to influence their perceptions of Private Moon's character. The morally laden speech, particularly terms like "immorality" and "degeneracy," could evoke emotive responses from the members of the court. Emotional engagement can be a powerful factor in persuasion. By associating same-sex acts with negative character traits and moral standing, Lt. Keller indirectly framed Private Moon's moral and biological character in a way that would impact the court's perceptions.

It is important to note that the effectiveness of Lt. Keller's approach depended on the composition and attitudes of the court. While some members might be more swayed by scientific reasoning, others may be influenced by moral considerations. Many might have been influenced by both in varying degrees. Successful persuasion often involves tailoring arguments to resonate with the diverse perspectives of the court members. His approach would seem to have covered all the proverbial bases.

However, Captain Coughlan's defense of Moon, to be presented the next day, would also exploit the court's attitudes. His approach would focus on not only raising questions about Keller's logical premises but also by presenting his own reasoning about the relationship between masculinity vis-à-vis morality and "natural" sexuality, something that might resonate with the court members who valued a strong, hegemonic masculine ethos.

Notes

1 Testimony Harvey Simpson (hereafter Simpson), General Court-Martial of Private Laurance E. Moon, Martial, Records of the Judge Advocate General, Record Group 153, National Archives and Records Administration, Washington, D.C. (hereafter Moon Court-Martial RG 153, NARA), 19.
2 Simpson, Moon Court-Martial RG 153, NARA, 19.
3 Krafft-Ebing, *Psychopathia Sexualis*, 1.
4 Jeffery Weeks, *The Language of Sexuality* (London: Routledge, 2006), 118.
5 Weeks, *Sexuality*, 19–20, 118; Chauncey, "Christian Brotherhood," 199.
6 Simpson, Moon Court-Martial RG 153, NARA, 19–20.
7 Simpson, Moon Court-Martial RG 153, NARA, 9–10.
8 Simpson, Moon Court-Martial RG 153, NARA, 17.
9 Simpson, Moon Court-Martial RG 153, NARA, 6.
10 Simpson, Moon Court-Martial RG 153, NARA, 6–7.
11 Simpson, Moon Court-Martial RG 153, NARA, 24.
12 Simpson, Moon Court-Martial RG 153, NARA, 7.
13 Simpson, Moon Court-Martial RG 153, NARA, 24.
14 Simpson, Moon Court-Martial RG 153, NARA, 7–8.
15 Simpson, Moon Court-Martial RG 153, NARA, 8.
16 Bronski, *Queer History*, 84–85.
17 Simpson, Moon Court-Martial, RG 153, NARA, 18.
18 Simpson, Moon Court-Martial, RG 153, NARA, 12.
19 Testimony of Joseph Bernard (hereafter Bernard), Moon Court-Martial, RG 153, NARA, 28–29.
20 Testimony of Private Robert J. Allen (hereafter Allen), Moon Court-Martial, RG 153, NARA, 72.
21 Bernard, Moon Court-Martial, RG 153, NARA, 29–30.
22 Bernard, Moon Court-Martial, RG 153, NARA, 31.
23 Bernard, Moon Court-Martial, RG 153, NARA, 30.
24 Norton, *The Myth of the Modern Homosexual*, 8–15; Chauncey, *Gay New York*, 205.
25 Bernard, Moon Court-Martial, RG 153, NARA, 31–32.
26 Bernard, Moon Court-Martial, RG 153, NARA, 33–34.
27 Allen, Moon Court-Martial, RG 153, NARA, 72.
28 Allen, Moon Court-Martial, RG 153, NARA, 73–74.
29 Defense, Closing Argument, Moon Court-Martial, RG 153, NARA, 184.
30 Bernard, Moon Court-Martial, RG 153, NARA, 38.

31 Testimony of George Ross (hereafter Ross), Moon Court-Martial, RG 153, NARA, 39–40.
32 Ross, Moon Court-Martial, RG 153, NARA, 41.
33 Ross, Moon Court-Martial, RG 153, NARA, 41.
34 Ross, Moon Court-Martial, RG 153, NARA, 42.
35 Ross, Moon Court-Martial, RG 153, NARA, 45.
36 Ross, Moon Court-Martial, RG 153, NARA, 53.
37 Testimony of Hughey Hollins (hereafter Hollins), Moon Court-Martial, RG 153, NARA, 54. RG 153, NARA.
38 Bernard, Moon Court-Martial, RG 153, NARA, 34–35.
39 Hollins, Moon Court-Martial, RG 153, NARA, 59–60.
40 Hollins, Moon Court-Martial, RG 153, NARA, 55.
41 Hollins, Moon Court-Martial, RG 153, NARA, 56.
42 Hollins, Moon Court-Martial, RG 153, NARA, 57–58.
43 Hollins, Moon Court-Martial, RG 153, NARA, 57.
44 Hollins, Moon Court-Martial, RG 153, NARA, 58.
45 The methodology was created from two sources: Mohsen Ghasemi Ariani, Fatemeh Sajedi, and Mahin Sajedi, "Forensic Linguistics: A Brief Overview of the Key Elements," *Procedia: Social and Behavioral Sciences* 158 (2014), 222–225 and Malcom Coulthard and Alison Johnson, "An Introduction to Forensic Linguistics: Language in Evidence," *The International Journal of Speech, Language and the Law* 15, no. 2 (2007), 275–280.
46 Latent Semantic Analysis (LSA) is a tool that helps demonstrate how words are related to each other in big blocks of text. It works by looking at how words that mean similar things often show up together and checks patterns where words reside in the text. It uses mathematical representations to create a unique map showing how these words are connected. This map can reveal hidden meanings and help people understand what words conceptualize. See Thomas Lanauer, Peter Foltz, and Darrell Laham, "Introduction to Latent Semantic Analysis," *Discourse Processes* 25, nos. 2–3 (1998), 259–284.
47 Non-Negative Matrix Factorization (NMF) is a process that helps decode large data sets of information. NMF looks at these large sets of words and breaks them down into smaller pieces, finding the main themes or ideas hiding in the text. NMF filters out negative or non-important elements in its process, making it easier for us to understand and determine what is important in the large data set. NMF is helpful in finding key ideas in large data sets. NMF finds applications in document clustering, topic modeling, and feature extraction, offering a way to represent text data in terms of latent semantic structures, revealing meaningful patterns within high-dimensional datasets, providing valuable insights. See Mohamad Hasan Bahari, Najim Dehak, Hugo Van hamme, and Lukas Burget, "Non-Negative Factor Analysis of Gaussian Mixture Model Weight Adaptation for Language and Dialect Recognition," *IEEE/ACM Transactions on Audio, Speech, and Language Processing* 22, no. 7 (2014), 1117–1129.

5 The Case for the Defense

The court reconvened the next day, and Judge Advocate Keller announced that the prosecution rested its case. Lieutenant Keller had made significant progress but left ample material for Captain Coughlan to shape Moon's defense. The character of the key witnesses was likely to be questioned by Coughlan, and Keller's presentation had further opened the door, nearly catching Simpson in a lie. The plan was to undermine not only Simpson's character but also Bernard's, while simultaneously promoting Moon's exemplary reputation among the troop and the officers of the post. Coughlan would emphasize Moon's skills as a soldier, his superior manliness, and his popularity while undermining the credibility of Simpson and Bernard, who possessed none of those qualities.

Coughlan first called Private Robert J. Allen. Allen had been Moon's roommate at the *Shaw and Powell Hotel* in Gardiner when the second encounter with Bernard occurred. In his account of that evening, he and Moon secured their room after the minstrel show, and then, around midnight, he claimed,

> we went down in the red-light district, and it was so crowded there I lost track of him. He was outside dancing. When I came out about an hour later, he was gone, or he might have been there over in one of the other houses. He wasn't in the one I was in.

While Allen was occupied, Moon found him and knocked on the door, asking him to go back to the hotel, but Allen ignored him. "It must have been about 2 o'clock, the last time he knocked on the door and it must have been about half-past two or three o'clock when I got up in the hotel."[1] When he returned, he claimed he saw "Private Bernard and Private Moon in bed sleeping." His account differed only in minor details to that point, but from there, he deviated further by denying that he had gotten in bed with Bernard and Moon. "I lit a cigarette, and then I woke Private Bernard up and told him to go into his own room. . . . Then I took off my clothes and went to bed after Private Bernard went to his bed." This lifted any suspicion of "immoral" activity from himself. He also recounted the next morning's drinking sequence differently from Bernard as well.[2]

Anticipating any potential moral questions about the sleeping arrangements, Coughlan asked: "How is that you went to sleep in a bed with another man?"

DOI: 10.4324/9781003530756-6

Allen replied, "Well, I had the intention of sleeping in another place, but my money ran out, so I had to come back to the hotel."

Coughlan continued, "Is that a common occurrence in Gardiner, for men to go two to a bunk?"

"Yes sir," replied Allen.

"Have you ever slept with him before?" continued Coughlan.

"Yes sir," admitted Allen. Then, Coughlan went to the heart of the issue.

"Have you ever noticed anything abnormal or unnatural about him?" Coughlan was striking at Keller's assumptions about natural sexuality.

Allen replied, "No sir."[3]

"Has the accused ever made any immoral advances towards you?" queried Coughlan along a more moral line.

"No sir."

Coughlan continued, "Did you ever suspect it of him? Did you ever see anything about him being peculiar in this respect?"

Allen countered with, "No, sir. Just found him like an ordinary man." By "ordinary man," Allen clearly meant heteronormative male.

Here the wording used to describe Moon became very evident. Captain Coughlan, an officer, was asking about Moon's essential character. Of course, he hoped that he could elicit responses favorable to Moon when he asked if anything was "abnormal or unnatural about him." Rather than the traditional "unnatural act" of sodomy, he was looking at Moon's whole character. The use of these terms in that way harkens to the growing scientific language used by sexologists and social purity reformers that was slowly creeping into the public's consciousness. Coughlan understood that the other members of the court, all educated officers, were looking at Moon through a lens of the growing influence of these labels that were becoming increasingly accepted in the general culture.

On the other hand, the enlisted men were using very different language. Hollins had heard there was a "cocksucker" in the troop and asked Bernard about it. Simpson, even if his testimony was a little spurious, also called Moon a "cocksucker." The enlisted men were defining Moon more narrowly through an action, "cock sucking," rather than through a broader condition of simply "being" someone who is "abnormal" or "unnatural." If he was "abnormal" or "unnatural" in one way, it was a general assumption about his overall state of being as assumed by the language of the officers.

Clearly, there was a negative connotation to each label and definition, but the "middle class" oriented officers' view of the world differed significantly from the more "working class" enlisted men.[4] The enlisted men seem more interested in a narrow definition that avoided the broader implications of the "unnaturalness" of being beyond the simple act. Using the single act as the moniker for Moon left open the possibility of him being "normal" or acceptable in other ways beyond this particular act. Given Hollins' and Ross' joking after the incident with Simpson, and Allen's possible causal response, there seemed a certain level of tolerance despite the rumors and gossip about it. It would appear there was a continuum of unacceptability. Surely, such acts were outside social norms, eliciting rumors, gossip, and some social discomfort, but not necessarily worthy of ostracism or direct condemnation by other enlisted men.[5]

These linguistic differences reflect the concept of "normal exception" and highlight the value of microhistorical methodology, which focuses on smaller units to reveal the nuanced ways individuals express their lived experiences. By narrowing the scope, microhistory uncovers the complex dynamics of personal relationships within specific settings, showing how behaviors deemed abnormal by broader norms can be normalized within certain groups. There is a clear divide between officers and enlisted men in their constructions of sexuality. The officers, with greater social authority, labeled same-sex acts as "immoral" or "abnormal" character traits, pathologizing these behaviors and linking them to deviance and unfitness for service. In contrast, enlisted men were less rigid, focusing on the act itself – "cock sucking" – without attaching broader moral judgments or strict categorizations. This more flexible view challenged the emerging binary constructions of sexual identity favoring a more queer paradigm. The same act was interpreted through different lenses, depending on one's social position, illustrating how what appeared deviant to one group may have been more acceptable, at least to a degree, for another.

Captain Coughlan then tried to portray Moon as being popular among his comrades, so much so his moral character could not be impinged. He asked Allen the question he would ask other witnesses, all with the same or similar response. "Are you a particular friend of Moon's?" Allen responded that he was. "You still consider Moon worthy of your friendship, do you?"

"Yes sir," replied Allen.[6]

Were the accusations and suspicions about Moon enough to inflict a pariah status upon him? Clearly, the answer was no. Coughlan asked the same question to seven other witnesses, including five sergeants. Sometimes, he made sure to let the court know these men knew what Moon had been charged with by adding the question, "Do you know what he is charged with?" That made no difference. Every witness stated it made no difference in their relationship with him.[7] Even Bernard stated that "Moon always was a good fellow. I never had any trouble with him," and Simpson had claimed, "There is not a man in the troop that thought more of him before this occasion. . . . Even at that, I had nothing against him, only this thing."[8]

In fact, Moon was so popular that members of the troop raised money for his defense. Private Allen noted that he started a subscription to raise money and hire a civilian lawyer to defend him against the charges. "How many men contributed to that?" asked Coughlan.

Allen responded, "I don't know the exact number of men, but we raised fifty dollars," which is about the equivalent of $1280 dollars in 2024.[9] Coughlan pressed on the number of men who contributed, and Allen suggested between 20 and 25, almost a third of the reported strength of Company F at the time.[10] If same-sex acts were seen as a threat to the later army since it would undermine unit cohesion, that did not necessarily seem to be the case with Moon in 1912. Instead, they rallied around the private.

On cross-examination, Lt. Keller focused on details about the exact time in the evening the events occurred, who was in what room and when. He also asked several questions about the next morning's imbibing of whiskey, and especially who drank from the bottle first. Allen was clear that Moon took the first drink. "Why does that stick so plainly in your mind that Moon took the first drink out of that bottle?"

"I just happened to notice it, and it came to mind as soon as he was accused of this thing," responded Allen.

Keller pressed him on other details to which Allen was unclear. Keller challenged him, "You seem to have forgotten everything except that Moon took the first drink out of the bottle. I fail to see how this sticks in your memory."

"It was only natural," said Keller, "because he was accused of a crime later on and I thought of them things that occurred."

The bottle incident was important enough that on the re-direct question, Coughlan wanted to give Allen a chance to clarify. "What was in the bottle you drank out of that morning?"

Allen said, "Whiskey."[11]

Apparently, that answer was sufficient, and Coughlan went in another direction, seeking to clarify the sleeping arrangements to mitigate any hint of impropriety. "In your experience, staying overnight in Gardiner, is it or is it not customary for men to visit around in different rooms?"

"Yes, sir, it is, with the soldiers in the post," confirmed Allen. With that, Coughlan turned the questioning over to the court.

Members of the court continued to press about who drank from the bottle and when. They also asked if Allen had seen Moon in the red-light district with women, which Allen confirmed. One member asked, "What did you think about Bernard being in your room when you came in that night?"

Allen responded, "I didn't think anything of it. I supposed they were drinking and both of them fell asleep."

The questions continued, "Were they both undressed?"

"I didn't notice Private Bernard, but Private Moon just had his shoes off. . . . Both of them were covered up."

"Is there a man in the troop that you know of who has traveled around with the accused more than you have?" asked the court.

"No, sir. I don't think there is."[12] If anyone would have had suspicions, it would have been Allen. After a few more questions by other members about the chronological details and the drinking the next morning, the court concluded its questioning.

Then Captain Coughlan took the defense in an entirely unexpected direction. He decided the best way to prove Moon's sexual desires were "normal" was to call in the local sexual experts. Two prostitutes from Gardiner made the six-mile trek to Fort Yellowstone and testified on Moon's behalf. They were introduced to the court and sworn in. The first to testify was Adelaide Lester. Coughlan asked her occupation. "I am a sporting woman," she answered. Lester had been a practitioner for several years, moving to Gardner after spending time in the copper-smelting town of

Anaconda, where she had gotten herself into trouble by taking $50 from a drunken client.[13] He then established that Moon had visited Gardiner and engaged in what the court would consider "natural" sexual activity between a man and a woman.

Q: Did Private Moon visit you very often?

A: He has visited me several times.

Q: Has he or has he not had sexual intercourse with you?

A: He has.

Q: About how often?

A: Well, every time he was down [in town].

Q: To the best of your recollection, when was the last time?

A: Not so very long before this trouble came up.

Q: During this intercourse, or during your intimacy with him, did you ever notice anything abnormal or unnatural in him towards you or any other person?

A: No, I never did.

Q: Was his intercourse in the natural manner, or otherwise?

A: It was.[14]

The first-hand account that Moon had engaged in "natural" sexual activity was helpful, but it did not establish that Moon had not engaged in "abnormal" sexual acts unless it could be established that a person would not or could not do both. Coughlan asked, "In the red-light district in Gardiner, have you ever heard anything about the accused as to his being abnormal in any way?"

She answered, "No sir, I have not. . . . I was surprised when I heard it."

"Do you know what the accused is charged with?" asked Coughlan.

"I certainly do," responded the sporting woman confidently.

With the fact that Moon had engaged in sex with women established, the Captain then boldly asked for her opinion on the matter, as an expert practitioner, which would establish the foundation that "normal" and "abnormal" sex were mutually exclusive of each other. "In your profession, your occupation," he asked, "you would probably know, or would have heard whether or not degenerate persons of this character ordinarily cohabit with sporting women. Do they do so?" Lester did not quite understand the question, so Coughlan rephrased it. "Do persons of this character, who are what the accused is alleged to be, are they found of women in a natural way?"

The sporting woman answered assertively, "No, I have never heard of such a thing." She added, "I have never heard of a man of that kind would have anything to do with women at all, and I think I have met all kinds of men. I have been out for about seven years now."[15]

In addition to trying to establish the mutual exclusivity of sexual choices, the whole exchange reveals several insights into the mindset of participants. Coughlan uses the words "degenerate" and "character" to describe what "the accused is alleged to be." The move from the previously used "abnormal" and "unnatural," to more distant, scientific, and all-encompassing terms describing the someone who committed these acts as a "degenerate" person, a term that emphasizes more of the negative moral qualities of the whole individual, is quite telling. Especially when tied to the term "character," we see the slow establishment of the presumed negative moral stereotypes associated with people who engaged in same-sex acts or the newly established "homosexual" status of a person.

Keller then cross-examined Ms. Lester. Hoping to show that it was plausible that Moon's desires could have changed, Keller directed her to "State as definitively as you can the last time you had intercourse with [Moon]."

"I could not because I do not know," answered Lester. But Keller's hopes were dashed when she added, "It was just a little while before this trouble came up that he was down." Keller tried to push her to admit it had been a while, but the sporting woman insisted it had been a matter of only a few weeks or months. Keller's questioning was brief, and he turned the witness over to the court. The court asked only a few questions, mostly repeating many of Coughlan's questions about any rumors of Moon, but her testimony remained consistent.

Coughlan next had Myrtle Gregg, another "sporting woman" of nine years, sworn in. She confirmed that she, too, knew "Moony" and had had sex with him, never noticing anything "abnormal or unnatural in him." Coughlan then asked another question, again adding insight into the development and acceptance of the concept of homosexuality. "Do persons of that class have any desires towards women?" People who engage in same-sex activities were now considered part of a "class," a taxonomic social group that, in his previous questioning, was "abnormal," "unnatural," with a "degenerate character."

The sporting woman accepted the premise of the implied understanding of Coughlan's questions and answered only slightly less definitively. "Never that I knew of. I never knew of any. They generally don't like women."

Coughlan also asked if there were any rumors about Moon among the other women, which there were not. As with Ms. Lester, he called upon her expert knowledge of things sexual. "In your experience, have you ever known of a case where a man was attracted to women that was charged with the thing that the accused is charged with?"

She answered firmly, "No sir, I don't think I ever have."[16]

Coughlan then opened the next line of his defense: the discrediting of the prosecution's primary witnesses, especially in comparison to Moon. "Do you know a soldier in this garrison by the name of Simpson?" Ms. Gregg admitted she did. "What sort of man is he when he is drinking?"

"He is pretty rough as a rule," she answered. When asked about Moon's demeanor in town, she replied that "he has been a perfect little gentleman every time I was there."[17] On cross-examination, Keller only asked how long Gregg had worked in Gardiner before turning questioning over to the court. Like their questioning of

Lester, the court pressed Gregg on any rumors about Moon, to which she maintained there were not any. They asked more about her impressions of Simpson. Gregg said she did not "know any rougher or dirtier character in the district than Simpson when he is drinking."[18]

Coughlan then recalled Adelaide Lester back to the witness stand, apparently having forgotten to ask about the character of Simpson and Bernard. He asked her the same questions about them, and she responded: "They usually get drunk every time they come down." So much so that they were

> so disgusting to me when they are drunk that I shut the door [to the crib] and let them go . . . they think they are real smart and I know [Simpson] came in one evening and he wanted me to go to bed with him and I told him all right and I wanted the money and he said "No, the fellow in the next room will pay you," – I think it was George Shearer – and he said "No," he will pay you, and I said "You don't think I am going to anyone else to collect my bills?" So, he got pretty sore at me and never did come to see me anymore.[19]

The "sporting women's" testimony seemed to reinforce the officers' hetero-homo paradigm, embodying a more rigid view of sexuality that aligned with binary classifications. Both groups tended to assume that sexual preference was a zero-sum proposition, believing that individuals could occupy only one position on the spectrum of sexual identity – either heteronormative or deviant – and that their entire character was reflected in these classifications. Interestingly, despite their closer social class affiliation with the enlisted men, these sporting women did not exhibit the same flexible queer understanding of sexuality. This alignment with middle-class officers may have stemmed from the sporting women's desire for social acceptance and legitimacy within a society that often marginalized their identities. By adhering to the moral and sexual norms upheld by the officer class, they may have sought to elevate their status and gain favor in a hierarchical structure that valued traditional concepts of femininity and morality. In contrast, enlisted men placed greater emphasis on the act itself rather than the labels attached to it, allowing for a broader understanding of sexual expression that defied rigid categorizations. This divergence in perspectives can be attributed to the distinct social contexts in which these groups operated.

The next expert witness was Major H.D. Bloombergh, M.D., the post surgeon. The "sporting women" supported the idea that if a person had a same-sex inclination, they would not or could not be attracted to the opposite sex. The recent culture had slowly been adopting that belief and Coughlan had little reason to doubt that the post's physician would suggest anything different. He started with the question, "Major, what is your experience as to sexual perversion?"

Bloombergh hesitated with "Extremely small in both a professional way and from reading." Undeterred, the questioning continued.

"Will you state to the court whether a sexual pervert would be inclined to have his pleasure in the natural manner or not?" Now Coughlan was assuming another state of "being" for people who held same-sex attractions, namely that of a "pervert."

Again, Bloombergh qualified his answer with, "I am inclined to the belief that the sexual pervert secures his gratification in an unnatural way and not as a rule in the natural manner."

Coughlan continued and asked if it was "probable at all that a person could be both, that is, both natural and unnatural in this gratification of his desires?" Finally, Bloombergh, realizing he was definitely out of his depth, answered: "My experience is not sufficient to enable me to give an opinion on that point."[20]

The defense was stumbling, and Coughlan asked no more questions. Judge Advocate Keller seized the moment on the cross-examination. "Do you consider yourself an expert witness in this case?"

Bloombergh answered, "I certainly do not."

Keller then asked that his testimony be stricken from the record as it was merely opinion.

Coughlan tried to salvage the situation by claiming Bloombergh was not called as an expert. Interestingly enough, after a five-minute recess, the court reconvened, allowed the doctor's testimony to stand, and overruled the Judge Advocate's objection.[21] However, Bloombergh's hesitation was striking compared to the testimony of the "sporting women," who spoke with the conviction of experts, never hesitating or qualifying their answers. The physician, on the other hand, qualified and hesitated in all his answers. Even though the idea of the "homosexuality" as a medical condition was only starting to take hold in parts of the scientific community and later accepted in the culture at large, that did not translate into widespread knowledge among all physicians.

Bloombergh's hesitations challenge certain assumptions about the emergence of homosexual identity at the turn of the 20th century. While some historians argue that the medical literature of the late 19th century marked a significant reconceptualization of homosexuality, Moon's court-martial suggests a more nuanced view. Medical discourse, often seen as pivotal in shaping homosexual identities, not only had limited influence on working-class communities of the enlisted men but even on the command's practicing surgeon. He relied more on his own admitted personal beliefs, reinforcing the idea that individuals who engaged in same-sex acts would not necessarily engage in heteronormative acts, which happened to reinforce the "sporting women's" opinion. This contrasts with the Newport Naval Station scandal of 1919, where the sailors believed that individuals could engage in sexual activity with "queers" (which had a negative identity implication at the time) without themselves being or becoming "queer," showing a discrepancy between popular notions and "scientific" knowledge.[22] Given Ross and Hollins' seemingly equivocal statement after Simpson described what happened in the cook's room, this may have been the case with the enlisted men in Troop F as well.

The interplay between the rigid sexual classifications upheld by officers and the more flexible understandings of enlisted men illustrates the value of integrating microhistory and queer theory in historical analysis. By examining the intersectionality of these contrasting perspectives, we can better understand how societal norms shape individual identities and relationships. This approach echoes the foundational works of classic microhistorians like Carlo Ginzburg, whose studies reveal the complexities of individual lives against broader historical contexts, and Judith Brown and Natalie Zemon Davis, who emphasize the nuances of gender and social dynamics in their analyses of ordinary lives. Ginzburg's exploration of the "normal exception" concept, for instance, underscores how seemingly marginal figures illuminate significant historical patterns, while Davis's focus on women's experiences challenges prevailing narratives and highlights the fluidity of identity. Together, these methodologies allow us to appreciate how Moon's case contextualizes sexuality and power dynamics intersect in specific social settings, ultimately enriching our understanding of historical events and the experiences of marginalized groups. This dual framework not only uncovers the nuances of individual experiences but also challenges the binary constructs that have historically shaped our understanding of sexuality, demonstrating the importance of an inclusive and intersectional perspective in historical scholarship.

As the case of the defense progressed, Coughlan's defense strategy then moved on to exactly how and why the charges were brought against Moon while establishing his popularity within the troop, proving his excellent aptitude as a soldier, and firmly establishing and emphasizing his masculinity. Questions would also probe for a motivation of why Simpson would make these accusations against Moon. Coughlan first called upon Private William Bass to testify that there seemed to be a bit of tension in Moon and Simpson's relationship. Bass also noted that Moon was popular and a personal friend, even in light of the charges against him.[23] Private Irvin Harris testified that Moon was helpful and friendly, but one day, Sergeant William Hinshaw warned Harris to stay away from Moon. "All he said to me was to keep away from Private Moon. I tried to find out what it was, but he wouldn't tell me."[24]

When Hinshaw was called to the stand, he confirmed Harris' testimony. A few days before, he had heard from another sergeant about talk among the troops that Moon had engaged in a same-sex act. For reasons unknown, he singled out Harris with a warning to stay away from Moon at the firing range (Figure 5.1). "I just simply told Private Harris that he was to keep away from Moon, that I didn't want him to be seen around with him like he was the day before. This was the second day since I had come into the knowledge of what he has been charged with."[25] The defense counsel then asked Hinshaw if he was a "good friend" of Moon's. Hinshaw replied that he was "merely a troop acquaintance."

"Have your friendly relations undergone any change since the charges have been put against him?" Coughlan asked.

"No sir, none whatsoever," replied Hinshaw.[26]

When Moon heard that Hinshaw had ordered Harris to avoid him, Moon confronted Hinshaw, who would not be specific about his reasons. Moon then asked Hinshaw for permission to go to his commanding officer about the matter. Hinshaw later reflected on this spirit to fight the rumors so passionately and changed his mind about the guilt of Moon.

> I don't know what really did cause me to change my mind, except Moon has been in the troop quite a while, since the fall of 1910, and during all that time

Figure 5.1 Soldiers at the Fort Yellowstone rifle range, date unknown. Maintaining their marksmanship was important for the soldiers. The rifle range was approximately three miles (4.83 kilometers) from the post and one mile from Gardiner.

Source: Photographer unknown, NPS photo 11551.

> I have known him, he has never been any such kind of man, and looking over his actions during all the time he has been in the troop, I couldn't believe it, in fact, I made up my mind then that it wasn't so, and his action in reporting the matter to the Troop Commander himself and wishing to stand trial for it convinced me that an innocent man would take steps to do that.[27]

Under cross-examination, Lt. Keller asked if anything might change Hinshaw's mind about Moon. "I wouldn't change my opinion now unless I actually seen it."[28]

The court then asked questions of the sergeant regarding Moon's accusers, searching for motives of why some soldiers would besmirch the popular Moon. "What do you think of [Simpson] as a soldier?"

Hinshaw answered,

> I don't think he is a reliable soldier at all. He is a good soldier at times when he is not drinking, when he lets it alone entirely, but that is very seldom. . . . He is always using profane language that is of the worst kind. He is about the most foul-mouthed man I ever heard, when he is drinking. Every word he utters is an oath nearly.

The court pressed on. "How is he personally when he is drunk, about his person?"

Hinshaw answered,

> I don't know whether I can call him dirty or not. I can give you an instance. [One night] he had been eating candy and had it smeared over his face, hands, and clothes. . . . He was roaming around quarters all evening, and I had to tell him to go to bed.

They then asked, "He was dirty and disgusting looking that night?"

Hinshaw simply responded, "Yes sir."[29]

If the court itself was looking for a juxtaposition against the clean-cut, popular Moon, they found it in Hinshaw's description of Simpson. Other witnesses, such as First Sergeant Henry Bauder, described Simpson as "an excellent worker" when sober but "doubtful" when he drank, which was very often.[30] Even the troop commander, Captain E. A. Hickman, described Simpson in unflattering terms.

> Private Simpson at all times is a loud-mouthed soldier. He talks incessantly whenever he gets a chance, drunk or sober. He is at times a violent drinker and he is one of the dirtiest drunks I have ever had anything to do with; dirty in person, foul-mouthed, and dirty and low as a human being can get from the effects of liquor. I don't think I have a man in the troop that compares to him for filth when he is drinking. He is a splendid cook when not drinking and does his work well in the kitchen, but every so often I have to take him out of the kitchen and confine him to break up his periods of drunkenness.[31]

Even his "good friend," Sergeant George Ringer, admitted that Simpson "isn't sober very often that I know of, sir, and he is a nuisance when he is drinking. You cannot rely upon him."[32] He added that Simpson had a predilection for "dirty stories and dirty songs and everything is dirty about him."[33]

Bernard's character was more ambiguous. First Lieutenant Jonathan M. Wainwright claimed he would "judge [Bernard] to be a very ordinary soldier, nothing beyond the ordinary."[34] Sergeant Bauder claimed that he had not "had much opportunity to study that man," but Captain Hickman characterized Bernard as "an ignorant foreigner of some kind; I don't know exactly what nationality, but if I were giving him a discharge prior to this present confinement, I would have given him a character of good." This was curious since Bernard was born and raised in Ohio. Hickman continued that "I have known of his being drunk several times, and tried him, I think, within the last three months as Summary Court Officer for absence without leave and drunkenness."[35] While such characterizations were not as utterly negative as Simpson's, they were hardly positive. On the other hand, people saw Private Moon in an overwhelmingly positive light.

The defense called Commissary Sergeant Charles Swanson to testify about Moon's character. A year before the alleged incidents, Moon had worked extra duty with Swanson in the Commissary and actually slept there. Swanson claimed that Moon "performed his duties in an excellent manner." When asked if he ever noticed “anything abnormal or unnatural in his movements,” Swanson said no and added Moon had an

> excellent character, in fact, he is one of the best men I have known in the service in my entire service, which is about twenty-two years. He is efficient, sober, and always attentive to his duties, and performed them cheerfully.

When asked about his honesty, Swanson replied, “I think he is perfectly honest.”[36]

Captain Coughlan called Captain Edwin Hickman, the commander of Troop F, to the stand. However, Hickman was also a member of the court, emphasizing how different a court-martial was from a civilian trial. Hickman, who detailed Moon to the Commissary, added that Swanson

> repeatedly spoke to me of [Moon] being quick to learn and apt in his work, and that he regarded him as an excellent man in connection with his commissary duties. I asked to have him relieved from the Commissary in order to place him in the orderly room and train him as a troop clerk, and he was getting along well in his duties as troop clerk. . . . He seemed to learn quickly anything that was required of him.[37]

He went on to say that he “expected if he made as good a troop clerk [as he was a commissary clerk], to have made him a corporal in the near future.”[38]

Hickman was not alone in his assessment of Moon. First Sergeant Henry Bauder

> found that Private Moon was an excellent man in every respect. He is a model young man, as much as I have had to do with him. In fact, I never saw a better man in my service . . . [he had] always done his duty right up to the handle. Clean and neat in dress and never to my knowledge was reprimanded in the troop. . . . He was always considered as the star of the troop.[39]

In fact, Moon was such a good soldier he was being considered for promotion. The contrast with the foul-mouthed, dirty, and unreliable Simpson could not be more evident.

Swanson, Bauder, and Hickman’s repeated choice of words, that Moon was “an excellent man,” reveals that his masculinity was very much on trial and an essential element of his defense. Part of that display of masculinity was Moon’s athletic prowess. He regularly placed in the troop’s athletic competitions in rings, high jump, long horse, parallel bars, and the lightweight boxing division.[40] As Captain Hickman noted, “[he] probably won as many points as any man for the troop in the athletic line.”[41] The emphasis on this athletic prowess was significant since by the late 19th-century athletics in schools, colleges, and the military was used to instill masculine qualities and allow public displays of it in a form of Darwinistic competition for others to admire and emulate.[42]

At the same time, Moon’s recent performance just before the trial had slipped from the previous competition. The court asked First Sergeant Bauder, “did you notice any marked change in Private Moon's condition as an athlete along about just before the meet? A falling off in his form?" The question seems to imply that if his athletic performance had fallen off, then his masculinity would have as well, leading to the possibility that the charges against him may, in fact, be true. Perhaps they were implying there was a germ or disease theory of the moral depravity of same-sex acts. Maybe they implied that Moon had "become" morally or even physically "sick." Bauder confirmed that recently Moon "wasn't as well developed as he was the year previously." However, he provided the more practical explanation that it "was on account of the man being on extra duty [in the commissary and then the orderly room] and he didn't have the time to take exercise and train himself up for the meet." The court pressed the issue. "Did you notice any marked change at any time while he was preparing for the meet this year, a falling off in his development, a loss of interest just before the meet?" Bauder replied, "No sir. It always seemed to me that he took the same interest."[43] Captain Hickman had concurred and took responsibility for Moon's lower form.

> His form was not as good as it had been in the previous meets, but in my opinion, that was due solely to the fact that I was not able to get him for practice. He was in the Commissary and he couldn't get off regularly. There was certainly nothing in his form that would show a lack of moral or physical stamina other than lacking the practice.[44]

Hickman tied Moon's athletic ability to his morality. Physical displays of masculinity demonstrated moral superiority in Hickman's mind.

Having established that Moon was an exemplary soldier who was morally upstanding and that at least one of his accusers was morally questionable, the defense then tried to find the motivation for why Moon was accused of these acts. Captain Coughlan asked Captain Hickman:

> From your experience as an officer serving with troops, have you ever noticed that good soldiers who attend to their duties properly, who were decent, were the object of taunts and jeers from the worthless members of the command?. . . Would you consider that as a motive for the charges against the accused at present?

Hickman responded that Moon was so talented that even though he was on the fast track to promotion, it did not create jealousy in the troop.

> [I]t has occurred to me that the prominence that the accused has attained from the day he was a recruit up until the time he was finally placed in the orderly room might have engendered the ill-will or jealousy of other members of the troop who were not as quick and apt as he is, or members of the troop who had had considerable more service than he has had, which is a bare possibility, as a means of creating some dislike against him. I saw no evidence of that, . . . He did undoubtedly receive considerable recognition by being placed on extra duty in the Commissary Department, giving him practically a

> sergeant's pay. He was a prominent figure in the troop in all entertainments at the post and the athletic meets, and he stepped from the Commissary Department into the troop orderly room as a clerk with the knowledge, I think, pretty well abroad in the troop that he was to be made a non-commissioned officer in the near future.[45]

Keller could make little headway in his cross examination of the witnesses who all claimed Moon was exemplary in both character and military skill. The pinnacle of the defense came when Moon took the risky move of testifying on his own behalf to vehemently deny all the incidents.

Moon started by recounting the day at the shooting range when Harris told him that Sergeant Hinshaw had told Harris to stay away from him. Moon gave his impression of Sergeant Hinshaw's, First Sergeant Bauder's, and First Lieutenant Keller's reactions as he moved up the chain of command to squelch the rumors, which he claimed he still did not know the substance of. He only found out about the accusations the next day when he was confined to the guardhouse by Lieutenant Keller.[46]

Next, Moon recounted the supposed first encounter with Simpson. He was working in the Orderly Room when Captain Hickman sent him to get menus from the kitchen. Earlier in the day, he told Simpson that he would also get some bills of fares (the receipts for provisions). Around 7 or 8 p.m., Simpson came into the room and said, "I got those bills of fare now if you want them."

Moon rose and went with Simpson to the kitchen. Along the way, Simpson offered Moon some canned pineapples. "I'll have some pineapple," Moon replied, "but don't bother to open any."

"I have some open," Simpson claimed.

Simpson went through the kitchen to the cook's room, where he put a bowl of pineapple on a chair. The two sat on the bunk and started chatting. Suddenly, Simpson poured something in the bowl and said, "That will make a good chaser."

"I don't want to drink too much," quipped Moon, "as Sergeant Bauder would smell my breath and I would have to report where I got the whiskey." Simpson minimized the danger and started to question Moon about things in the Orderly Room and some of the summary (or minor) courts-martial within the troop. Moon said he was not allowed to discuss such things. Simpson pressed Moon for information while also pushing Moon to drink the whiskey. Moon stood to leave when, unexpectedly, there was some rustling at the door. Simpson opened a drawer and quickly turned out the light. A couple of people came in, Moon could not see who, and Simpson told them to leave. Moon left the room and glancing back, he could see with light from the open door into the kitchen. Simpson closed the drawer and grabbed some menus. Moon walked by Hollins and Ross, who were sitting at the table in the kitchen.[47]

When Moon returned to the Orderly Room, First Sergeant Bauder told him to type a cleaner muster roll, which would take about an hour. Moon looked at his watch; it was approximately 8:05, which meant he had only been with Simpson for about 5 minutes. Moon also decided not to report Simpson for the whiskey because

"I wasn't certain of this man's intentions." He was also worried about his reputation in the troop and that the "men would ridicule me as they I know I do drink," and to report Simpson would seem very hypocritical.[48]

Moon then talked about the supposed incident on the road from Gardiner. He and a group were returning from town when Moon and Bernard, only acquaintances at best, started a conversation about Bernard's family. Bernard began to struggle, and Moon tried to help him by running with him. He said he was only trying to help,

> Because I seen he was in that condition [ie-falling down drunk] . . . and I tried to run him a little while on the road to sober him up . . . I saw no one else attempt to do it [help him], and it was just kindness on my part, just as I would for anyone else.[49]

The incidents in the hotel room were complete fabrications, as was the supposed second incident at Simpson's bunk. He could find no reason why Simpson or Bernard would make such accusations.[50]

On cross-examination, Judge Advocate Keller probed Moon's story, looking for inconsistencies. He questioned why Moon was in Simpson's room, how long he was there, and, most importantly, why it was dark. "What did [Simpson] put [the light] out for?"

"I don't know, sir," answered Moon. "He grabbed the bottle (of whiskey) and switched the light out all of a sudden."

"What did you think he did it for?"

"I don't know, sir," insisted Moon. "I thought perhaps he was hiding the whiskey there and that someone was coming in to reprimand him."[51]

Keller probed details about where Moon was in the room, what Simpson was wearing, whether Moon could see who came in the room, and other details, which Moon answered in as innocuous a way as possible. Keller then wanted clarification on Moon's popularity in the troop and why Simpson and Bernard would say these things if they were not true. Moon continued to plead ignorance; he simply did not know why.[52]

When Keller was done, the court members took their turns asking questions. One member asked, "Has Cook Simpson told a dirty lie about you?" to which Moon responded, "Yes, sir." The court then challenged Moon's masculinity on the issue. "Has it ever occurred to you to thrash him? . . . Why have you not done that?"

Moon, claiming to be the virtuous soldier, preferred good order. "Because I didn't want to put myself into any trouble, sir."[53]

Like Keller, some members sought details to find any inconsistencies. They asked about the order of events for the various incidents, everyone's level of sobriety, and why the lights were turned out in the cook's room. Moon insisted he did not know. "I thought he was doing it to hide the whiskey and that he was afraid that someone would come in there and reprimand him," Moon again answered.

"Did he make an unnatural proposition to you?" asked a court member.

"No, sir. I had no conversation with him, only about the drinking, about the pineapple, about the Orderly Room, and the charges."

"Did you ever have any reason to suppose that Cook Simpson would permit any person to commit an immoral act on his person?"

"No, sir," answered Moon.[54]

After more questions about the details of the road between Gardiner and the post, the court excused Private Moon. Given that it was 5:30 p.m., the court adjourned for the evening and agreed to reconvene at 1:45 p.m. the next day.

The forensic analysis of Captain Coughlan's defense, cross-examinations, and closing arguments reveals that his strategy took a nuanced approach in relation to Lt. Keller's assertions about same-sex acts (Figure 5.2). Rather than outright challenging the scientific and moral premises put forth by Lt. Keller, Coughlan acknowledged and seemed to accept these premises as the core conceptualization. However, his defense extended these assumptions by introducing an observable performative aspect that could be challenged, especially given Private Moon's widely positive masculine behaviors and reputation. This addition implied that there might be a theatrical or visible element to same-sex acts that would be contradictory to contemporary hegemonic masculine behaviors, introducing a layer of complexity but one that could be observed, reported on, and potentially contradicted by the witnesses.

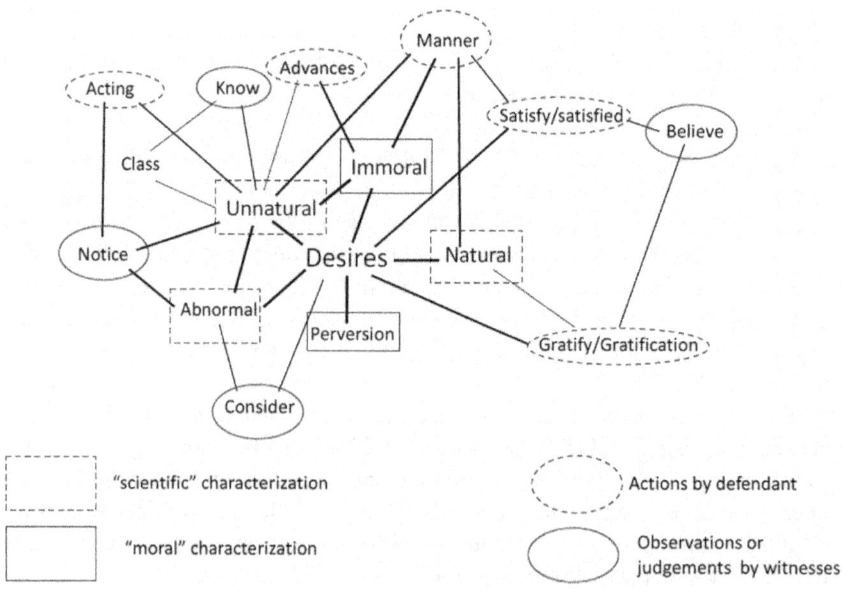

Figure 5.2 Conceptual word cloud of Captain Coughlan's presentation of the same-sex acts or offenses for which Moon was accused. The core concept was presented as his "desires." The forensic analysis indicates that Coughlan accepted Lt. Keller used two primary paradigms, "scientific" and "moral/ethical," to characterize the acts but extended them to presumed actions that could be observed and judged by the witnesses. The larger the word, the more it was used. The darker the line, the more the connecting words indicate a higher frequency of use together.

Source: Image created by the author.

The language model suggests Captain Coughlan's questions directed the witnesses' attention to these observational aspects. They were asked to state whether they "noticed" Private Moon's actions ("manners," "advances," or "acting") mainly in the more scientific language value ("abnormal" or "unnatural," with the implied meaning of "unmasculine"). However, he did not wholly neglect the moral elements ("immoral," also with the implied meaning "unmasculine"). This approach sought to ground the bulk of the discourse in objective evidence and eyewitness accounts, aiming to provide a more tangible representation of Moon. However, certain observable actions by the Moon might span both scientific and moral language. Moon's "manner" could be either "natural" or "immoral." He could also make an "immoral" or "unnatural" sexual "advance" to another.

The testimony of the "sporting women" supported his case. The alignment of the two prostitutes' testimony with the officers' rigid heteronormative perspective, despite their working-class status, reflects broader social dynamics. Although they operated on society's margins and willfully violated them, they were still influenced by dominant late Victorian moral frameworks, which shaped views on sexuality. By supporting this binary in their testimony, these women reinforced their position within prevailing norms, distancing themselves from the stigma attached to same-sex acts. Gender expectations and respectability politics also shaped their responses. Even as marginalized figures, they faced pressure to conform to societal norms in a public legal setting. Aligning with heteronormative ideals allowed them to maintain a degree of legitimacy and avoid association with Moon's alleged deviance.

Finally, their testimony reflects broader efforts to gain respectability and navigate class mobility. Though their profession placed them outside acceptable norms, adopting more mainstream views on sexuality helped preserve[55] or improve their standing. This shows the complex interplay between survival, respectability, and conformity to dominant norms, even for those at society's fringes. Their testimony demonstrates how class, gender, and societal pressures shaped views on sexuality in the military. It also reveals how marginalized individuals navigated these dynamics by aligning with dominant perspectives to maintain credibility and avoid exclusion.

Additionally, Captain Coughlan navigated the moral dimension by asking witnesses to make judgments about what they "considered" or "knew" about Moon's actions. The hypothetical judgments presented to Dr. Bloombergh about what he "believed" were the ways certain people "satisfied" or "gratified" sexual desire again begged the question of judgment on actions. Questioning the actions of Private Moon, whom witnesses nearly universally claimed were "normal," was an attempt to highlight the subjectivity inherent in moral assessments of his actions. Since Moon was well known to be a good soldier who displayed a well-regarded masculine ethos, the questions of morality were begging for a negative response to reinforce his moral character. Science and morality are not necessarily independent, but by intertwining scientific, performative, and moral aspects, Captain Coughlan crafted a defense strategy that sought to bring clarity and positive interpretations of Moon's physical and moral character into the discourse, raising doubts in the court's mind as to Moon's ability to commit such acts. The defense witnesses portrayed Private Moon in an overwhelmingly positive way. Captain Coughlan must have felt confident about his case so far.

Notes

1 Testimony of Private Robert Allen (hereafter Allen), General Court-Martial of Private Laurance E. Moon, 73. RG 153, NARA.
2 Allen, Moon Court-Martial RG 153, NARA, 70–72.
3 Allen, Moon Court-Martial RG 153, NARA 72–73.
4 For more discussion on how the discourse about homosexuality was affected between middle-class education and working-class realities, see Norton, *The Myth of the Modern Homosexual*, 19–28.
5 Even in other contexts in the West and especially the army in the West, working-class and enlisted men could have sex with other men without gaining pariah status based on certain cultural factors. Peter Boag, "Sexuality, Gender, and Identity in Great Plains History and Myth," *Great Plains Quarterly* 18, no. 4 (Fall 1998), 335.
6 Allen Moon, Moon Court-Martial RG 153, NARA, 81.
7 Testimony of Private Robert McAleer (hereafter McAleer), Moon Court-Martial RG 153, NARA, 85; Private Irvin Harris (hereafter Harris), Moon Court-Martial RG 153, NARA, 103; Private William Bass (hereafter Bass), Moon Court-Martial RG 153, NARA, 106–107; Sergeant William Hinshaw (hereafter Hinshaw), Moon Court-Martial RG 153, NARA, 108–109; Sergeant Charles Swanson (hereafter Swanson), Moon Court-Martial RG 153, NARA, 126–127; Sergeant Henry Bauder (hereafter Bauder), Moon Court-Martial RG 153, NARA, 131–132; Sergeant George Ringer. (hereafter Ringer), Moon Court-Martial RG 153, NARA, 175.
8 Testimony of Private Joseph Bernard (hereafter Bernard), Moon Court-Martial RG 153, NARA, 36; Testimony of Private Harvey Simpson (hereafter Simpson), Moon Court-Martial RG 153, NARA, 12.
9 Allen, Moon Court-Martial RG 153, NARA, 80–81; For monetary conversion, see http://www.in2013dollars.com/1912-dollars-in-2023?amount=50.
10 Allen, Moon Court-Martial RG 153, NARA, 81.
11 Allen, Moon Court-Martial RG 153, NARA, 74, 76.
12 Allen, Moon Court-Martial RG 153, NARA, 76–78.
13 "Miss Lester Discharged," *The Anaconda Standard* (Anaconda, MT), September 14, 1907, 9.
14 Testimony of Adelaide Lester (hereafter Lester), Moon Court-Martial RG 153, NARA, 86–87.
15 Lester, Moon Court-Martial RG 153, NARA, 88–89.
16 Testimony of Myrtle Gregg (hereafter Gregg), Moon Court-Martial RG 153, NARA, 89–92.
17 Gregg, Moon Court-Martial RG 153, NARA, 92.
18 Lester, Moon Court-Martial RG 153, NARA, 90.
19 Gregg, Moon Court-Martial RG 153, NARA, 92.
20 Testimony of H. D. Bloombergh (hereafter Bloomberg), Moon Court-Martial RG 153, NARA, 100–101.
21 Bloombergh, Moon Court-Martial RG 153, NARA, 101.
22 Chauncey, "Christian Brotherhood," 204.
23 Bass, Moon Court-Martial RG 153, NARA, 106–107.
24 Harris, Moon Court-Martial RG 153, NARA, 103.
25 Hinshaw, Moon Court-Martial RG 153, NARA, 108.
26 Hinshaw, Moon Court-Martial RG 153, NARA, 111.
27 Hinshaw, Moon Court-Martial RG 153, NARA, 111–112.

28 Hinshaw, Moon Court-Martial RG 153, NARA, 112.
29 Hinshaw, Moon Court-Martial RG 153, NARA, 121.
30 Testimony of First Sergeant Henry Bauder (hereafter Bauder), Moon Court-Martial RG 153, NARA, 130.
31 Testimony of Captain E. A. Hickman (hereafter Hickman), Moon Court-Martial RG 153, NARA, 139.
32 Ringer, Moon Court-Martial RG 153, NARA, 176.
33 Ringer, Moon Court-Martial RG 153, NARA, 176.
34 Testimony of First Lieutenant Jonathan M. Wainwright (hereafter Wainwright), Moon Court-Martial RG 153, NARA, 121.
35 Bauder, Moon Court-Martial RG 153, NARA, 134; Hickman, Moon Court-Martial RG 153, NARA, 139.
36 Swanson, Moon Court-Martial RG 153, NARA, 126–127.
37 Captain E. A. Hickman, General Court-Martial of Private Laurance E. Moon, 137. RG 153, NARA.
38 Hickman, Moon Court-Martial RG 153, NARA, 137–138.
39 Bauder, Moon Court-Martial RG 153, NARA, 131–132.
40 Bauder, Moon Court-Martial RG 153, NARA, 138.
41 Bauder, Moon Court-Martial RG 153, NARA, 138.
42 Nye, "Western Masculinities in War and Peace"; Bungaard, *Muscle and Manliness*, 109; Oriard, *Reading Football.*
43 Bauder, Moon Court-Martial RG 153, NARA, 135.
44 Hickman, Moon Court-Martial RG 153, NARA, 142.
45 Hickman, Moon Court-Martial RG 153, NARA, 138–139.
46 Hickman, Moon Court-Martial RG 153, NARA, 145.
47 Hickman, Moon Court-Martial RG 153, NARA, 146–147.
48 Hickman, Moon Court-Martial RG 153, NARA, 147–148.
49 Testimony of Laurance E. Moon (hereafter Moon), Moon Court-Martial RG 153, NARA, 158, 169.
50 Moon, Moon Court-Martial RG 153, NARA, 149–151.
51 Moon, Moon Court-Martial RG 153, NARA, 153–154.
52 Moon, Moon Court-Martial RG 153, NARA, 158–160.
53 Moon, Moon Court-Martial RG 153, NARA, 168.
54 Moon, Moon Court-Martial RG 153, NARA, 161–165.
55 Michael Foucault, *The History of Sexuality: An Introduction, Volume I* (Vintage Books, 1990), 24–27, 38–40; Judith R. Walkowitz, *Prostitution and Victorian Society: Women, Class, and the State* (Cambridge: Cambridge University Press, 1982), 11–73.

6 Closing Arguments and Deliberations

On the next and final day of the court-martial, Friday, July 12, the defense called only two witnesses, Private William Smith and Sergeant George Ringer. The questions for both centered around the character of Privates Simpson and Bernard, reinforcing previous testimony that Simpson was an untrustworthy, chronic drinker and that Bernard was an equally unreliable soldier, both of whom must have been jealous of Moon's good reputation. Sergeant Ringer, who characterized himself as a "friend" of Simpson's despite his shortcomings, believed that the verbose Simpson merely "started [a rumor] and it got beyond his control; it spread so in the troop, someone took hold of it, and he had to stick to his story." When asked why he would continue to support his story, Ringer responded, "It should have showed up in the troop what kind of man he was, spreading them kind of rumors." Both Smith and Ringer claimed to remain good friends with Private Moon despite the charges brought against him.[1] With that, the defense rested its case.

The court president then asked Captain Coughlan if he would like to make a final statement when submitting his case. In the introduction to his closing comments, Coughlan started by discrediting the key witnesses for the prosecution while reminding the court of Moon's stellar reputation:

> Mr. President: from the nature of the testimony given in this case, it will not be necessary for me to spend much time in argument. The basis of the prosecution rests entirely on the unsupported testimony of two witnesses, Simpson and Bernard, both of whom acknowledge having been drunk during the occasions of the election commission of the offenses. Their testimony in this respect was only plainly corroborated but nearly all of the witnesses for the defense and the prosecution. This fact in itself is sufficient to adjudge them unworthy of belief about anything connected with the case. The witness, Simpson, has shown to be a confirmed drunkard, a course, foulmouthed individual, and drunk or drinking nearly all the time. Is it any wonder that such a vile imputation against a clean, upright, and manly soldier emanates from him? The witness, Bernard, is also a habitual and interpret user of intoxicants, and his disregard of his duty is only plainly a matter of record.[2]

DOI: 10.4324/9781003530756-7

Coughlan then reminded the court of an incident involving a Private Knight, someone apparently rumored to have performed heterosexual oral sex on a prostitute in Gardiner. Even with that case, Coughlan could build on Moon's reputation to face the investigation and court-martial:

> During the testimony here, an almost parallel case has cropped out, or practically the same imputation was launched against a member of the command by the idle words of a prostitute in Gardner, Montana. The unfounded rumors were floating around until they were crushed by a member of his organization. But here, the accused, at the first information, estimated investigation in order that he might face his accusers and be justified in a fitting manner by the law.[3]

Coughlan's comparison of Knight's "parallel case" of heterosexual oral sex reveals an interesting vision of how Moon's case was viewed. The fact Moon performed oral sex on people of the same sex was perhaps not the only "immoral" element of his actions. The non-procreative act was perhaps as equally damning as was the growing societal anxiety of same-sex acts.[4]

Coughlan then summarized his case with eight enumerated and detailed summaries that continued to discredit the prosecution's key witnesses and promote Private Moon. Some of the inconsistencies with the actual testimony were small. Still, clearly, Coughlan hoped that taken together and in conjunction with other evidence would effectively juxtapose the good reputation of Moon with the seemingly unreliable characters of Simpson and Bernard:

The attention of the court is invited:

1. To the statement of Simpson that he, with Hollins, set a trap to catch the accused, when as a matter of fact, Hollins does not claim any knowledge of such a pact.
2. Simpson's statement that Hollins had several drinks that day or evening, while Hollins states positively that he did not have a drink that day or evening.
3. The statement to Hollins by Simpson when the former entered the room with Ross to catch the accused: "Don't come in on me like that, old trapper," while Hollins states that Simpson's words were "get out, old trapper, I am sleeping." Had Simpson laid a trap to catch the accused, why should he, himself, block any attempt at the disclosure of wrongdoing, by his own words, or why should his two scouts, Hollins and Ross, neglect such an opportunity by failure to switch on one of the electric lights in the room? The prosecution has failed to show that either Hollins or Ross saw the accused in Simpson's room that night, even after the alleged plans of Simpson and Hollins to accomplish that very thing.
4. Attention is also invited to the statement of Bernard that there was no light in the room where he and the accused of sleeping upon the entrance of the Private Allen. The latter states the light was on, and also the curtains up, on the big window in the room, which was situated on the ground floor and in plainview from the sidewalk.

5. The positive statement of Bernard that he did not drink from the same bottle after the accused the next morning, and the likewise positive statements of Private Allen that he did do so.
6. The statement of Bernard that after the election commission of the offense, he avoided the accused when he admitted later that he had danced with the accused in the gymnasium. What a closer contact or what closer expression of intimacy could be wished for to show unbroken friendship in view of the nature of the charges.
7. Bernard's statement to Sergeant Hinshaw after the date of the legend commission of the offense that he, Bernard, knew of no wrongdoing on the part of the accused. With reference to the statement of Bernard that he was so drunk that he did not know what he was doing during the legend commission of the offense is against him by the accused, and in view of the discrepancies in his testimony, cited above, it is a wonder that any creams at all should be placed in his testimony. With regard to the latter, attention is invited to the testimony of Lieutenant Wainwright, Judge Advocate of the General Court, that tried Bernard in 1911 for being off post. The former stated that, to the best of his recollection, Bernard was sworn in on his own behalf. His plea was "not guilty." The outcome of the trial was acquittal for Bernard. It is clear that the latter, under oath, made such statements as to his innocence of the charge that the court found him "not guilty." After the trial, stung with remorse, he informed Sergeant Bergdahl that he had been off post and Sergeant Bergdahl, according to the troop commander, was a soldier of excellent character. I repeat, should the testimony of Bernard be considered at all in this case?
8. Attention is invited to the statement of Bernard against the accused of the occurrence on the road between Gardiner, Montana, and the post. You all know that this distance is about 5 miles. Now consider the time of year, which is given as about March 2, the middle of the night, the thermometer down around zero, the ground covered with snow. Is it reasonable to suppose that anyone would choose an occasion of this cone for the gratification of his desires, or would it be physically impossible?

   So much for the two witnesses concentrating the entire fabric of the prosecution.[5]

If the testimony of the prosecution's key witnesses were discredited and Moon's positive reputation established, Coughlan then moved to establish the premise that it would be impossible for someone with Moon's upright character to have committed such "unnatural" and "immoral" acts. First, even though his own witness actually faltered on the stand, he called upon Dr. Bloomberg's testimony:

> With reference to the testimony of Major Bloombergh, the post surgeon, on sexual perversion, the testimony of all concerned, in the matter of the gratification of desires in the normal and abnormal or unnatural male adult, were such an individual in existence, that is, who satisfied his desires in the natural way and then desired abnormalities in this respect, you were nothing short of a sexual monstrosity and a fit subject for exhibition in a medical museum.[6]

This might have been a valiant attempt to salvage Dr. Bloombergh's testimony since the surgeon was much less definitive than Coughlan suggested. Did he truly believe the court would not remember the surgeon's faltering and indefinite responses? Or was he trying to provide a sliver of rhetorical evidence that would give the court just enough to add to their own confirmation bias that people who seek their "gratification" one way cannot find it another? Nonetheless, Coughlan was playing on the general assumption that sexual attraction and gratification was a binary hetero-homo model, discarding any possibility of a more queer spectrum, so much so that they would have been considered "a sexual monstrosity." The moral implications were evident as well. Heteronormative, procreative sex was "natural" and therefore "moral," while same-sex, by definition non-procreative, was "unnatural" and therefore "immoral," and those who may have desires to engage in it as well as heteronormative pleasure were a hyperbolic monstrosity.

Coughlan then reminded the court of Moon's exemplary moral character and behavior in the face of these unpleasant charges by the witnesses already deemed unreliable at best:

> In connection with the defense, special attention of the court is invited to the conduct and actions of the accused when the rumors of his alleged immoral acts reached his ears. He immediately informed his First Sergeant and requested an investigation, not only from the latter but from his troop and post commander. Had the accused been guilty of what he is charged, it is only reasonable to infer that he would've attempted to desert during the three or four days after the investigation while he still had his liberty.[7]

For good measure, Coughlan wanted again to cast doubt on the details of Simpson's account, possibly to establish his generally poor character:

> First Sergeant Bauder testified that on the ninth, the accused went to Simpson's room for his bills of fare and that he, the accused, was absent from the orderly room for five or 10 minutes. Consider the time employed and going in from the orderly room to Simpson's room and return and see whether or not it were physically possible for the commission of this act in the short space of time without detection. The accused returned and worked in the orderly room until midnight.[8]

Surely, the court would question why Simpson and Bernard would allege such actions against the upright Moon. Having established that Simpson and Bernard were not reliable witnesses with questionable characters at best, Coughlan went on to suggest that their petty jealousy of Moon's exemplary service would drive them to besmear his good name while allowing him to take more verbal shots at the witnesses:

> The motive for the imputation of this unnatural crime against the accused is close at hand. Rumors circulated in idle and maudlin moments from unclean minds and foul mouths of Simpson and Bernard had gained such headway

> that the latter, alarmed at the prospect of standing trial and the consequences for the defamation of a man's character, sought protection in charging the accused directly with a crime in the hope of his conviction.[9]

As he reached his conclusion, he wanted to remind the court of Moon's stellar character once again. He called not only upon his reputation among the men in his troop and the non-commissioned officers but also upon the testimony of Moon's troop commander, who was also, not incidentally, a member of the court deciding Moon's fate:

> From the testimony of Captain Hickman, Sergeant Bauder, post commissary Sergeant Swanson, and others, it is readily seen that Private Moon is an excellent soldier, obedient, honest, upright, and truthful; an all-around athlete, and as the First Sergeant states: "the star of the troop." Notwithstanding the present immoral imputation, still retaining the trust and friendship of the best men in the troop.[10]

Coughlan used the masculine language of the time to describe Moon's character. How could an athletic and "excellent soldier," who was "obedient, honest, upright and truthful," commit these acts? He was an "all-around athlete," clearly demonstrating his positive morality and masculinity. If actions reveal character, Coughlan was suggesting Moon could not commit anything but moral and natural acts. But before he closed, he took one more swipe at the prosecution's key witnesses, just for good measure.

> Contrast these excellent attributes with the aforementioned characteristics of Simpson and Bernard, having well in mind the testimony of their troop commander, and the counsel will not be afraid of a finding unfavorable to the accused.
>
> The accused, through his counsel, desires to thank the court for the careful consideration given to his case. He leaves his case in the hands of the court.[11]

With that, Captain Coughlan sat down. The court President asked the Judge Advocate if he would like to summarize his case. Having the final word gave the Judge Advocate an advantage since Lieutenant Keller's arguments would be the last thing the court would hear before they began their deliberations. However, Keller must have realized that Coughlan had landed a few severe blows that he would need to address. The defense only needed to raise questions rather than form a fully cohesive argument, and Coughlan certainly had raised questions. But the biggest questions were about the character of the people involved more than the actions that brought Moon to trial. Lieutenant Frank Keller would need to engage in some serious damage control before he could summarize his case. With that in mind, the Judge Advocate rose and addressed the court:

> May it please the court: the Judge Advocate submitting this case desires to make a brief review of the evidence before the court and also to take

> exception to numerous statements included in the address by the counsel, which were not substantiated by evidence.[12]

First was the damage control. Coughlan must have raised some seriously concerning points about Simpson and Bernard's reputations for drunkenness in the era of temperance moving to prohibition, for that was where Keller felt the need to start:

> The statement of the counsel in his address that drunkenness was admitted on the part of Private Simpson is, in my opinion, unsubstantiated by evidence. All who saw him stated, and he testified before the court, that he was not drunk on this occasion; some stated he had been drinking, and the accused himself on the witness stand stated that Simpson was not intoxicated and knew nothing about his drinking.
>
> The evidence before the court to show that Bernard was drinking on the occasions that have been testified to does not indicate that he was intoxicated on April 20, 1912; that was also testified to by the accused himself.[13]

With a weak transition at best, Keller tried to pivot the court's attention from his key witnesses suggested moral shortcomings to Moon's. Coughlan, calling upon the wide-ranging testimony of soldiers and officers at the post, had effectively built a positive image of Moon that Keller would need to counter. If Coughlan used positive masculine terms to describe Moon's character, Keller tried to question that very masculinity by reframing Moon's actions, or more accurately, his inactions, again calling upon the rumors of Private Knight's heterosexual oral sex:

> I might refer to the similar charges made against another man of this troop at the same time, which has been brought before this court, and referred to in testimony, that a Private Knight. I wish to draw a contrast between the way that matter was handled and the way the present case was handled. The rumor was started, as stated by the counsel for the accused, by a prostitute. The prostitute was one of the witnesses for the defense, and it would not seem to be becoming to impeach his own witness. However, Knight, who is not supposed to be an athlete, squelched all these charges with a solid thrashing, and nothing more has been said about it, and counsel tries to make a contrast with an athletic young star, who allows such charges to go on in the troop by his physical inferiors.[14]

Given Keller's own history of fighting at West Point to toughen up a cadet who was seen as lacking the ideal masculine, giving someone "a solid thrashing" was a natural touchpoint to prove one's masculinity. Given the culture at West Point at the time and the fact that most of the officers on the court were tied to the academy and its culture, Keller could reasonably assume that this would at least open the possibility in their minds that Private Moon might not quite be the paragon of manhood that Coughlan suggested, even if he was more athletic and "physically superior." However, in so doing, Keller also tacitly acknowledged that the court would assume physical prowess was generally considered a "moral" virtue.

After that, Keller returned to reforming the reputation of one of his key witnesses, Bernard, again, this time in more detail:

> With reference to the testimony before the court, I will mention that the testimony offered by the prosecution has been in regard to the facts, it has been offered in the affirmative, as opposed to testimony offered by the defense in the negative, with one single exception, and that was the accused himself. No single fact brought out by the prosecution has been denied. The best witnesses the defense has offered testified to the good character and the veracity of every witness, with the exception of Bernard. The attempt to impeach Bernard's testimony has fallen flat for the reason that no single point of his testimony has been denied. His general veracity has not been attacked. His testimony before this court is entitled to as much consideration as anyone else's. It has been shown that Private Bernard testified to an untrue fact before the court in his previous trial, and the mere fact that he went to his acting First Sergeant and asked that a correct understanding be had between himself and his troop commander is evidence of his honest intention.[15]

Lastly, Lieutenant Keller addressed the motivation question that Coughlan raised. Given the serious consequences of admitting to the acts under oath, he found merely jealousy among soldiers unconvincing and felt the court would think so as well:

> During this trial, every effort on the part of the court, the council, and the Judge Advocate has been made to find a motive, if such there be, for charging the accused with this offense. The only motive that can be brought out is that of justification. There has been testimony offered to show that the accused has been in friendly relations with every member of the troop, and I leave it to the court to decide whether these men who are in the accusers could concoct such a scheme against any men.

Then, to close, Keller once again took a last swipe at Moon's masculinity as he submitted his case with another condemnation about the lack of violence to settle the matter:

> I will leave it to the court to decide whether any athletic individual would stand very long without resorting to fisticuffs for such an accusation were they not true.[16]

With all due false humility, he then laid Moon's fate in the hands of his fellow officers on the court:

> I will state that it is not my motive to force the conviction in this case, nor is it in any other case in which I am Judge Advocate. I'm merely presenting evidence as it appears to me and reviewing it in as fair away as I can, and it is according to the evidence you decide the case.[17]

At the conclusion of Judge Advocate Keller's remarks, the court members retired to another room to deliberate. They had four days' worth of testimony from 22 witnesses and 186 pages of transcripts to review. The logical arguments made by both the prosecution and the defense relied on assumptions about the social construction of masculinity, morality, and the nature of sexuality that were neither tested, challenged, or questioned. However, each case was also presented by army officers for army officers making up the court. Therefore, the logic shows how officers in the early 20th century were conventionalizing these three concepts and how they related to their minds, and how it led to prejudicial thinking that would dominate the military's thinking on queer soldiers for the rest of the century.

Both cases in Moon's court-martial followed basic syllogistic reasoning. Syllogism is a logical reasoning method that involves drawing conclusions from two propositions, known as premises, based on their relationship with a third proposition, known as the conclusion. There are certain assumptions, known as axioms, for each premise. Argumentation follows a structured format where the major premise establishes a general rule, the minor premise provides a specific example, and the conclusion logically follows from the premises. The origins of syllogism arise in ancient Aristotelian thought but have evolved over time to incorporate different modal sets. Modal syllogism incorporates different modalities, such as possibility and necessity, into the premises and conclusions. It allows for the evaluation of statements with modal operators, like "possible," "necessary," or "impossible," and explores the relationships between these modalities to draw valid deductions about the given propositions.[18] The basic paradigm often used for syllogism is:

Major premise (e.g., all humans are mortal)
Minor premise (e.g., Socrates is human)
Conclusion (e.g., Socrates is moral)

First Lieutenant Keller first presented the basic facts that Moon committed a same-sex act, corroborated by his witnesses, Simpson and Bernard. However, he did not directly demonstrate how those acts were "prejudice to good military discipline." To do that, there was a syllogistic argument about masculinity vis-à-vis individuals who engaged in same-sex acts (i.e., queer individuals):

Major Premise: Masculine men are heteronormative.
Minor Premise: Queer individuals are not heteronormative.
Conclusion: Queer individuals are not masculine.

That was one of the assumptions commonly understood in his argument among the other officers of the court. They all assumed that hegemonic masculinity, heteronormative sexuality, morality, and good soldiering were all the same. The major premise had the problem of reducing the concept of masculinity to a single, narrow definition, ignoring the diversity of traits and identities that can be encompassed within masculinity. This oversimplification undermined the validity of the argument by failing to account for the complexity of human experiences and identities.

This would remain the core argument of the military for the rest of the 20th century and into the first years of the 21st century. Yet, it is all based on assumptions that should have been challenged or tested. The problem with syllogisms is the logic overshadows the importance of critically examining or verifying the underlying assumptions. In this case, failing to do so led the army to the noun form of prejudice, or "preconceived opinion not based on reason or actual experience," that queer individuals would continue to face in the United States for the next century.

Yet, it would be largely accepted within the military at the time, so Keller shaped his logic accordingly. The core of his primary argument is based on the following:

Major Premise: Good soldiers are masculine.
Minor Premise: Moon was not masculine.
Conclusion: Moon was not a good soldier (ergo prejudicial to good military discipline).

Despite his efforts to suggest Moon's masculinity was lacking for not "thrashing" his accusers, the defense's witnesses across the trial had endorsed Moon's masculine performance and described him as a good soldier. The "sporting women" also attested to his heteronormative sexual behaviors. Consequently, despite having witnesses admitting to the acts themselves, Keller's logic and the assumptions behind them were fundamentally flawed.

Coughlan likewise used syllogism in his defense of Private Moon. His underlying assumption was that morality and hegemonic masculinity were directly tied to each other. Therefore, after establishing Moon's positive moral character, the core of his argument involved two congruent syllogistic arguments that worked symbiotically together. The first was:

Major Premise: Masculine men are moral.
Minor Premise: Private Moon is masculine.
Conclusion: Private Moon must be moral.

The second was:

Major Premise: Moral men are heteronormative.
Minor Premise: Private Moon is moral.
Conclusion: Private Moon must be heteronormative.

This was also supported by the testimony of the "sporting women" who recounted that Moon had "regular" sexual relations with them and the others who testified how athletic Moon was and that he was an outstanding soldier.

In both these syllogistic arguments, the Achilles's heel lies in their major premises, which oversimplified complex concepts like morality and masculinity or heteronormativity. The first argument brushes aside the reality that people have diverse moral beliefs and that being masculine does not automatically mean being morally upright. The second one boldly assumes that all morally sound individuals neatly fit into heteronormative boxes, disregarding the rich tapestry of moral identities and the possibility of challenging society's accepted or preferred sexual norms while still being ethical. Both arguments might strike a chord with fellow military members, reflecting prevailing attitudes of the time. Yet, they fall short of capturing the nuanced reality of human behavior and the intricate interplay between identity, morality, sexuality, and societal expectations. Instead, they offer a tidy but flawed view of complex issues, ultimately weakening their logical foundations but nonetheless remaining the dominant argument for excluding queer people from the military for a century.

It was not just the logic that was revealing. The wording used throughout the trial revealed the intersectionality of same-sex acts across class lines during this time of subtle change in social attitudes about sexuality and masculinity.[19] The differences in the words used by the enlisted men and officers indicate that the assumptions of the officers were, in fact, challenged to a degree by the enlisted men. For them, the tie between heteronormative sexuality, masculinity, and morality may not have been as strong. The incongruity of the words and their implied meaning demonstrated the tension that existed in society as the binary homo-hetero paradigm was emerging.

The enlisted men used fewer words with a narrow meaning to describe what Moon would be if the charges were true. The words were significant as they revealed the concept behind them and were coded so the speaker and listener could mutually understand what the word meant and social attitudes about it.[20] The narrowly defined "cocksucker" described an act, and while that act was outside traditionally accepted social norms, it was limited to Moon's sexual choices. Simpson, Ross, Hollins, and Bernard describe Moon in this way. Interestingly enough, the receivers of the act, Simpson and Bernard, were not described with similar terms, perhaps indicating slightly less stigma associated with passively receiving rather than actively performing the action. This would explain why Simpson was excited that "the party" (ie-Moon) was coming the night of his first encounter, why he seemed relatively open about soliciting Moon, and even willingly bragged and joked about it afterward with Hollins and Ross. The working-class mentality was distinct, and in other contexts in America, under the right circumstances, men could have sex with other men without achieving pariah status.[21]

On the other hand, the non-commissioned and commissioned officers used very different words to describe the suspected Moon. Theirs had a broader definition that extended beyond the simple act itself. "Unnatural" and "abnormal" went past Moon's actions and could be applied to him as a whole person, both biologically and his moral character, emphasizing the perceived overall holistic deviance than the more narrowly applied action term. Though the emerging medical term "inversion" was not used, it too was a more widely defined term that conflated one part of an individual into more broadly applied negative stereotypes.[22] The absence of the more medically used discourse is telling, as is the Post Surgeon's admitted limited knowledge and experience. Seven years later, in the investigation at the Newport, Rhode Island Naval Station, the officers likewise did not use the medical terminology in their findings, preferring the popular term "queer" instead.[23] However, with

Private Moon's court-martial, such popular terms were not used, and instead, a sort of middle ground was expressed.

The popular terminology would not have worked for Lieutenant Keller, who was prosecuting the case. The urban "queer" subcultures of the time emphasized the effeminacy and a striking opposition to hegemonic masculinity. Men in those communities often ostentatiously breached traditional masculine displays as a signal to others, and terms such as "pussyfoot," "sissy," "fairies," and "pogues" emphasized that fact.[24] It was clear that Moon could not be put into this category as he was a "star" in the highly masculine military culture. The terms used in his court-martial, whether "cocksucker," "abnormal," "unnatural," or "pervert," had understood meanings behind them. The people who used them had some concept in their heads that corresponded to the sense of the word they chose to use, as did the people who heard those words. What they implied was part of the culture that had not yet come to grips with categorizing and stereotyping people based on same-sex attraction or acts. Moon did not fit into their expected effeminate stereotypes.

These linguistic distinctions illustrate the concept of "normal exception" and underscore the value of microhistory, which focuses on smaller units to reveal how individuals navigate their lived experiences. In the case of Private Moon's court-martial, this approach sheds light on the divide between officers and enlisted men in their constructions of sexuality. Officers, with greater authority, labeled same-sex acts as "immoral" or "abnormal," pathologizing them and linking such behaviors to deviance and unfitness for service. Enlisted men, however, took a more pragmatic view, focusing on the act itself – "cock sucking" – without attaching broader moral judgments. This flexible stance reinforces the queer theory challenges to the emerging binary constructions of sexual identity, illustrating how the same act could be interpreted as deviant by one group and relatively normal by another, depending on social position.

The contrasting views of sexuality between the officers and enlisted men in Private Moon's case reveal a deeper divide in their conceptions of what constituted a good soldier (see Figure 6.1). While the officers, with more moral and legal power, adhered to a rigid framework that linked masculinity to sexual morality, seeing same-sex behavior as a direct challenge to military discipline and character, the enlisted men appeared less concerned with these moral judgments. For the enlisted ranks, camaraderie and competence in the field outweighed personal conduct off-duty, leading to their acceptance of Moon despite the accusations. Through the court-martial process, the officers sought to impose their stricter, more moralistic view of soldiering, using the trial as a tool to reinforce their belief that same-sex behavior was not only a threat to military masculinity but was a personal failing, threating the military's cohesion and order. This clash over what made a soldier "fit" for duty highlights the broader tensions between the officers' desire for conformity and control, and the enlisted men's more flexible, pragmatic understanding of military life.

The forensic linguistic modeling of each group's conceptualized Private Moon and shows how they expected individuals to conform to heteronormative masculine and sexual norms. The collates extracted from the enlisted men's text provide valuable insights into their perceptions and attitudes toward Private Moon. One

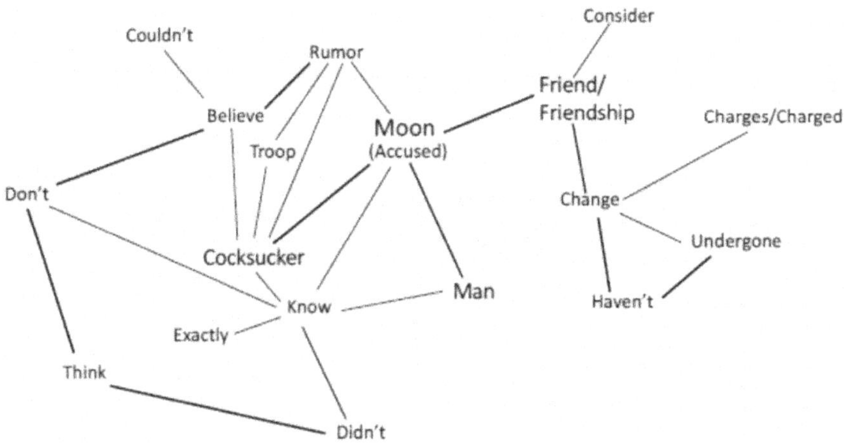

Figure 6.1 Collates conceptualizing the impression of Private Moon from the testimony of the enlisted men.

Source: Image created by the author.

notable observation is the recurring use of the term "friend" in reference to Private Moon. They consistently portray him in friendly terms. However, the presence of associated words like "haven't," "changed," and "consider" implied that despite the allegations, their bond with Moon remained steadfast.

On the flip side, Private Moon found himself branded with the derogatory label of "cocksucker." But this term was more about his actions than his whole moral makeup. People kept using phrases like "didn't," "couldn't," and "don't," which hinted at their doubts about Moon being deserving of such a harsh title. It was as if they could not reconcile that sexual act with his otherwise exemplary masculine persona. The word "rumor" kept popping up, making it seem like this accusation was based more on gossip than on solid facts. And by tossing in the word "man" alongside Moon's name, it seemed like folks expected him to live up to some masculine ideal. Overall, it painted a picture of skepticism and hearsay rather than solid proof or firsthand experience.

The collates provide a revealing insight into how the enlisted men saw Private Moon, showing a mix of closeness, doubt, and disrespect. They often called him "friend," and they remained so, hinting a level of acceptance even in light of the accusations of being a "cocksucker," which they found hard to believe. Either there was a level of acceptance in his sexual choices or Moon's masculine character was so established they could not believe the accusations. Possibly, it was both.

Similar to the enlisted men, the non-commissioned officers' language implied they had a friendly rapport with Private Moon, unaffected by the accusations against him (see Figure 6.2). But what stood out were the words "excellent" and "man," which seemed to define the core characteristics of how they conceptualized him. "Man" suggests a strong, masculine identity, highly valued for someone in

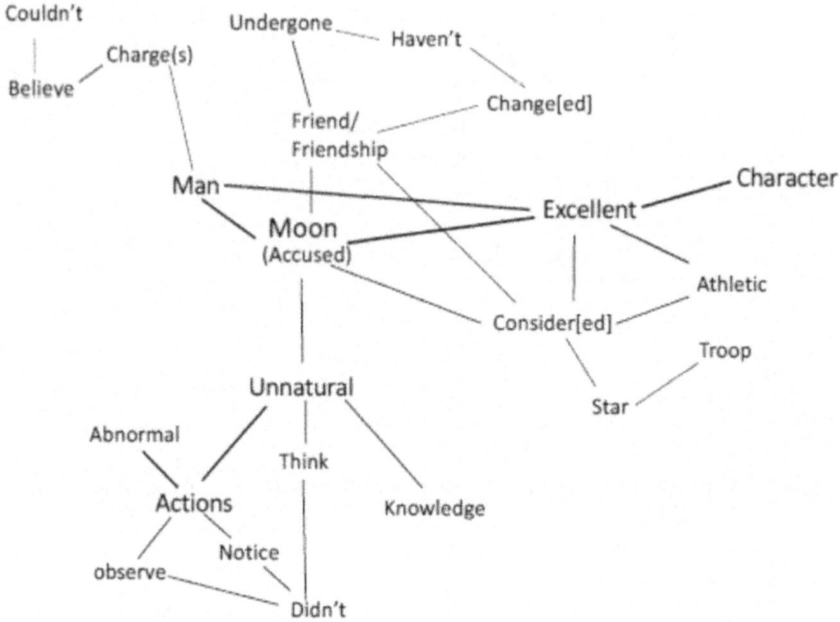

Figure 6.2 Collates conceptualizing the impression of Private Moon from the testimony of the non-commissioned officers.

Source: Image created by the author.

the military. Pairing "man" with "excellent" highlights his exceptional masculine qualities, whether in his actions, character, or abilities.

The word "excellent" was central to the conversation, often linked with terms like "character," "considered," and "athletic." When "excellent" was paired with "character," it hinted that Private Moon's standout moral qualities went beyond just being good at his job. It suggested he embodied traits like integrity, discipline, and moral strength. The use of "considered" hinted that his excellence had been thoughtfully recognized, maybe through evaluations from peers or higher-ups. And connecting it with athleticism hinted at his physical strength, adding to his image of masculinity.

Another thread unfurled in the testimonies, punctuated by the word "unnatural," a clear nod to the allegations against him. "Unnatural" was not just about his actions; it painted Moon as somehow at odds with the very fabric of "nature" itself. This broader interpretation hinted at a moral failing rather than just specific deeds, as did the testimony of the enlisted men. It hinted that any departure from traditional heteronormative and hegemonic masculinity should have been glaringly obvious. The tight link between "actions," "abnormal," "notice," and "observe" underscored the intense scrutiny of the non-commissioned officers. The use of "didn't" outright denied any observable deviation from expected norms in Private Moon's behavior. In essence, they were not just watching Moon; they were evaluating him and concluded he fit their understanding of an "excellent man" and described him accordingly.

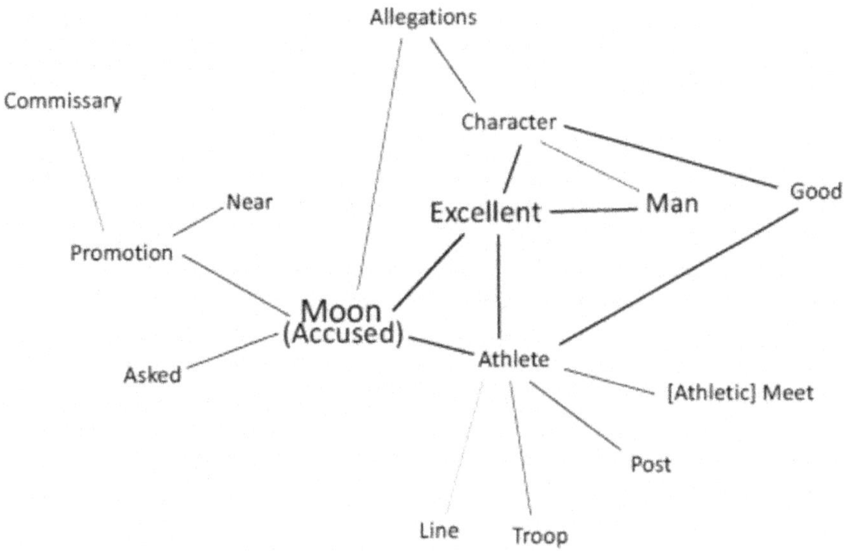

Figure 6.3 Collates conceptualizing the impression of Private Moon from the testimony of the commissioned officers, many of whom were also members of the court who would deliberate Private Moon's fate.

Source: Image created by the author.

The commissioned officer's portrayal of Private Moon homed in on the connection between Moon and the labels "excellent" and "athlete" (see Figure 6.3). This connection was not just superficial; it hinted at a crucial facet of Moon's identity, shining a spotlight on his physical prowess and hinting at his significant role in the military's perception of character, particularly through displays of masculine strength and dominance. Moreover, the term "excellent" was not just about performance; it was intricately intertwined with the concept of "character," suggesting that the officers' evaluation of Moon extended far beyond his actions, encompassing broader qualities like integrity, discipline, and morality. This linkage underscored the significance of Moon's conduct as a fundamental element of his character, especially within the context of military values that placed a premium on physical excellence and traditional masculinity.

Furthermore, the tie between Moon and the term "excellent" did not just denote a surface-level admiration but hinted at a deeper level of respect and recognition for qualities highly prized within the echelons of military leadership. This association was not solitary since it was intricately woven with other descriptors like "character" and "man," showcasing the complexity of how they conceptualized Moon's masculinity. The link to "character" suggested that Moon's excellence stemmed from attributes beyond mere physical prowess, further cementing his standing and reputation within the military hierarchy. Moreover, like the NCOs, the inclusion of "man" alongside "excellent" emphasized the gendered dimensions of Moon's identity, aligning with societal norms and expectations of masculinity within the military milieu.

The collates extracted from the texts provide valuable insights into the perceptions of not only Private Moon among different military social groups but they also shed light on their notions of masculinity and expected sexual norms. The enlisted men held Moon in high regard, evaluating the charges against him based solely on the narrowly defined actions associated with them. Conversely, both commissioned and non-commissioned officers focused on Moon's character, questioning whether it aligned with natural or abnormal standards. However, their perceptions were largely positive, with descriptors like "excellent" and "man" forming the core of their judgments, emphasizing his physical and moral masculinity in a favorable light. They emphasized Moon's behaviors, particularly his athleticism, which was clearly demonstrated, contrasting with the vague nature of the charges against him. Overall, there was a collective high regard for Moon's character and physical abilities, highlighting qualities such as integrity, discipline, and physical prowess that aligned with military expectations. These analyses offer nuanced insights into the multifaceted perceptions of Private Moon within the military community, revealing complexities in interpersonal relationships, masculine behavioral norms, and communication patterns among military personnel.

Collates are only one analytical tool to understand how masculinity, sexuality, and relationships interacted in the military environment. Sentiment analysis, another valuable forensic linguistic tool, provides insights into emotional dynamics and attitudes expressed by the prosecution, defense, witnesses, and even the members of the court, thus aiding in understanding the underlying unconscious emotional component of evaluating Moon. After the same preliminary processing testimonies for collation analysis, the sentiment analysis algorithm assigns sentiment scores to individual words and phrases, categorizing them as positive (+1), negative (–1), or neutral (0) based on predefined sentiment lexicons or machine learning models trained on labeled data. Additionally, sentiment analysis algorithms may consider linguistic features such as part-of-speech tagging within the context and syntactic structure of the data set to improve accuracy. Subsequently, sophisticated aggregation methods, such as weighted averaging or sentiment intensity analysis, account for the varying impact of different words or phrases on the overall sentiment. These methods may assign different weights to words based on factors such as their frequency, relevance, or intensity of sentiment. The sentiment scores are aggregated and averaged to determine the overall sentiment of the subgroup's text, which can vary from highly positive (maximum score of 1) to highly negative (maximum score of –1) or somewhere in between. The typical score is in a range between –0.05 and 0.05 since it would be unlikely for every word in a text to be entirely positive, negative, or even neutral.[25]

The results are presented in Figure 6.4. The prosecution's more negative sentiment score indicated an attempt to present an understandably more critical or accusatory narrative against Private Moon, while the defense's more positive sentiment score suggested an expectedly more optimistic or supportive stance. The Non-Commissioned Officers' notably higher sentiment score demonstrated a particularly emotive and favorable testimony, potentially influencing the overall tone of the proceedings. The "sporting women's" even higher score indicated a

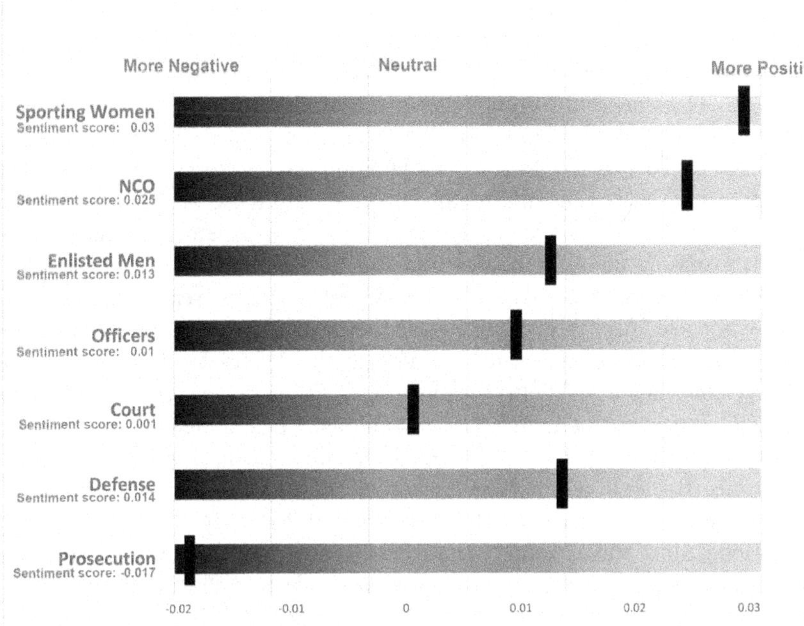

Figure 6.4 Graph summarizing the sentiment analysis scores of testimony in Private Moon's court martial.

Source: Image created by the author.

significant level of positivity, signaling a strong advocacy for Moon and conviction of their testimony. Overall, these sentiment analysis scores provide a nuanced understanding of the emotional dynamics within the courtroom, illuminating the attitudes and perspectives of the different parties involved in the case. It also re-enforces the level of support for the masculine ideals expressed in their collates regarding Moon in the different levels of the military's social hierarchy at the time.

Unlike a traditional trial where the jury remains silent, Moon's court-martial enabled the measurement of the jury's sentiments in two ways: first, through the words used during the court's questioning of the witnesses, and second, through the testimony of the court's officers who were called to testify. It is reasonable to assume that the sentiment scores of the court and officers could reveal glimpses of their potential bias for or against Moon and how the prosecution or defense's case might influence their verdict. If their cases had an emotional tone that was in line with the court's sentiment, it could strengthen their credibility and persuasive power.

These different roles of the court's officers were unique and surprisingly produced very different linguistic results depending on the role the officers were playing at the time. When acting as the court, the sentiment score of the officers was 0.001 or almost entirely neutral, with only the slightest positive tone. When the officers shifted from their roles as interrogators to witnesses, the aggregate score improved to 0.01 – a tenfold increase in a more positive direction. This score aligned more closely with Coughlan's defense sentiment score of 0.014 than with Keller's negative prosecution score of –0.017. The officer's testimony score may have indicated an existing bias in favor of Moon, perhaps reinforced by the other positive testimony of the enlisted men, non-commissioned officers, and sporting women. Coughlan's case needed only to work at exploiting that bias for a favorable verdict.

The proximity of Coughlan's sentiment score with those of the officers/court and the other witnesses potentially influenced the court's perception of the case. However, assuming that sentiment would solely determine the verdict would be wrong. The emotional tone and attitudes expressed by the different parties involved indirectly impacted how their arguments and testimonies were perceived. The sentiment analysis scores of the court's comments, the defense, and the prosecution could have contributed to shaping the overall perception of the case and potentially affecting the outcome, but many factors would likely determine the verdict.

Private Moon's case must have presented several problems for the court in their deliberations. By all accounts, he was a good, if not excellent, soldier; he was well-liked by his comrades; and yet, he did not seem to firmly be in the heteronormative model since the accounts of other men implicated in the trial had a ring of truth to them. Even though they did not articulate with the clarity of nearly a century of prejudice, the trial laid out many of the prejudicial arguments the U.S. Army gave in the late 20th century on why queer service members should not be able to serve in the military centering on perceived desirable heteronormative stereotypes of masculinity.[26] Yet, in 1912, the case of Private Laurance E. Moon proved that they could and that there was a fundamental flaw in the masculine warrior paradigm.

Even if the accusations were true, they demonstrate that they did not negatively affect his ability to soldier, unit morale, or even his displays of masculinity. Both Keller and Coughlan's syllogistic arguments and assumptions failed. Moreover, as seen with the reaction of soldiers like Hollins and Ross to Simpson's "proof," there may have even been a level of tolerance to same-sex acts and people who engaged in them, at least among the working-class enlisted men. However, 1912 was a very different time from the late 20th century, when the army had successfully aligned the enlisted men's perception more closely with the officer's binary hetro-homo binary and the masculine warrior paradigm. In the process, the inflexibility of resistance and punishment – both legal and social – from that norm became more severe.

The linguistic evidence of Private Moon's court-martial reveals a distinct clash between the officers and enlisted men regarding their conceptions of not only masculinity and sexuality but how that affected being a "good soldier." While the officers, guided by the rigid heteronormative and masculine-warrior expectations, sought to portray Moon's alleged same-sex behavior as a fundamental flaw in his character and ability to be a good soldier, despite being clearly competent at his duties and considered worthy of promotion because of them. The enlisted men, on the other hand, focused more practically on his actions as a soldier and the warm interpersonal relationships they had with him. For them, his competency and camaraderie remained intact despite sexual actions, and their linguistic choices consistently reflected terms like "friend," indicating their enduring bond with him. The enlisted men's emphasis on Moon's ability to perform his duties, rather than his adherence to sexual norms, illustrates a more pragmatic view of soldiering, one in which sexual behavior was secondary to how well someone carried out their responsibilities.

This practical stance stood in stark contrast to the officers' attempts to impose their more moralistic and categorical views through the court-martial process. The officers' language revealed a clear intent to enforce a unified version of their vision of military masculinity, in which same-sex behavior was seen as inherently "unnatural" and incompatible with the ideals of an "excellent man" or soldier. Their focus on terms like "character" and "unnatural" suggested that they viewed the charges against Moon not just as a reflection of a single action but as a deeper moral failure that, in their mind, could undermine military order. In doing so, they aimed to codify a more rigid understanding of soldiering, one that aligned closely with late Victorian ideals of masculinity and sexual purity. However, the enlisted men's reluctance to let the accusations change their perception of Moon hinted at a broader, quieter resistance to these evolving norms. While the officers used the trial to enforce a strict binary between acceptable and deviant sexual behavior, the soldiers' continued acceptance of Moon suggests a more flexible and tolerant culture, one in which acts could be separated from identity, and soldiering was defined by skill and camaraderie rather than strict adherence to heteronormative ideals. However, the officer's view ultimately prevailed with the codification of making sodomy officially illegal in the rewrite of the army regulations in 1916 and 1920, as well as the growing acceptance in and out of the armed forces with new categories and stereotypes centering around "homosexuality."

As the concept of "homosexuality," and by extension, homophobia, evolved and became more entrenched in both the military and popular mind, the situation changed. By the late 20th century, people defined as "homosexuals" had achieved a pariah status in the military with significant amounts of physical, psychological, and legal homophobic harassment.[27] However, it need not necessarily have been that way. Despite his same-sex predilections, Private Moon was seen by the non-commissioned and commissioned officers as the embodiment of military masculinity, and his character was seen as impeccable. The enlisted men saw him favorably as well and showed signs of accepting degrees of same-sex acts. Yet, between Moon's case in 1912 and the century-long fight to decriminalize sodomy and homosexuality in the military, the U.S. Army had constructed its own homophobic reality that became increasingly monolithic and antagonistic, barring thousands of talented soldiers and sailors like Moon from serving.

Notes

1 Testimony of Sergeant George Ringer, General Court-Martial of Private Laurance E. Moon, Records of the Judge Advocate General, Record Group 153, National Archives and Record Administration, Washington, D.C., (hereafter Moon Court-Martial, RG 153, NARA), 175–176; Testimony of Private William Smith, Moon Court-Martial, RG 153, NARA, 173.

2 Captain Timothy M. Coughlan (hereafter Coughlan), Defense Closing Statement, Moon Court-Martial, RG 153, NARA, 183–184.
3 Coughlan, Statement of the Defense, Moon Court-Martial, RG 153, NARA, 184.
4 Katz, "The Invention of Heterosexuality"; Krafft-Ebing, *Psychopathia Sexualis*, 56, 79; Shaw and Ferris, "Perverted Sexual Instinct," 185–204; Kiernan, "Perversion"; [Author unknown], "Perverted Sexual Instinct"; G. Frank Lydston, "Sexual Perversion, Satyriasis and Nymphomania," *Medical and Surgical Reporter* 61 (1889), 253–258; Hughes, "Erotopathia."
5 Coughlan, Statement of the Defense, Moon Court-Martial, RG 153, NARA, 184–186.
6 Coughlan, Statement of the Defense, Moon Court-Martial, RG 153, NARA, 186–187.
7 Coughlan, Statement of the Defense, Moon Court-Martial, RG 153, NARA, 187.
8 Coughlan, Statement of the Defense, Moon Court-Martial, RG 153, NARA, 187.
9 Coughlan, Statement of the Defense, Moon Court-Martial, RG 153, NARA, 187–188.
10 Coughlan, Statement of the Defense, Moon Court-Martial, RG 153, NARA, 188.
11 Coughlan, Statement of the Defense, Moon Court-Martial, RG 153, NARA, 188.
12 First Lieutenant Frank Keller (hereafter Keller), Judge Advocate Closing Statement, Moon Court-Martial, RG 153, NARA, 188.
13 Keller, Judge Advocate Closing Statement, Moon Court-Martial, RG 153, NARA, 188–189.
14 Keller, Judge Advocate Closing Statement, Moon Court-Martial, RG 153, NARA, 189.
15 Keller, Judge Advocate Closing Statement, Moon Court-Martial, RG 153, NARA, 189–190.
16 Keller, Judge Advocate Closing Statement, Moon Court-Martial, RG 153, NARA, 190.
17 Keller, Judge Advocate Closing Statement, Moon Court-Martial, RG 153, NARA, 190.
18 Susanne Bobzein, "Ancient Logic," in *Stanford Encyclopedia of Philosophy*, ed. Edward N. Zalta. Accessed January 12, 2023, https://plato.stanford.edu/entries/logic-ancient/; Christin Lundberg, *The Essential Guide to Rhetoric* (Boston: Bedford St. Martins, 2018), 37–39; Irving Copi, *Introduction to Logic*, 3rd edn. (New York: Macmillan Co., 1969), 190; Marko Malin, *Aristotle's Modal Syllogistic* (Cambridge: Harvard University Press, 2013), 23–34.
19 Weeks, "Sins and Diseases."
20 Steven Pinker, *The Stuff of Thought: Language as a Window Into Human Nature* (New York: Penguin Books, 2008), 282, 290–291.
21 Katz, *Love Stories*; Boarg, *Re-Dressing America's Frontier Past*, 335.
22 Bronski, *A Queer History*, 76–78, 83–85; Grossman, "Whitman in Your Pocket," 95.
23 Chauncey, "Christian Brotherhood," 205.
24 Kimmel, *Manhood in America*, 68–69; Norton, *The Myth of the Modern Homosexual*, 8–15; Chauncey, "Christian Brotherhood," 189–211, 189.
25 Eric Breck and Claire Cardie, "Opinion Mining and Sentiment Analysis," in *The Oxford Handbook of Computational Linguistics*, ed. Ruslan Mitkov (Oxford: Oxford University Press, 2018), 43–58; Lei Lei and Dilin Liu, "Conducting Sentiment Analysis," *Computational Linguistics* 48, no. 1 (2022), 68–92; Harish Duff Sharma and Parul Goyal, "An Analysis of Sentiment: Methods, Applications, and Challenges," *Engineering Proceedings* 59, no. 1 (2023), 68.
26 Rand Corporation, *Sexual Orientation*, xxiv.
27 Anon, *Uniform Discrimination: The "Don't Ask, Don't Tell" Policy of the U.S. Military* (New York: Human Rights Watch, 2003), 21–30.

7 Civilian Life Again

The court in Moon's case reconvened at 3:45 p.m. on July 12, 1912. Moon and the rest of the room rose. Major Wright led the court into the room and, after everyone was seated, read the verdicts: "Not Guilty" on all accounts.[1] However, even after Moon left the room, no doubt jubilant in his victory, the court continued their business. Both Privates Simpson and Bernard were charged with crimes for the same incidents, and their cases were to be heard immediately after Moon's case while the officers were still impaneled. The specifications charged that both had allowed "an unnatural and immoral act to be committed" upon them by Moon. Simpson had the added charge that he encouraged Moon to desert and avoid the charges.[2] Ironically, both men were represented by Captain Coughlan, Moon's counsel, who had effectively smeared them both to win Moon's acquittal. They were separately arraigned immediately after Moon's trial, both pleading "guilty" to the charges regarding the "unnatural and immoral" acts. Simpson pled not guilty to advising Moon to desert but was ultimately convicted on that charge three days later.[3]

However, their guilty pleas caused legal problems for Moon. How could the court accept that they were guilty of permitting the acts to have occurred upon them when the same court had acquitted Moon of committing those same acts? The legal paradox was obvious and begged resolution. Consequently, the court for Moon reconvened at 6:15 p.m. and changed their findings to "Guilty" on all charges.[4] Thus, in less than three hours, Private Laurance E. Moon was found both "Not Guilty" and "Guilty." The three men were to be dishonorably discharged from the service and sentenced to serve three years of hard labor for their "crimes." The Army's Judge Advocate General, however, remitted the period of confinement for all three.[5] At some point, a curious handwritten note by an unknown author was added to the jacket of Moon's court-martial file. It stated, "This should be remarked upon as absolutely against the policy of the dept," without referencing what that implied (see Figure 7.1).

After discharge, Joseph Bernard moved back to Youngstown, Ohio. He worked as a truck driver for the Armour D. Company, married but continued to live for a while with his extended family. He registered for the draft just before World War I, listing himself as exempt from service because he had a "father, mother, wife to support and was dishonorably discharged."[6] Little can be found about Joseph Bernard after that until his death on January 28, 1955.[7]

DOI: 10.4324/9781003530756-8

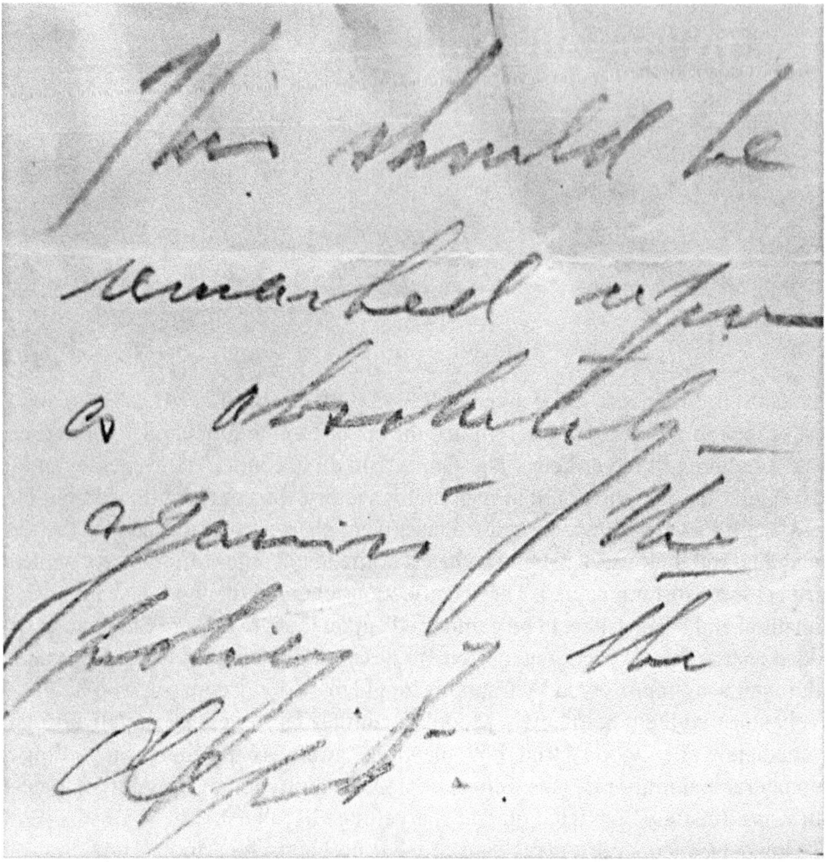

Figure 7.1 A handwritten note stating "This should be remarked upon as absolutely against the policy of the dept." When the note was added and by whom is unclear as is what "this" is referring to. Included on the cover of Private Moon's Court Martial filed in the National Archives and Record Administration.

Harvey Simpson made his way to the copper mines of Butte, Montana, working in the infamously poor and dangerous conditions of the Speculator Mine.[8] He married Sarah E. Gilbert in November of 1916 in a "pretty home wedding."[9] During World War I, he filled out a draft card but did not claim exemption, and it does not appear he was ever drafted. His marriage to Sarah seems to have begun to turn sour when, in 1924, he published an advertisement in the paper stating: "I will not be responsible for bills contracted by my wife. HARVEY SIMPSON."[10] By at least 1927, his marriage failed as Sarah wed Harry Woodthorpe. Listing no family, Simpson checked into Butte's Murray Hospital on May 2, 1929, for pulmonary tuberculosis and silicosis, dying two months later at the age of 48.[11]

Laurance Edgar Moon returned to his hometown of Baltimore, where many of his brothers and sisters still lived, as well as his estranged wife Annie, to whom he was still technically married. Moon found work as a clerk for the Baltimore and Ohio Railroad, but the former promising young soldier began a series of difficulties that marred his life after he left the army. His time in the service would not be forgotten and, in many ways, seems to have remained influential until his death. Yet, Laurance's struggles stand in marked contrast to his comrades' image of him as "the star of the troop" during his time at Fort Yellowstone.

Laurance's father, Thomas, was still a sea captain living in Norfolk, Virginia. His older brother, William, followed in his father's footsteps and went to sea, but he lived in Baltimore while his eldest brother, George, was a bartender. Annie, Laurance's estranged wife, also lived in Baltimore but appears to have had a bit of an unsettled life. On February 17, 1915, she ran screaming into West Fayette Street after Joseph Brozowski stabbed her.[12] Annie and Laurance would remain estranged but officially married until May 2, 1917, when she petitioned and was granted a divorce on the grounds of abandonment. "He did not want to support me and would not work," she said and claimed he left after two weeks when her mother complained to him about not paying board. The newspaper account said "that she asked her husband to come back, but he told her he did not want to live with her," consequently, they lived apart for over ten years, two of which Laurance was in the army posted in far off Yellowstone National Park.[13] Just over two weeks after getting the divorce, Annie applied for a marriage license to wed Charles J. Hall.[14]

The rest of the Moon family underwent other changes as well. Laurance's older sister by ten years, also named Annie, had passed away in 1909, shortly before Laurance had entered the army. Not long after Laurance was discharged in 1912, her husband, Harry Barnett, died, leaving their three children, Ellen, Annie, and Harry Jr., as orphans in Baltimore. The Moon matriarch Ellen, living with her husband Thomas in Norfolk, VA, applied to become their legal guardian and was approved after her husband provided a $600 bond.[15] Tragedy struck again in 1915 as Laurance's older brother Roland also died after an unknown but protracted illness.[16]

If Laurance thought that the heroic glow of his father was in the past, he was mistaken. Dramatically, Captain Thomas O. Moon's lightship sunk in a storm in January 1915, and he and the crew had to be rescued. In 1916, the 55-year-old Thomas O. Moon captained the *Charles F. Mayer* towing the barge *Poilu* across the war-ravaged waters of the North Atlantic. Even though the voyage was relatively uneventful as "Captain Moon did not come in actual contact with submarines," Norfolk's *Virginia-Pilot* newspaper ran a lengthy, two-column story about the trip with an endearingly dramatic title "Towed Barge to France, Captain Moon Home Again: Adventure-Loving Sea-Rover Now Says He Would Like to Make a Voyage in German Merchant Submarine." Moon's enthusiasm was clearly evident. "He stated last night with a sparkle in his eye," the reporter recalled, "that he would not mind in the least making a trip to Germany on one of the Kaiser's blockade-running submarines and would be ready to go at any time."[17]

Unaware to Laurance, the military updated and modernized the Articles of War just before the United States entered the war. The original regulations had originally been written in 1806 and only slightly revised in 1874 and 1908. The 1916 revisions were a major rewrite and implemented on March 1, 1917. For the first time, they included a specific and direct reference to sodomy four years after Laurance had been convicted for the act. Article 93 declared that any servicemember engaging in assault to commit sodomy would be criminally charged. But in 1920, when Congress approved another modified version of the Articles, sodomy became a crime in itself, separate from the offense of assault. The new definition declared simple sodomy was subject to court-martial and possible dishonorable discharge. The article was seen as a way to maintain order and discipline in the military by preventing sexual misconduct.[18]

The introduction of Article 93 was met with only limited criticism from some quarters. However, the military doubled down in the coming years and established standards that made individuals unfit for service who exhibited effeminate tendencies and "sexual perversion."[19] Wrongfully assuming the link between military masculinity and sexual choice, military psychiatrist Albert Abrams articulated the general assumptions and justification for excluding gays from the military that would stand for nearly a century.

> Homosexuality must be confronted as a fact, and not as a theory. In recruiting the elements which make up our invincible army, we cannot ignore what is obvious and which will militate against the combative prowess of our forces in this war and the deterrent post-bellum influences. From a military viewpoint, the homosexual is not only dangerous, but ineffective as a fighter. . . . It is imperative that homosexualists be recognized by the military authorities.[20]

Undoubtedly, Laurance Moon was unaware of these revisions, nor would he have likely cared if he had been. He also probably would not have identified as this new "homosexual" since the concept had only arisen and became popularly accepted after his time in the army and since he also enjoyed sexual gratification from women.

When the United States entered the war, Congress passed the Selective Service Act of 1917, which required all men between the ages of 21 and 30 to register for military conscription or the draft. The act was seen as a necessary measure to quickly expand the armed forces and bolster the country's military efforts in Europe. Laurance dutifully filled out his Draft Registration Card in 1917, but on line 12, he claimed an exemption for having been dishonorably discharged (Figure 7.2).[21] Nevertheless, he was drafted back into the service on June 24, 1918. Laurance obediently reported to Camp Meade, MD, and again found himself in the army, assigned to a Detached Causal Development Battalion. Interestingly enough, Laurance likely ran into at least one familiar face as his old friend from Fort Yellowstone, Robert Allen, was in the same battalion. Allen, however, was not the ideal soldier since records list him as Absent Without Leave (AWOL) three times in eight months.[22] Even with familiar company, Laurance continued to argue that his court-martial six years earlier made him ineligible for service, and he "refused to consider himself a soldier or accept pay."[23] If the army did not want him in 1912, why should they want him now? Despite the military's official policies against gays serving during the 20th century, it historically reduced the enforcement of that policy in order to meet the manpower needs during times of war.[24] Moon being drafted back into service should not, therefore, be surprising.

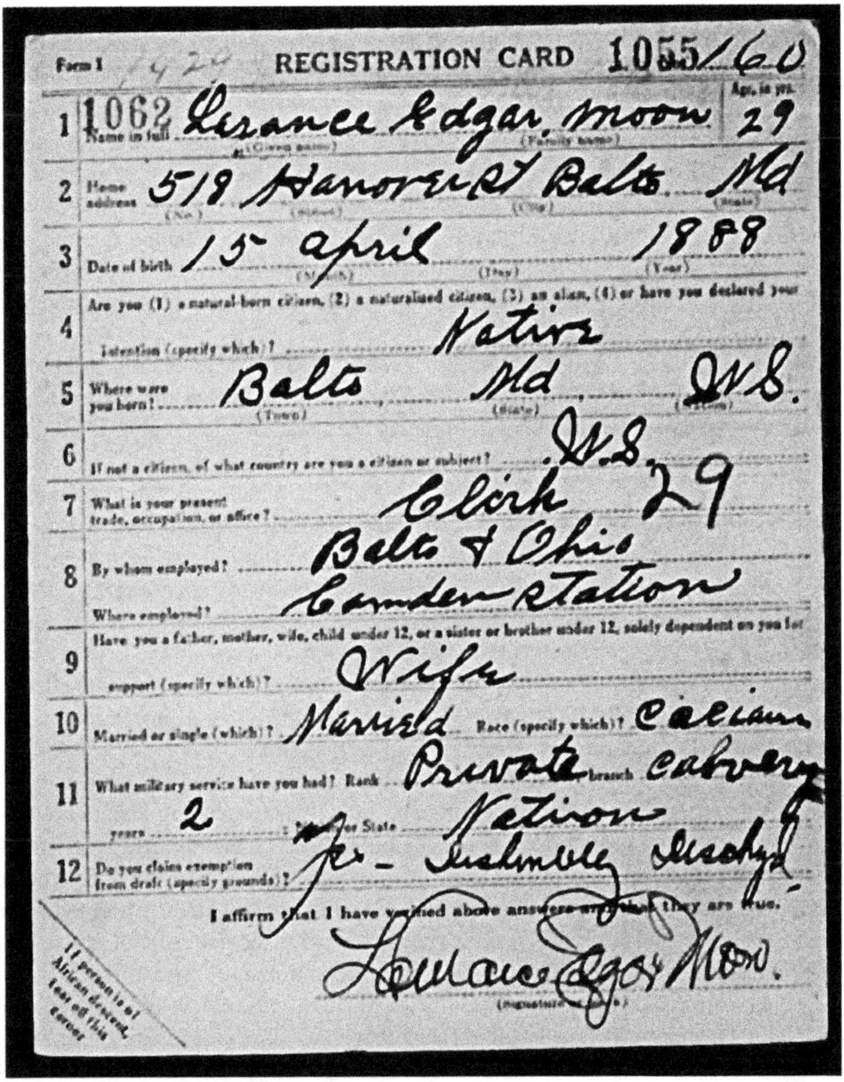
Form 1 REGISTRATION CARD 1055/60

1 1062 Name in full Lerance Edgar Moon (Given name) (Family name) Age, in yrs. 29

2 Home address 519 Hanover St Balto Md (No.) (Street) (City) (State)

3 Date of birth 15 April 1888 (Month) (Day) (Year)

4 Are you (1) a natural-born citizen, (2) a naturalized citizen, (3) an alien, (4) or have you declared your intention (specify which)? Native

5 Where were you born? Balto Md U.S. (Town) (State) (Nation)

6 If not a citizen, of what country are you a citizen or subject? U.S.

7 What is your present trade, occupation, or office? Clerk 29

8 By whom employed? Balto & Ohio Where employed? Camden station

9 Have you a father, mother, wife, child under 12, or a sister or brother under 12, solely dependent on you for support (specify which)? Wife

10 Married or single (which)? Married Race (specify which)? Caucasian

11 What military service have you had? Rank Private branch Cavalry years 2 Nation or State Nation

12 Do you claim exemption from draft (specify grounds)? Yes – Dishonorably discharged

I affirm that I have verified above answers and that they are true.

Laurance Edgar Moon (Signature or mark)

If person is of African descent, tear off this corner.

Figure 7.2 World War I draft card of Laurance Moon. In Box 12, he claimed an exemption due to being dishonorably discharged.

While the army investigated Moon's complaints, the war ended. With no need to look into the matter further, the army honorably discharged Laurance on December 2 "by reason of demobilization."[25] Soldiers who were discharged on the same day were given a travel allowance to return home. The Final Payroll Muster listed Laurance as eligible for $0.63, but his name was lightly crossed out, and he was the only person in the document where that happened. This seems consistent with his refusing to consider himself a soldier or receive pay. Yet, despite claiming to have refused his honorable discharge later in life, the document listed Private

Laurance E. Moon among the soldiers "honorably discharged," giving Moon the rare status of having been both acquitted and convicted in a court-martial in the same court martial and being both dishonorably and honorably discharged.[26]

Once again, Laurance Moon returned to civilian life. Sometime between his divorce from Annie in 1917 and the 1920 census, he had married a woman named Charlotte or "Lottie" and was employed as a chauffeur for a cigar manufacturer. In 1919, his father, the intrepid Captain Thomas O. Moon, retired and moved with Laurance's mother back to Baltimore, buying a house on Wilkens Avenue. His older brother William also lived in Baltimore and worked as a ship's engineer. His oldest brother George remained in Norfolk but had given up bartending and was now a sea captain in his own right.[27]

While there is no way of knowing, it would have been interesting to know if Laurance had read an article in the January 25, 1920, edition of *The Baltimore Sun* titled "Newport Rector Alleges 'Vicious Methods' in Vice Probe."[28] The article described the now-infamous Newport Naval Station sex scandal. The scandal stemmed from several drunken parties, some of which included "illicit activities" such as same-sex sodomy by sailors at the Newport YMCA, often involving underage boys. These activities were exposed by a U.S. Navy investigation that revealed widespread same-sex acts but was highly controversial for encouraging "undercover" sailors to investigate the allegations by willfully engaging in sodomy themselves to apprehend the suspects. The scandal caused an uproar in the United States and led to the resignation of some of the Navy's top leaders and the court-martial of many of the offenders. The affair also prompted the Navy to introduce stricter regulations governing the sexual behavior of its personnel.[29]

Like Moon's court-martial, the Newport controversy offers valuable insights into the history of sexuality, use of language and labels in creating mental models, challenging certain assumptions about the emergence of the "homosexual" identity. While some historians argue that the late 19th century marked a significant reconceptualization of homosexuality, both Moon's case and the Newport evidence suggest the need for a more nuanced view. Medical discourse, often seen as pivotal in shaping homosexual identities, took time to permeate general society and clearly had limited influence, particularly on working-class communities even decades later. Furthermore, they highlight the complexity of sexual identity formation. Terms like "pervert," "abnormal," "unnatural," and "queers" were used differently across various social contexts in the scandals, demonstrating the multifaceted nature of sexual categorization in the first two decades of the 20th century.[30]

The controversies also shed light on the interaction between masculine behaviors and sexual identity formation, challenging the notion of a straightforward correlation between the two. The defining factor in the Newport scandal was the effeminate behaviors of certain "gang" members derogatorily labeled "queer." Moon's case was the other side of the same coin where definitely masculine behaviors were idealized despite same-sex desires. The cases reflect broader societal debates over the boundaries of acceptable masculinity and the definition of sexual deviance and identities that arose from those definitions in the early years of the century. Yet, given the many echoes of his court-martial, if Laurance Moon had even read about the Newport case, how would he have reacted? The historian will never know if he was even aware of the incident and, if he was, how he would respond to it.

Even with a new bride and his extended family nearby, the 1920s would be a challenging decade for Laurance on several levels, once again contrasting with the promising image of him during his time in the army at Fort Yellowstone. In early 1923, Laurance had left his chauffeur job, and he was listed in the Baltimore City Directory as a salesman. However, early that same year, Moon found himself very publicly in legal trouble once again, albeit in the civilian legal system. Even though his marriage to Lottie would last until her death in 1963, there were signs of significant struggles. In the early spring, Lottie had a dream that "all was not well between her husband and Marie Bushman, 14 years old, a girl who had been employed to help with the housework," the *Baltimore Sun* reported. Lottie told young Marie about her dream, who in turn told Mrs. Moon that Laurance had tried to sexually assault her. Lottie had Laurance arrested and brought before a criminal court. By the time of the trial, Lottie had second thoughts as she "testified she was excited at the time and did not know what she was doing." As the jury deliberated, "she sat in the courtroom softly crying." Ultimately, Laurance was found "not guilty," and the bailiff had to "prevent Mrs. Moon from embracing her husband until the paper for his release had been prepared."[31]

As the 1920s progressed, things began to accelerate for Laurance. On August 3, 1926, Harry Barnett, his nephew by his deceased sister Annie, died in a tragic beach accident. The 20-year-old Barnett had been a member of Company B of the Fifth Maryland National Guard Regiment and went with two of his troopmates to Virginia Beach, where they were swept out to sea along with a local physician. Their bodies were missing for over a day before washing ashore. Young Harry's funeral was held at his grandfather's house, that of Thomas O. Moon. Laurance was counted amongst his survivors in Harry's obituary.[32] Tragedy almost struck again later that year when Laurance's father, Thomas, was lost at sea during a storm for over six days. The resolute mariner had come out of retirement to captain a boat called the *Buccaneer*, owned by the exclusive Buccaneer Club of New York. The ship was an old three-masted barkentine re-serviced as a type of floating night club for the exclusive members to escape the restrictive confines of prohibition by sailing beyond U.S. territorial waters to meet rum runners and allow its members to drink freely. A storm hit the boat around September 18, 1926, and for six days, it was not heard from and feared to have sunk. However, the battered ship did return to port, and all were safe, giving Thomas Moon at least one more daring tale to add to his repertoire of sea adventures.[33]

Yet, six months later, actual tragedy did strike as Laurance's eldest brother, George, died. The cause was not listed, but the funeral once again was held at their father's home. Laurance was again numbered among his brother's survivors.[34] The impact of these family deaths and near deaths is impossible to gauge. However, Laurance began a series of curious actions that would profoundly impact his life. Were they connected? At best, we can only speculate, but in the late 1920s, Laurance's actions show signs of extreme emotional distress, and his court-martial a decade and a half before seems to have been a part of it in some way.

By early 1928, Laurance contacted Senator Millard E. Tydings of Maryland regarding the court-martial. The nature and substance of his communication with Tydings are unknown since the only record of it is from letters from Army staff responding to it that were inserted into Laurance's court-martial record. A search in the Adjutant Generals Office Records and the Judge Advocate General's Office Records in the National Archives as well as the Millard Tydings Papers at the University of Maryland revealed no additional documents or even reference to it. Tydings apparently had written to the Army's Adjutant General, Major General Lutz Wahl. Wahl's office sent the request to the Judge Advocate General's Office (JAGO), where it was received on March 9, 1928. The Judge Advocate General, Major General J. A. Hull, looked into the case. His letter responding to Wahl does give some insight into Laurance's request. Moon asked Tydings to implore the army to have his court-martial "reopened for the hearing of certain evidence which Moon states he possesses and which he claims will disprove his guilt of the charges of which he was convicted and sentenced by general court-martial."[35]

Why, after 16 years, did Moon want his case reopened? What new evidence could he possess that would have convinced the Judge Advocate to overturn his conviction? Even though he did not recognize his service in 1917, the army considered him "honorably discharged," so why did this case mean so much to him now? The answers are unknown and made little difference to the Judge Advocate General. In his response to the Wahl, Hull stated the facts of the case, including the odd scenario of being found "Not Guilty" and then "Guilty" on the same day but claimed it was not against policy. Hull also noted the handwritten comment on Moon's court-martial paperwork: "This should be remarked upon as absolutely against the policy of the dept." Who wrote that cryptic note and why was not known, even to Hull. Were they referring to the shift from not guilty/to guilty? If it was against policy, why did the conviction stand? Or were they referring to the charges against Moon? Again, more mysteries.

In the end, as far as the Judge Advocate General was concerned, none of it mattered.

> Neither the penciled memorandum above quoted, nor the record contains anything to show what the memorandum pertained to or by whom it was written. While it might have pertained to the action of the court in considering its findings, there is nothing to show this to be the fact.

He went on to add that according to the "Manual for Courts-Martial and Army Regulations effective at the time of the trial . . . there was nothing irregular in the action of the court in reconsidering its findings of not guilty and substituting, therefore, findings of guilty." Thus, the Judge Advocate concluded

> Moon's trial and sentence having been legal and that part of the sentence pertaining to the dishonorable discharge and forfeiture having been carried to execution, the War Department is now without authority to reopen the case for the purpose of hearing evidence or of withdrawing or altering the dishonorable discharge which Moon received.

Adjutant General Wahl summarized Hull's comments in slightly more diplomatic terms for the letter to Senator Tydings. He strategically did not reference the handwritten note to that was also inserted in Moon's court-martial file to ensure the matter remained closed.[36]

The following summer, an interesting personal advertisement appeared in *The Baltimore Sun* by Laurance's wife, Lottie. "My husband stated in the *Sun* papers on July 28, 1929, that he would not be responsible for my debts. Please be advised that I have been self-supporting since January 11, 1919, and responsible for my own debts."[37] The posting was curious since the 1920 census did not list Lottie as being employed. The advertisement by Laurance she referenced also cannot be found. But clearly, once again, there seemed to be tension within Laurance's marital relationship.

By the fall of 1929, Laurance's emotional state seemed to have worsened as he wrote several angry and threatening postcards to prominent figures, including the Attorney General of the United States. The matter was deemed serious enough that the case was referred to U.S. Attorney W.W. Woodcock in Baltimore. On November 6, 1929, Woodcock asked for a warrant to arrest Laurance because he

> did unlawfully and knowingly deposit for mailing and deliver, a certain postcard address to "William D. Mitchell, United States Attorney General, Washington, D.C." upon which card is contained terms or language of a libelous, scurrilous, defamatory and threatening character, and which card was mailed at Baltimore, Maryland.

U.S. District Judge J. Frank Supplee, Jr. signed the warrant, and it was executed on November 21, 1929, by Mr. M.D. Traub, Special Agent for the Department of Justice. Moon was held on a $500 bond.[38]

Laurance's legal troubles once again garnered public attention. On Friday, November 21, the day of his arrest, *The Baltimore Sun* ran a short story about Moon's actions under the title "Held for Threats to Cabinet Officer. L.E. Moon Accused of Sending Slanderous Postal Cards to W.D. Mitchell." According to the *Sun*,

> Moon had been warned . . . against sending such cards and letters, after several had been sent to prominent persons in the last six months, and that he had been warned at least twice that such practices would get him in trouble.

However, Laurance "refused to comply and dispatched the card to Mr. Mitchell" and was "charged with violating that section of the United States penal code which prohibits sending obscene, libelous, slanderous, and threatening matter though the mail." The story was sensational enough that it was picked up by other newspapers across the state.[39]

The matter was brought before a federal grand jury on December 5, and Moon was indicted. The grand jury inquest provides additional details on the "libelous, scurrilous, defamatory and threatening character" of Laurance's correspondence and tantalizes historians but leaves them only thirsting for more. Moon disparaged the U.S. Attorney General by addressing the card to the

Dishonorable William D. Mitchell [emphasis added]
Attorney General of the United States
Washington, D.C., USA

In the text, Laurance blamed Mitchell and other unnamed individuals for some extreme but unknown personal and domestic struggles.

> You filthy bunch of political crooks (the
> intelligentsia of our country), you have ______[*expletive deleted?*]
> near tortured the life out of me.
> You have got to give me recognition the
> ensuring week or it is MURDER I commit.
> Your dirty, undermining work has turned
> my own household into enemies.
> THE MT VERNON LIFE INSURANCE COMPANY
> One of the Criminal Depots.
>
> L.E. Moon[40]

What could the U.S. Attorney General have done that would make Laurance believe he estranged him from his family? What would a life insurance company have to do with it? Was Moon expecting but not receiving a payout from his brother George's death? Were his recent efforts to reopen his court-martial related to whatever Laurance referenced with this card? Were the recent string of deaths and near-death experiences in the extended Moon family enough to prompt Laurance to try and get a life insurance policy for himself, only to be rebuffed because of a dishonorable discharge now nearly two decades old? Would that be why he tried to reopen the court-martial 16 years later? Or is this latest incident utterly unrelated to trying to overturn the court-martial? The record is provocative yet frustratingly silent, raising many more questions than answers. However, it clearly demonstrates that Laurance's emotional state seemed desperate.

Perhaps the enigmatic connections that Laurance spelled out in his cryptic message to the Attorney General were clouded by the impenetrable fog of genuine mental illness and, therefore, entirely opaque to anyone else. That certainly seemed like a possibility to Judge Supplee. On January 4, 1930, Judge Supplee issued an Order of the Court for the U.S. Marshals "to remove Laurence [sic] Edgar Moon from the Baltimore City Jail to the Mental Hygiene Clinic at 622 W. Lombard Street" so he could "be examined by Doctor M.S. Guttmacher, and thereafter to be returned to the Baltimore City Jail."[41] Of course, his evaluation is not part of the public record. Still, we can assume it was not positive because, on January 23, 1930, District Attorney Woodcock filed a motion of *Nolle Prosequi* (meaning "will not prosecute"). Laurance Moon, the motion claimed, "has been examined by two physicians of the Mental Hygiene Society of Maryland and has been declared insane in accordance with the laws of the State of Maryland, and a request made for his release to the State Authorities in order that he may be committed as an insane person." Moon was subsequently transferred to the Spring Grove Hospital for the Insane in Centerville, MD, and remanded to the custody of Dr. Leo Wallace, MD.[42]

What the exact diagnosis was and how long he stayed at Spring Grove Hospital is not clear. By the time the 1930 census was conducted at Spring Grove on April 14 to 21, Laurance was not listed as a patient. Interestingly enough, neither he nor Lottie were listed in Baltimore or elsewhere in the country. They apparently fell through the cracks of the census-taking process. Regardless, Laurance's recent dramatic fall had taken its toll, and perhaps his complaint that things had "turned" his own "household into enemies" might, in fact, have been true. When Laurance's father died in 1937, his obituary recounted his daring exploits. Still, it ended with: "Surviving are two sons, Chief Engineer William I. Moon of the Tolchester Ferry across the Chesapeake Bay and Captain Robert T. Moon of Norfolk, Va., and three daughters." Laurance's name was conspicuously absent.[43]

That same year, Laurance once again worked as a salesman in Baltimore, but by 1940, the U.S. Census listed him as a caretaker at a cemetery alongside his wife, Lottie. However, his wages were listed only at $400 a month, while Lottie was making $520 as the cemetery's superintendent. They had a border living with them, 52-year-old Mary Darby, who eclipsed them both working as a clerk for a railroad at $1700 a month.[44] Laurance's caretaking days ended when the U.S. entered World War II. In 1942, the Selective Service conducted its fourth registration, also known as the "Old Man's Registration," since it collected information on the wartime skills of men born between 1877 and 1897. Thus, at the age of 54, Laurance once again had to register for the draft. He did not claim exemption this time and listed his employment as a clerk for the Bethlehem Shipyard.[45]

By the beginning of the war, more changes occurred in the military regarding their relationship with people who enjoyed same-sex acts. In 1941, the Army Medical Corps declared homosexuals and those "with homosexual proclivities" as having "psychopathic personality disorders" and unsuitable for service. However, as was always the case in U.S. history, the exclusions would be loosely enforced in order to meet wartime manpower needs.[46] The U.S. Articles of War were modified again in 1950 as the new Uniformed Code of Military Justice went into effect, but the same exclusion was included in Article 125, which stated "any person subject to this chapter who engages in unnatural carnal copulation with another person of the same or opposite sex or with an animal is guilty of sodomy. Penetration, however slight, is sufficient to complete the offence."[47] Once again, it is unlikely Moon would have known nor cared about such changes.

After the war, the record becomes exceedingly scarce for both Laurance and Lottie. Sadly, the 1950 census, taken on April 21, once again listed Laurance as a patient at Spring Grove Hospital for the Insane. When he came, how long he was there, and for what reason is unknown. Lottie lived with her cousin Alice E. Culler and still worked as a superintendent of an unnamed cemetery.[48] After that, the record was silent until June 6, 1963, when Lottie passed away. Her obituary listed no children, only a niece named Mary Streib. Despite her and Laurance's struggles,

Lottie was remembered as Laurance's "beloved wife." Four and a half years later, on January 2, 1967, Laurance passed away at the age of 78.[49] Whether or not he finally recognized his honorable discharge from the army in 1917, it nonetheless granted him the right to be buried among his comrades at the Baltimore National Cemetery. The "star" of Troop F, First U.S. Cavalry in 1912, finally received the honor he rightfully deserved for his dutiful service despite the prejudice he faced.

Notes

1 General Court-Martial of Private Laurance E. Moon, Records of the Judge Advocate General, Record Group 153, National Archives and Record Administration, Washington, D.C., (hereafter Moon Court-Martial, RG 153, NARA), 190.
2 General Court-Martial of Private Harvey G. Simpson, Records of the Judge Advocate General, Record Group 153, National Archives and Record Administration, Washington, D.C., (hereafter Simpson Court-Martial, RG 153, NARA), 3; General Court-Martial of Joseph Bernard, 3. RG 153, NARA.
3 Simpson Court-Martial, RG 153, NARA, 3.
4 Moon Court-Martial, RG 153, NARA, 191.
5 Moon Court-Martial, RG 153, NARA, 191; Simpson Court-Martial, RG 153, NARA; Court-Martial of Private Joseph Bernard, Records of the Judge Advocate General, Record Group 153, National Archives and Record Administration, Washington, D.C.
6 "United States World War I Draft Registration Cards, 1917–1918," NARA microfilm publication M1509, Ancestry.com (hereafter U.S. World War I Draft Cards), s.v. Joseph Bernard.
7 U.S. Social Security Application and Claim Index, 1936–2007. Ancestry.com, s.v. Joseph Bernard.
8 U.S. Census, 1920, Butte City, Silverbow County, Montana, database with images, *FamilySearch.org*, https://familysearch.org/ark:/61903/1:1:K7XX-R2T (hereafter U.S. Census); U.S. World War I Draft Cards, s.v. Harvey Simpson.
9 "Simpson-Gilbert," *The Anaconda (Montana) Standard*, December 3, 1916, 25.
10 *The Butte (Montana) Miner*, July 31, 1924, 11.
11 "Montana, County Marriages, 1865–1950," database with images, *FamilySearch*, https://familysearch.org/ark:/61903/1:1:F37K-DH5, December 7, 2014; Harvey G. Simpson and Sarah E. Gilbert, November 30, 1916; citing Marriage, Silver Bow, Montana, county courthouses, Montana; FHL microfilm 1,906,954; "Montana, County Births and Deaths, 1840–2004," database with images, *FamilySearch.org*, https://familysearch.org/ark:/61903/1:1:QKNR-CN85, August 4, 2017; Harvey G. Simpson, July 2, 1929; citing Death, Butte, Silver Bow, Montana, United States, various county recorder offices; FHL microfilm 2,311,841; "Montana, County Marriages, 1865–1950," database with images, *FamilySearch.org*, https://familysearch.org/ark:/61903/3:1:S3HT-DZR9-YG5?cc=1609797&wc=M61M-7ZS%3A120254101, 21 May 2014, 004350511 > image 122 of 532; county courthouses, Montana.
12 "Ran Screaming Into Street," *Evening Sun* (Baltimore, MD), February 18, 1915, 14.
13 "Deserted Bride, She Says," *The Baltimore Sun*, May 3, 1917, 5.
14 "Marriage Licenses," *The Baltimore Sun*, May 22, 1917, 4.
15 "Qualified as Guardian," *Virginian-Pilot* (Norfolk, VA), December 4, 1814, 8.
16 Roland G. Moon, *The Virginian-Pilot* (Norfolk, VA), October 19, 1915, 3.
17 "Towed Barge to France, Captain Moon Home Again," *The Virginia-Pilot* (Norfolk, VA), September 4, 1916, 7.
18 Naoko Wake, "The Military, Psychiatry, and 'Unfit' Soldiers, 1939–1942," *Journal of the History of Medicine and Allied Sciences* 62, no. 4 (2007), 464–465; Eskridge, 100–101, 172–173.

19 Lehring, *Officially Gay*, 81–82.
20 Albert Abrams, "Homosexuality – A Military Menace," *Medical Review of Reviews* 24 (1918), 528–529.
21 *The Baltimore City Directory for 1917*. Accessed February 15, 2022, https://lib.guides.umd.edu/c.php?g=327119&p=2197762 (hereafter, *Baltimore City Directory*); Laurance Edgar Moon, United States World War I Draft Registration Cards, 1917–1918. NARA Microfilm Publication M1509.
22 The payroll of Detached Casuals Development Battalion, November 1 to December 2, 1918. National Personnel Records Center, National Archives and Record Administration, St. Louis, MO.
23 Major General J. A. Hull, Judge Advocate General to Senator Millard E. Tydings, February 29, 1928. General Court-Martial of Private Laurance E. Moon, RG 153, NARA, enclosure.
24 Lehring, *Officially Gay*, 107–110.
25 Major General J. A. Hull, Judge Advocate General to Senator Millard E. Tydings, February 29, 1928. Moon Court-Martial, RG 153, NARA, enclosure.
26 Major General J. A. Hull, Judge Advocate General to Senator Millard E. Tydings, February 29, 1928. Moon Court-Martial, RG 153, NARA, enclosure; Payroll of Detached Casuals Development Battalion, November 1 to December 2, 1918. National Personnel Records Center, National Archives and Record Administration, St. Louis, MO.
27 *The Baltimore City Directory for 1919*; U.S. Census, 1920, Baltimore County, Maryland.
28 "Newport Rector Alleges 'Vicious Methods' in Vice Probe," *The Baltimore Sun*, January 25, 1920, 8.
29 Lawrence R. Murphy, "Cleaning Up Newport: The U.S. Navy's Persecution of Homosexuals After World War I," *Journal of American Culture* 7, no. 3 (1984), 57–64; Chauncy, "Christian Brotherhood," 189–221; Berube, *Coming Out Under Fire*, 134; Lawrence R. Murphy, *Perverts by Official Order* (New York: Haworth, 1988), 97–121.
30 Chauncy, "Christian Brotherhood," 193–195, 204–205. For discussions on how medical discourse shaped the creation of a homosexual identity, see Michael Foucault, *The History of Sexuality: An Introduction*, translated by Robert Hurley (New York: Pantheon Books, 1978); Mary McIntosh, "The Homosexual Role," *Social Problems* 16 (1968), 182–192; Kenneth Plummer, ed., *The Making of the Modern Homosexual* (London: Hutchinson, 1981). More recent works consider nuances of how medical literature was only one part of a dynamic process. See Thomas Laqueur, *Making Sex: Body and Gender From the Greeks to Freud* (Cambridge, MA: Harvard University Press, 1990); Chauncey, *Gay New York*. Jonathan Ned Katz, *The Invention of Heterosexuality* (Chicago: University of Chicago Press, 2007); Asti Hustvedt, *Medical Muses: Hysteria in Nineteenth-Century Paris* (New York: W.W. Norton & Company, 2011).
31 "Dream Caused Wife to Arrest Husband," *Baltimore Sun*, April 19, 1923, 28.
32 "Bodies of Doctor and Soldier Cast Ashore Near Cape," *The Virginia-Pilot*, August 5, 1926, 1.
33 "Buccaneer Club Ship Missing for 6 Days," *Democrat and Chronicle* (Rochester, NY), September 24, 1926, 31.
34 George O. Moon, *Baltimore Sun*, March 22, 1927, 5.
35 Judge Advocate General (hereafter JAG), Maj. General J. A. Hull to U.S. Army Adjutant General (hereafter Adj. Gen.), Maj. General Lutz Wahl, Moon Court-Martial, RG 153, NARA, enclosure.
36 Hull to Wahl, Moon Court-Martial, RG 153, NARA, enclosure.
37 Laurance E. Moon, *The Baltimore Sun*, August 30, 1929, 21.
38 The affidavit, complaint, or information for a warrant, 16 November 1929, United States of America vs. Laurance E. Moon, Criminal Docket 13397, District Court of the United States for the District of Maryland, National Archives and Records Administration, Philadelphia, Pennsylvania.

39 "Held for Threats to Cabinet Officer. L.E. Moon Accused of Sending Slanderous Postal Cards to W.D. Mitchell." *The Baltimore Sun*, November 22, 1929, 30; "State News of the Day as Told by Reporters," *The Daily Times* (Salisbury, MD), November 22, 1929, 1.
40 Grand Jury Inquest, December 5, 1929, United States of America vs. Laurance E. Moon, Criminal Docket 13397, District Court of the United States for the District of Maryland, National Archives and Records Administration, Philadelphia, Pennsylvania.
41 Order of the Court, United States of America vs. Laurance E. Moon, Criminal Docket 13397, District Court of the United States for the District of Maryland, National Archives and Records Administration, Philadelphia, Pennsylvania.
42 Order of the Court, January 23, 1930, United States of America vs. Laurance E. Moon, Criminal Docket 13397, District Court of the United States for the District of Maryland, National Archives and Records Administration, Philadelphia, Pennsylvania
43 "Capt. Moon, 86, Dies at Home in Lansdowne, Md.," *The Times Dispatch* (Richmond, VA), January 5, 1935, 15.
44 *Baltimore City Directory for 1937*; U.S. Census, 1940, Ward 16, Baltimore City, Baltimore County, Maryland.
45 Laurance Edgar Moon, "United States World War II Draft Registration Cards," NARA Microfilm Publication M1939.
46 Lehring, *Officially Gay*.
47 Harry Stack Sullivan, "Selective Service Psychiatry," *Psychiatry* 4 (1941), 442, 451; Wake, "Military Psychiatry," 465; Berube, *Coming Out Under Fire*, 2, 276–277; Lehring, *Officially Gay*, 75–76; Peter D. Jacobson, "Sexual Orientation and the Military: Some Legal Considerations," in *Out in Force: Sexual Orientation and the Military*, eds. Gregory M. Herek, Jared B. Jobe, and Ralph M. Carney (Chicago: University of Chicago Press, 1996), 39–64.
48 U.S. Census 1950, Spring Grove State Mental Hospital, Baltimore County, Maryland.
49 "United States Census, 1940, Ward 16, Baltimore City, Baltimore County, Maryland; U.S. World War II Draft Cards, s.v. Laurance Edgar Moon, 1942, https://www.findagrave.com/cgi-bin/fg.cgi?page=gr&GRid=1006527.

Conclusion

Two and a half years after Laurance Moon passed away, on June 28, 1969, police raided a popular gay bar in New York City's Greenwich Village. Police raids and harassment frequently targeted the Stonewall Inn due to vice laws criminalizing homosexuality. As police conducted the raid, patrons of the Stonewall Inn unexpectedly resisted with a ferocity that took the police by surprise. Tensions escalated, and the crowd outside the bar grew in numbers, with onlookers and passersby joining the protest. People threw objects at the police, chanted slogans, and refused to disperse. The resistance continued for several days; demonstrators demanded an end to police harassment and to the larger criminalization of homosexuality. The riots were characterized by a spirit of defiance as the LGBTQ+ community pushed back against the systemic oppression they faced. The events at Stonewall ignited a broader movement for LGBTQ+ rights and became a catalyst for organizing and activism, inspiring subsequent protests, marches, and the formation of advocacy groups dedicated to fighting for equality and ending discrimination against the LGBTQ+ community.[1]

While the Stonewall riots were not the first instance of LGBTQ+ resistance, they marked a significant turning point, symbolizing a collective determination to challenge societal norms and demand change. The riots and the subsequent activism that followed were instrumental in shaping the modern gay rights movement and pushing for greater visibility, acceptance, and equal rights for the community, including those serving in the U.S. military. The impact of the riots on gays in the armed forces was evident in subsequent years as LGBTQ+ individuals and their allies fought for their right to serve openly. Grassroots organizations, such as the Servicemembers Legal Defense Network (SLDN), emerged to challenge discriminatory policies and advocate for equality in the military. The activism and awareness generated by the Stonewall riots contributed to a glacially slow but sizable shift in societal attitudes, eventually leading to policy changes.[2]

In 1975, Leonard Matlovich, a highly decorated Air Force Tech Sergeant who had served with distinction in Vietnam and always had the highest performance reviews, came out of the closet while still on active duty in a very public way. He declared his sexual orientation to *Time Magazine*, becoming the first openly gay service member to challenge the military's ban on homosexuality publicly. Despite facing subsequent discharge, Matlovich fought for his reinstatement, arguing for equal rights, and challenging the military's discriminatory policies. His case garnered significant attention and raised awareness about the issue of gays in the military.[3]

The government had put forth various justifications to support the ban on homosexuals serving in the military, echoing Lt. Keller's syllogistic arguments against Moon. Gay men and lesbians were deemed unfit based on mental and physical grounds, which Matlovich was trying to disprove and was subsequently reinforced by other numerous examples of gays who honorably served in the military. Even the American Psychological Association had renounced same-sex orientation as mental illness, but the military continued to hold on to that justification.[4] During the 1950s, Senator McCarthy and others had alleged that homosexuals posed a national security risk, but this was refuted by the Navy Crittenden Report, which found that alcoholics and adulterous heterosexuals posed greater security concerns.

The Crittenden Report, written in 1957, was kept secret, even from Tech Sgt. Matlovich, until 1976.[5] Officially called "Report of the Board Appointed to Prepare and Submit Recommendations to the Secretary of the Navy for the Revision of Policies, Procedures and Directives Dealing with Homosexuality," it was commissioned by the U.S. military in response to growing concerns about homosexuality within its ranks. The report, compiled by Air Force Colonel James Crittenden, concluded that homosexuality posed no inherent risk to military effectiveness and recommended that individuals should not be automatically barred from military service solely based on their sexual orientation. It dismissed the idea that homosexuals constitute a security risk but nonetheless did not advocate for an end to anti-gay discrimination because "the service should not move ahead of civilian society nor attempt to set substantially different standards in attitude or action with respect to homosexual offenders."[6]

The Matlovich case was only the first of many lawsuits in the 1970s and 1980s by service members challenging the ban on gays in the military in light of the growing gay rights movement after Stonewall. However, the military doubled down on its resistance to lifting its ban on gays. In 1982, the Department of Defense issued DoD Directive 1332.13, which stated:

> Homosexuality is incompatible with military service. The presence of such members adversely affects the ability of the Armed Forces to maintain discipline, good order, and morale; to foster mutual trust and confidence among the members; to ensure the integrity of rank and command; to facilitate assignment and worldwide deployment of members who frequently must live and work in close conditions affording minimal privacy; to recruit and retain members of the military services; and in certain circumstances, to prevent breaches of security.[7]

However, much to the Pentagon's chagrin, the controversy over the gay ban would not go away. In 1988, the Department of Defense ordered another study on the issue from the Defense Personnel Security Research and Education Center (PERSEREC), which only reinforced the conclusions of the Crittenden Report thirty years earlier. "Since [1957] no new data have been presented that would refute [the] conclusion that homosexuals are not greater security risks than heterosexuals."[8] The report also noted that:

> One of the most powerful reasons for rejecting change has to do with the imagery of the combat soldier. Although unsupported by evidence, the belief is widely held that men must be rugged, tough, and macho to achieve success in battle. In the belief system of current traditional military authorities, homosexual men cannot be rugged, tough, and macho. The stereotype of homosexual men centers on the feminized male who is unable to perform masculine tasks. It is interesting to note that this stereotype continues to flourish even though female personnel now perform all manner of military tasks except combat, and it is well known that such "macho males" as motorcyclists of the Hell's Angels type and many tough prisoners in correctional setting engage in homosexual behavior.[9]

Private Moon's case in 1912 only reinforced the PERSEREC conclusion, and displays of gendered masculine behavior and a preference for same-sex gratification are not inextricably connected. Laurance Moon was definitely a capable, even masculine, soldier who at least occasionally enjoyed sexual acts with other men. It did not interfere with his ability to be a good soldier. However, at least among the officer class, there was a growing manifestation of the heteronormative masculine paradigm that queer soldiers like Moon faced growing prejudice based on biased and ill-informed assumptions. Even though the enlisted men of Moon's troop seem to have had a more open attitude, the officers had more social and legal power, particularly in the service but also outside of it, and it is not surprising their view became the dominant view. Historian Gary Lehring contends that once that view became criminalized in the military, discrimination and homophobia against LGBTQ+ people also became institutionalized in the civilian American culture at large.[10]

Over the 20th century, the officers' moral conception of same-sex gratification, grounded in a rigid hetero-homo binary, became the dominant interpretation both within and outside the military. The "normal exception" revealed in Moon's court-martial demonstrates that, initially, enlisted men held a more flexible, less morally defined view of same-sex acts, focusing on the behavior itself without attaching strict moral labels. However, as the military grew more bureaucratic and aligned with broader societal norms, the officers' perspective – labeling same-sex acts as "immoral" or "abnormal" – became more widely enforced, gradually influencing the views of enlisted men as well. This shift stemmed from the military's increasing emphasis on discipline, order, and conformity, reflecting civilian anxieties about sexual deviance. As the binary notion of "homosexuality" solidified, its clarity and rigidity appealed to the military's need for control, contrasting with the earlier, more fluid understanding among enlisted men. The officers' moralizing framework provided an easily enforceable standard that aligned with institutional goals, and as the U.S. military set broader societal precedents during wartime and social change, this interpretation spread beyond its ranks. By pathologizing and oversimplifying same-sex desire, the military reinforced a binary understanding of sexuality, entrenching the stigmatization of non-heteronormative behaviors for much of the century.

The PERSEREC report also noted that the only real resistance to lifting the ban on gays in the military was purely a social construction. "The unreasoned resistance to learning or interacting with homosexuals has led to the formulation of the concept of *homophobia*," they concluded. And they conceded that homophobia was, like all phobias, "connoting unreasoned fear and avoidance of certain classes of objects." It seemed particularly strong in men, the report concluded. "Some men experience uneasy feelings when in close proximity to other men who are identified as homosexuals. It is as if such nearness could pollute one's identity." It had also become endemic in "the conventional attitude structure of American males. It is based on entrenched religious beliefs, folklore, and stereotypes" as well as "the strong motivation" to "disown the possibility of having homosexual interests." In the highly masculinized military, homophobia, based on nothing more than pure, unreasoned prejudice and fear, was, in fact, the true enemy both in 1912 and for the century after. However, by the 1980s, homophobic "attitudes are connected to the heroic and positively valued image of the powerful, virile heterosexual male and the degraded and negatively valued image of the powerless, weak, feminized, homosexual male," according to the report.[11]

In Moon's case, homosexuality was not yet fully defined or stereotyped by society at large, at least by the enlisted men in his troop. By denying him and others the queer space outside of the hetero-homo binary, the growing dominance of the officer class's construct helped push the acceptance of the heteronormative masculine paradigm that the PERSEREC report identified. By giving it the name "homosexual," it acquired meaning, a definition with parameters and mental substance, to find a convenient and efficient way to convey that meaning (with all its stereotypes) to others. It became a "pointer" of sorts for the rest of the world to understand an assumed common sense of social substance for those to which the label was applied.[12]

However, at the same time, that now-defined paradigm also spawned a yin to its yang when hostility and homophobia rose in response to the new concrete homosexual construct and its unmasculine meaning. In the queer space found in the "normal exception" of Moon's court-martial demonstrates how men could explore expressions of sexuality with other men among the working class. However, as the military leadership and society increasingly sought to order, medicalize, strengthen, and oversimplify conceptual understandings of same-sex attractions, the person who engaged in sodomy was no longer judged by their actions alone, but rather by their actions became indicative of their entire moral character. Such behaviors were seen as morally dangerous aberrations in larger societal frameworks but were, in fact, benignly normalized within specific subcultures. But through the 20th century, the officers' more morally rigid concepts prevailed and became endemic.

This shift reinforced the rigid binary of sexual identity, further marginalizing those who fell outside the newly established norms, and transformed what had been a more benignly fluid understanding of same-sex behavior into a stigmatized identity marker. They were labeled, and thus, society thrust upon them an identity with which they had little control other than to negotiate their reactions to it.[13] Without the label and the assumed stereotypes associated with it, homophobia would not have existed in the way it developed, and the military's prejudice against gays that the PERESERC report idcntified might not have been as entrenched.

In the 1992 presidential campaign, Democratic candidate Bill Clinton brought the issue to a head and promised to end the exclusion of gays in the military. Once elected, he met with his Joint Chief of Staff, General Colin Powell, to discuss the issue. Powell vociferously resisted lifting the ban, but President Clinton told him, "I made a campaign promise, and I sure want to keep it." Yet, he added, "I also took an oath last week as commander in chief, and I have to consider the well-being of the armed forces." Powell recollected that the discussion was "respectful but tense." He was "increasingly disappointed that this issue had been allowed to become the new administration's first military priority." Still, he also felt "the President had given us a fair hearing. He knew where the military stood, and he had shown a willingness to compromise."[14] The issue then proceeded to Capitol Hill, where hearings were held to explore lifting the ban. There, homophobia, in not so many words, took center stage under the guise of military efficiency.

On May 11, 1993, Senator Sam Nunn, Chair of the Senate Armed Services Committee, called witnesses to testify on the ban. In the afternoon, rank-and-file service personnel, some of whom were gay, would testify to lifting the ban. But in the morning, the lead-off witnesses would testify about the detrimental effects such a move would have. The presumed star witness would be recently retired army four-star general Norman Schwarzkopf, still in the public's adoration for his victory in the 1992 Gulf War and his captivating briefings with strong camera presence. Also testifying would be Marine Corps Major Kathleen Bergeron, Navy Command Master Chief David Bourne, who happened to be Black, and Marine Corps public relations specialist Colonel Frederick Peck. The selection of witnesses was meant to convey the diversity of opinions against lifting the ban and undermine the comparison to previous integration battles in the military around women and African Americans. With a woman, a Black man, a public war hero, and an articulate and charismatic public relations officer, they presented their case, full of the prejudicial stereotypes that had developed through the 20th century.

General Schwarzkopf began by admitting that many gay and lesbian service members had served honorably in the past. Doing so, he avoided the claim that they do not make good soldiers and that a service member's sexuality was not what was important to him, but rather, it was the openness of their behavior. He felt that given the unique conditions of the military, openly gay individuals would affect "unit cohesion." "As I've said before," he said, "homosexuals have served in the past and done a great job of serving their country and can do so in the future. It is a question of open homosexuality in a unit that causes this breakdown of unit cohesion."[15] The other members of the panel agreed throughout the rest of the hearing. Schwarzkopf added, "We have the finest armed services we've ever had in the history of America, I will confess to you I have a lot of trouble trying to figure out why we're fixing something that clearly isn't broken" and that lifting the ban would "have a serious impact upon the quality of our armed forces. I think, in fact, we will end up with a second-class armed force for quite some time in the future."[16] The prejudicial ban on gays, in the general's mind, had made the U.S.

Army the dominant force in the world. His biased, unchallenged, and unopposed assumptions were that the stereotyped heteronormative masculine warrior would presumably be undermined by openly gay personnel. This was the heart of what the PERESERC report stated was homophobia's "uneasy feeling [some men feel] when in close proximity to other men who are identified as homosexuals. It is as if such nearness could pollute one's identity." Since the identity of the military was collectively the heterosexual masculine warrior, the fear was they could pollute the organization like a virus.

Colonel Frederick Peck's testimony was perhaps the most poignant of all the panelists. He towed the party line that openly gay soldiers and sailors do not fit within the military culture. "It's not the worth of the individual we are talking about here," he claimed. "We're not saying that because people are too short or too tall, or mentally deficient, or physically deficient somehow or another, that their personal worth is something less. We're just saying they don't fit in."[17] Peck said the military is a unique and special environment within American society. "Serving in the military is not a right, it is a privilege. . . . We have a right in the military to discriminate."[18] And, as it turned out, the policy was very personal for Colonel Peck. With very little explanation but a presumed understanding that gays would pollute the masculine military complex, he said, "If the ban on gays and lesbians serving in the military were to be dropped, I would counsel all three of my sons to stay out of the military, absolutely."[19] Colonel Peck's testimony then became even more emotional as he talked explicitly about his son Scott.

Figure C.1 Colonel Frederick Peck, USMC, testifying before Congress in 1993 on the military's ban on homosexuals, where he admitted his own son was gay. CSPAN.

Scott Peck was a senior at the University of Maryland Baltimore County. He had been writing several op-ed pieces in the student newspaper about the injustice of the military's ban on gays. His father, stationed in Somalia, was keenly aware of the fever pitch the issue was reaching and asked for information from his son to explore the subject in greater depth. When the colonel returned to the States just days before testifying, Scott informed him that his writing was more than just political opinions; he was gay. "I knew when I was in first grade that I was attracted to men," Scott later recalled. He was very nervous to tell his father. "We are talking about a Marine colonel who is Republican on top of that," he said. The conversation went well, all things considered. They settled on a "gentlemen's agreement" to agree to disagree on the military ban. However, "My father said that homosexuality was genetic and was not a chosen lifestyle, and he had no religious or moral objection to homosexuality," Scott told reporters. He understood why his father still had to speak his truth to the Senate committee about the ban. "My father is one of the few individuals who has an ethical code and always seems to live by it."[20]

At the hearing, Colonel Peck told the senators, "If [Scott] were to come into the recruiter's office, it would be the recruiter's dream come true – 6-foot-1, blue-eyed, blond hair, great student." That sentence revealed how significantly the prejudicial military masculine stereotype was ingrained that an athletic Aryan male ideal was the epitome of a soldier. It is also curious how Major Kathleen Bergeron, seated at the end of the table from Peck, might have responded to the slight that men are the recruiter's "dream come true," and not women or Command Master Chief David Bourne to Peck's adoration of a white racial ideal. Then Peck nervously started rubbing his hands together and added, "If he were to go and seriously consider joining the military . . . I would have to actively fight it" because "my son Scott is a homosexual, and I don't think there's any place for him in the military." He quickly added, "I love him as much as I do any of my sons. I respect him. I think he's a fine person."[21] His son was touched. "You can't ask much more than to have your father accept you in front of the U.S. Senate," Scott said.[22]

Colonel Peck then elaborated on why he felt so strongly that the military was not the right place for Scott, and it revealed how far the embracing of the military's heteronormative masculine culture had come since Moon's case in 1912 as well as the growth of the concurrent homophobia. "I've spent 27 years of my life in the military, and I know what it would be like for him if he went in. And it would be hell. I would be very fearful that his life would be in jeopardy from his own troops." Coldly and matter-of-factly, he told the senators that "he would be at grave risk . . . I'm not saying that that's right or wrong, or whatever. I'm just telling you that's the way it is. . . . Fratricide is something that exists out there, and there are people who would put my son's life at risk in our own armed forces."[23] While Peck's impressions might have been exaggerated, even if he did actually believe them, it is far from Private Moon's case 80 years earlier. If merely being a gay soldier threatened Scott Peck's life if he became a soldier, Moon's case before the institutionalization of military homophobia demonstrates that it was not the case given his popularity within his troop.

In 1994, the military compromised with politicians in the infamous "Don't Ask, Don't Tell" policy that allowed gays to serve in the armed forces so long as they did so in the proverbial closet to make the heteronormative service members more comfortable. That remained the standard policy for almost the next 20 years. Groups of service members continued to fight for lifting the ban entirely and allowing them to serve openly. Rather than using the rhetoric of a civil rights issue, they met the military on their chosen battleground. If the military felt the ban was effective because of military effectiveness, the new tactics demonstrated the cost, both in monetary terms and in the loss of essential skills, that the ban cost. As the nation embarked on the prolonged Afghan and Iraqi wars in the early 21st century, both costs became evident to the military brass.

Combined with the rapidly shifting acceptance of queer individuals by American society at large, President Obama began to look at ending the ban entirely. At an address to the Human Rights Campaign in 2009, he told gay service members and veterans, "It's not for me to tell you to be patient any more than it was for others to counsel patience to African Americans petitioning for equal rights half a century ago." He had resurrected the Civil Rights analogy, which had not been effective in 1993, but then also added practical considerations about military effectiveness with expelling gay and lesbian service members, which had been a more effective strategy. "We cannot afford to cut from our ranks people with the critical skills we need to fight. We should be celebrating their willingness to show such courage and selflessness on behalf of fellow citizens, especially when we are fighting two wars."[24] The ugly era of at least official military prejudice ended on September 20, 2011, when Congress finally passed, and President Obama signed, the bill ending the "don't ask, don't tell" policy and the criminalization of same-sex acts by service members, 99 years after Laurance Moon was court-martialed.[25]

Despite the official decriminalization of LGBTQ+ identities, service members still face substantial challenges. Discrimination remains widespread, with LGBTQ+ individuals experiencing higher rates of harassment and unfair treatment compared to their non-LGBTQ+ peers. This discrimination spans public spaces, workplaces, housing, and even within the military itself. Transgender service members encounter particular difficulties as policies and attitudes toward gender identity differ significantly across military settings and states. Increasing state-level anti-LGBTQ+ legislation raises concerns about the safety and well-being of service members and their families. Laws restricting gender-affirming healthcare and regulating educational content create hostile environments, sometimes forcing military families to relocate to more supportive areas, disrupting their lives and careers. Furthermore, political debates and backlash against diversity and inclusion initiatives within the military contribute to a sense of instability and lack of support for LGBTQ+ service members. The end of "Don't Ask, Don't Tell" marked progress, but the fight for LGBTQ+ rights in the military is far from over.

Notes

1 Bronski, *A Queer History*, 209–210, 214, 219; John-Manuel Andriote, *Stonewall Strong: Gay Men's Heroic Fight for Resilience, Good Health, and a Strong Community* (Boston: Rowman & Littlefield, 2017), 101–105.

2 Berube, *Coming Out Under Fire*, 271–272; Shilts, *Conduct Unbecoming*, 283–285; Barry Adam, *The Rise of Gay and Lesbian Movement* (Boston: GK Hall & Co., 1987), 58.
3 "Armed Forces: Homosexual Sergeant," *Time*, June 9, 1975; "The Sexes: The Sergeant v. the Air Force," *Time*, September 8, 1975; "Armed Forces: No to Matlovich," *Time*, September 19, 1975.
4 Berube, *Coming Out Under Fire*, 160, 202; Lehring, *Officially Gay*, 57–60, 66–70.
5 E. Lawrence Gibson, *Get Off My Ship: Ensign Berg vs. the U.S. Navy* (New York: Avon, 1978), 256–267.
6 S. H. Crittenden, "Report of the Board Appointed to Prepare and Submit Recommendations to the Secretary of the Navy for the Revision of Policies, Procedures, and Directives Dealing with Homosexuality," Chairman S.H. Crittenden (Washington, D.C.: Government Printing Office, 1957), 30.
7 Department of Defense Directive 1332.14 (1982). Accessed January 12, 2023, https://usiraq.procon.org/sourcefiles/DOD-Directive-1332-14.pdf.
8 Theodore R. Sarbin and Kenneth E. Karols, *Nonconforming Sexual Orientation in the Military and Society* (Washington, D.C.: Defense Personnel Security Research and Education Center, PERS-TR-89–002, December 1988), 29. Accessed January 12, 2023, https://archive.org/details/NonconformingSexualOrientationintheMilitaryandinSociety.
9 Sarbing and Karols, "Nonconforming Sexual Orientation," 27–28.
10 Lehring, *Officially Gay*, 47–51, 72–74, 188–189.
11 Sarbing and Karols, "Nonconforming Sexual Orientation," 30.
12 Steven Pinker, *The Stuff of Thought: Language as a Window into Human Nature* (New York: Viking, 2007), 287–288.
13 McIntosh, "The Homosexual Role," 1892; Chauncey, "Christian Brotherhood," 203; Bronski, *A Queer History*, 95; Katz, "The Invention of Heterosexuality"; Lehring, *Officially Gay*, 44–47.
14 Powell and Persico, *My American Journey*, 572–573.
15 Testimony of U.S. Army General (ret.) Norman Schwarzkopf (hereafter Schwarzkopf), U.S. Senate Armed Services Committee, May 11, 1993. "Homosexuals in the Military, Part 1." Accessed November 24, 2021, https://www.c-span.org/video/?40573-1/homosexuals-military-part-1, 1:04:21 (hereafter "Homosexuals in the Military, Part 1," May 11, 1993. CSPAN).
16 Testimony Schwarzkopf, "Homosexuals in the Military, Part 1," May 11, 1993. CSPAN, 105:21; 1:57:51.
17 Testimony of Colonel Frederick Peck, USMC (hereafter Peck), "Homosexuals in the Military, Part 1," May 11, 1993. CSPAN, 27:23.
18 Testimony of Peck, "Homosexuals in the Military, Part 1," May 11, 1993. CSPAN, 58:37.
19 Testimony of Peck, "Homosexuals in the Military, Part 1," May 11, 1993. CSPAN, 27:54.
20 "A Marine Father, a Gay Son . . ." *Tampa Bay Times*, May 13, 1993, 1.
21 Testimony of Peck, "Homosexuals in the Military, Part 1," May 11, 1993. CSPAN, 28:19.
22 "A Marine Father, a Gay Son . . ." *Tampa Bay Times*, May 13, 1993, 1.
23 Testimony of Peck, "Homosexuals in the Military, Part 1," May 11, 1993. CSPAN, 29:01.
24 Barack Obama, "It's Not For Me to Tell You to Be Patient," Remarks to Human Rights Campaign Dinner, Washington, D.C., October 11, 2009, in *Vital Speeches of the Day* 75, no. 12 (December 2009), 543–545.
25 Michael B. Donley, Norton A. Schwartz, and James A. Roy. *Memorandum for ALMAJCOM-FOA-DRU/CC: Subject: Repeal of Don't Ask, Don't Tell (DADT).* September 20, 2011, https://web.archive.org/web/20120105175738/http://cdn.theatlantic.com/static/mt/assets/steve_clemons/Repeal%20of%20DADT.pdf.

Bibliography

Newspapers

Anaconda Standard (Anaconda, MT)
Baltimore Sun (Baltimore, MD)
Bismarck Tribune (Bismarck, ND)
Boston Globe (Boston, MA)
Butte Miner (Butte, MT)
Detroit Lancet (Detroit, MI)
Evening Sun (Baltimore, MD)
Portland Press Herald (Portland, Maine)
San Francisco Chronicle (San Francisco, CA)
San Francisco Examiner (San Francisco, CA)
Tampa Bay Times (Tampa Bay, FL)
The Times Dispatch (Richmond, VA)
Virginia Citizen (Irvington, VA)
Virginian-Pilot (Norfolk, VA)

Archival

American Psychiatric Association. Application for Leave to File Brief Amici Curiae in Support of the Parties Challenging the Marriage Exclusion, Case No. S1477999 in the Supreme Court of the State of California, 2012.

Department of Defense (DoD) Directive 1332.14 (1982). Government Accounting Office. Accessed January 12, 2023, https://www.gao.gov/assets/nsiad-92-98.pdf

Digitized Baltimore City Directories. University of Maryland, https://lib.guides.umd.edu/c.php?g=327119&p=2197762

Find a Grave Index, 1600s-Current. HeritageQuest.com, https://www.ancestryheritagequest.com/search/collections/60525/

Fort Yellowstone Cemetery Records. Yellowstone National Park Library (YNPL), Vertical File (V.F.).

General Orders and Memoranda, Record Group 393, Records of Continental Commands, Fort Yellowstone, General Orders and Memoranda, National Archives and Records Administration, Washington, D.C.

Grand Jury Inquest, December 5, 1929. United States of America vs. Laurance E. Moon, Criminal Docket 13397, District Court of the United States for the District of Maryland, National Archives and Records Administration, Philadelphia, Pennsylvania.

Letters Received, Fort Yellowstone, WY. Record Group 393, Records of Continental Commands, Fort Yellowstone, General Orders and Memoranda, National Archives and Records Administration, Washington, D.C.

Montana, County Births and Deaths, 1840–2004. Database With Images, FamilySearch, https://www.familysearch.org

Montana, County Marriages, 1865–1950. Database With Images, FamilySearch, https://www.familysearch.org

Order of the Court, January 23, 1930. United States of America vs. Laurance E. Moon, Criminal Docket 13397, District Court of the United States for the District of Maryland, National Archives and Records Administration, Philadelphia, Pennsylvania.

Order of the Court. United States of America Vs. Laurance E. Moon, Criminal Docket 13397, District Court of the United States for the District of Maryland, National Archives and Records Administration, Philadelphia, Pennsylvania.

Records of the Judge Advocate General, Record Group 153 National Archives and Record Administration, Washington, D.C.

Summary Court-Martial Records. Record Group 393, Records of Continental Commands, Fort Yellowstone, General Orders and Memoranda, National Archives and Records Administration, Washington, D.C.

Testimony of Colonel Frederick Peck, USMC. "Homosexuals in the Military, Part 1." May 11, 1993. Accessed November 24, 2021, https://www.c-span.org/video/?40573-1/homosexuals-military-part-1

The Affidavit, Complaint, or Information for Warrant, November 16, 1929. United States of America Vs. Laurance E. Moon, Criminal Docket 13397, District Court of the United States for the District of Maryland, National Archives and Records Administration, Philadelphia, Pennsylvania.

The Payroll of Detached Casuals Development Battalion, November 1 to December 2, 1918. National Personnel Records Center, National Archives and Record Administration, St. Louis, MO.

United States World War I Draft Registration Cards, 1917–1918. National Archives and Records Administration (NARA) Microfilm Publication M1509.

United States World War II Draft Registration Cards, Fourth Registration, 1942. National Archives and Records Administration (NARA) Microfilm Publication M1939.

U.S. Census 1890. U.S. Federal Census Collection, HeritageQuest.com, https://www.ancestryheritagequest.com/search/categories/usfedcen/

U.S. Census 1900. U.S. Federal Census Collection, HeritageQuest.com, https://www.ancestryheritagequest.com/search/categories/usfedcen/

U.S. Census 1910. U.S. Federal Census Collection, HeritageQuest.com, https://www.ancestryheritagequest.com/search/categories/usfedcen/

U.S. Census 1920. U.S. Federal Census Collection, HeritageQuest.com, https://www.ancestryheritagequest.com/search/categories/usfedcen/

U.S. Census 1930. U.S. Federal Census Collection, HeritageQuest.com, https://www.ancestryheritagequest.com/search/categories/usfedcen/

U.S. Census 1940. U.S. Federal Census Collection, HeritageQuest.com, https://www.ancestryheritagequest.com/search/categories/usfedcen/

U.S. Census 1950. U.S. Federal Census Collection, HeritageQuest.com, https://www.ancestryheritagequest.com/search/categories/usfedcen/

U.S. Social Security Application and Claim Index, 1936–2007. HeritageQuest.com, https://www.ancestryheritagequest.com/search/collections/3693/

U.S.S. Hercules II (YT-13). Accessed February 5, 2021, https://www.history.navy.mil/research/histories/ship-histories/danfs/h/hercules-ii.html

Virginia Military Institute Roster Database. Accessed March 10, 2021, https://archivesweb.vmi.edu/rosters/record.php?ID=4161

Published

"Armed Forces: Homosexual Sergeant." *Time*, June 9, 1975.

"Armed Forces: No to Matlovich." *Time*, September 19, 1975.

"NH 73908 CSS Nansemond (1863–1865)." *Naval History and Heritage Command.* Accessed November 17, 2022, https://www.history.navy.mil/content/history/nhhc/our-collections/photography/numerical-list-of-images/nhhc-series/nh-series/NH-73000/NH-73908.html.

"The Sexes: The Sergeant v. the Air Force." *Time*, September 8, 1975.

Abrams, Albert. "Homosexuality – A Military Menace." *Medical Review of Reviews* 24 (1918), 528–529.

Adam, Barry. *The Rise of Gay and Lesbian Movement*. Boston: GK Hall & Co., 1987.

Adams, James Eli. *Dandies and Desert Saints: Styles of Victorian Masculinity*. Ithaca: Cornell University Press, 1995.

Allsep, L. Michael, Jr. "The Myth of the Warrior: Martial Masculinity and the End of Don't Ask, Don't Tell." *Journal of Homosexuality* 60, no. 2 (2003), 384, 386–387.

Allsep, Michael L., Jr. "The Myth of the Warrior: Martial Masculinity and the End of Don't Ask, Don't Tell." *Journal of Homosexuality* 60, no. 3 (2016), 381–400.

American Psychiatric Association. *Application for Leave to File Brief Amici Curiae in Support of the Parties Challenging the Marriage Exclusion, Case No. S1477999 in the Supreme Court of the State of California*, 2012.

Anderson, Fiona. "A Trail of Drift and Debris: Traces of Whitman in the Correspondence Art of Ray Johnson." *Journal of American Studies* 49 (2015), 55–75.

Andriote, John-Manuel. *Stonewall Strong: Gay Men's Heroic Fight for Resilience, Good Health, and a Strong Community*. Boston: Rowman & Littlefield, 2017.

Anon. *Uniform Diswcrimination: The "Don't Ask, Don't Tell" Policy of the U.S. Military*. New York: Human Rights Watch, 2003.

Arkin, William, and Lynne R. Dobrofsky. "Military Socialization and Masculinity." *Social Issues* 34, no. 1 (1978), 151–168.

Barbezat, Michael D. "Bodies of Spirit and Bodies of Flesh: The Significance of the Sexual Practices Attributed to Heretics from the Eleventh to the Fourteenth Century." *Journal of the History of Sexuality* 25, no. 3 (2016), 387–419.

Bateman, Geoffrey. *Don't Ask, Don't Tell: Debating the Gay Ban in the Military*. Boulder, CO: Lynne Rienner, 2003.

Bederman, Gail. *Manliness and Civilization: A Cultural History of Gender and Race in the United States, 1880–1917*. Chicago: University of Chicago Press, 1995.

Belkin, Aaron. *Bring Me Men: Military Masculinity and the Benign Façade of American Empire, 1989–2001*. New York: Columbia University Press, 2012.

Benemann, William. *Male-Male Intimacy in Early America: Beyond Romantic Friendships*. New York: Routledge, 2006.
Berube, Allan. *Coming Out Under Fire: The History of Gay Men and Women in World War II*. Chapel Hill: University of North Carolina Press, 1990.
Betros, Lance. *Carved From Granite: West Point Since 1902*. College Station: Texas A&M University Press, 2012.
Bingham, Caroline. "Seventeenth-Century Attitudes Toward Deviant Sex." *Journal of Interdisciplinary History* 1 (1971), 447–468.
Blackburn, Gregory. "Army Men: Military Masculinity in Call of Duty." In *Masculinities in Play*, edited by Nicholas Taylor and Gerald Voorhees, 37–53. London: Palgrave Macmillan, 2018.
Boag, Peter. "Sexuality, Gender, and Identity in Great Plains History and Myth." *Great Plains Quarterly* 18, no. 4 (Fall 1998), 335.
Boag, Peter. *Re-Dressing America's Frontier Past*. Berkeley: University of California Press, 2011.
Bobzein, Susanne. "Ancient Logic." In *Stanford Encyclopedia of Philosophy*, edited by Edward N. Zalta. Accessed January 12, 2023. https://plato.stanford.edu/entries/logic-ancient/.
Borch, Christian. *The Politics of Crowds: An Alternative History of Society*. New York: Cambridge University Press, 2012.
Brady, Sean. "All About Eve? Queer Theory and History." *Journal of Contemporary History* 41, no. 1 (2006), 185–195.
Brasas, Juan Herrero. *Walt Whitman's Mystical Ethics of Comradeship: Homosexuality and the Marginality of Friendship at the Crossroads of Modernity*. Albany, NY: SUNY Press, 2010.
Braudel, Fernand. "History and the Social Sciences: The Longue Durée." In *On History*, translated by Sarah Matthews, 27–38. Chicago: The University of Chicago Press, 1980.
Bristow, Edward J. *Vice, and Vigilance: Purity Movements in Britain Since 1700*. Totowa, NJ: Rowman and Littlefield, 1977.
Bronfenbrenner, Urie. "Towards an Experimental Ecology of Human Development." *American Psychologist* 32, no. 7 (1977), 513–531.
Bronfenbrenner, Urie. "Environments in Developmental Perspective: Theoretical and Operational Models." In *Measuring Environment Across the Life Span: Emerging Methods and Concepts*, edited by S. L. Friedman and T. D. Wachs, 3–28. New York: American Psychological Association, 1999.
Bronfenbrenner, Urie, and Ann C. Crouter. "The Environmental Models in Development Research." In *Handbook of Child Psychology: History, Theory, and Methods*, edited by P. H. Mussen and W. Kessen, Vol. 1, 198, 357–414. New York: Wiley.
Bronski, Michael. *A Queer History of the United States*. Boston: Beacon Press, 2011.
Brown, Richard D. "Microhistory and the Post-Modern Challenge." *Journal of the Early Republic* 23, no. 1 (2003), 1–20.
Brucker, Gene. *Giovanni and Lusanna: Love and Marriage Renaissance Florence*. Berkeley: University of California Press, 2004.
Bungaard, Axel. *Muscle and Manliness: The Rise of Sport in American Boarding Schools*. Syracuse, NY: Syracuse University Press, 2005.
Butler, Judith. "Performative Acts and Gender Constitution: An Essay in Phenomenology and Feminist Theory." *Theater Journal* 40, no. 4 (1988), 519–531.
Butler, Judith. *Undoing Gender*. Boston: Routledge, 2004.
Campagne, John. "Walt Whitman, Our Great Gay Poet?" *Journal of Homosexuality* 55 (2008), 648–664.
Canterella, Eva. *Bisexuality in the Ancient World*. New Haven: Yale University Press, 2002.
Cartledge, Paul. "The Politics of Spartan Pederasty." *Proceedings of the Cambridge Philological Society* 207, no. 27 (1981), 17–36.
Cartledge, Paul. *The Spartans: The World of the Warrior-Heroes of Ancient Greece*. New York: Overlook Press, 2003.

Caslen, Robert L., Cindy R. Jebb, Daniel Gade, and Hope C. Landsem. *Getting to the Left of Sharp: Lessons From West Point's Efforts to Combat Sexual Harassment and Assault.* Carlisle, PA: Strategic Studies Institute, US Army War College, 2015.

Chambers, John Whiteclay, II. *The Tyranny of Change: America in the Progressive Era, 1890–1920.* New York: St. Martin's Press, 1992.

Chauncey, George, Jr. "Christian Brotherhood or Sexual Perversion? Homosexual Identities and the Construction of Sexual Boundaries in the World War One Era." *Journal of Social History* 19, no. 2 (Winter 1985), 189–213.

Chauncey, George, Jr. *Gay New York: Gender, Urban Culture, and the Making of the Gay Male World, 1890–1940.* New York: Basic Books, 1994.

Cocks, Harry G. "The Growing Pains of the History of Sexuality." *Journal of Contemporary History* 39, no. 4 (October 2004), 657–666.

Cohen, Thomas V. *Love and Death in Renaissance Italy.* Chicago: University of Chicago Press, 2004.

Connell, R.W. *Masculinities,* 2nd ed. Los Angeles: University of California Press, 2005.

Copi, Irving. *Introduction to Logic*, 3rd ed. New York: Macmillan Co., 1969.

Crenson, Matthew A. *Baltimore: A Political History.* Baltimore: Johns Hopkins University Press, 2007, 115–124, 316–328.

Crittenden, S. H. "Report of the Board Appointed to Prepare and Submit Recommendations to the Secretary of the Navy for the Revision of Policies, Procedures, and Directives Dealing With Homosexuality." Chairman S.H. Crittenden. Washington, D.C.: Government Printing Office, 1957.

Crozier, Ivan. *Sexual Inversion: A Critical Edition.* London: Palgrave Macmillan, 2008.

Cullum, George W. *Biographic Register of the Officers and Graduates of the U.S. Military Academy at West Point, New York Since Its Establishment in 1802*, Vol. IV, 1890–1900. Edited by Edward S. Holden. Saginaw, Michigan: Seeman & Peters, 1901.

Cullum, George W. *Biographic Register of the Officers and Graduates of the U.S. Military Academy at West Point, New York Since Its Establishment in 1802*, Vol. V, 1900–1910. Edited by Lieut. Charles Braden. Saginaw, Michigan: Seeman & Peters, 1910.

Cullum, George W. *Biographic Register of the Officers and Graduates of the U.S. Military Academy at West Point, New York Since Its Establishment in 1802*, Vol. VI, 1910–1920. Edited by Colonel Wirt Robison. Saginaw, Michigan: Seeman & Peters, 1920.

Cullum, George W. *Biographic Register of the Officers and Graduates of the U.S. Military Academy at West Point, New York Since Its Establishment in 1802*, Vol. VII, 1920–1930. Edited by Captain Wm. H. Donaldson. Chicago: R.R. Donnelley & Sons, 1930.

Cullum, George W. *Biographic Register of the Officers and Graduates of the U.S. Military Academy at West Point, New York Since Its Establishment in 1802*, Vol. VIII, 1930–1940. Edited by Lt. Col. E. E. Farman. Chicago: R.R. Donnelley & Sons, 1940.

Darling, Nancy. "Ecological Systems Theory: The Person in the Center of the Circles." *Research in Human Development* 4, no. 3 (2007), 203–217.

Davis, Natalie Zemon. *The Return of Martin Guerre.* Cambridge, MA: Harvard University Press, 1983.

DeCecco, John P., and John P. Elia. "A Critique and Synthesis of Biological Essentialism and Social Constructionist Views of Sexuality and Gender." *Journal of Homosexuality* 24, no. 3 (1993), 1–26.

Downing, Karen, Johnathan Thayer, and Joanne Begiato. "A Sailor's Progress." In *Negotiating Masculinities and Modernity in the Maritime World, 1815–1940*, edited by Karen Downing, Jonathan Thayer, and Joanne Begiate, 15. New York: Palgrave-Macmillan, 2021.

Dubbert, Joe. "Progressivism and the Masculinity Crisis." *Psychoanalytic Review* 61 (Fall 1974), 433–455.

Egan, R. Danielle, and Gail Hawkes. "Producing the Prurient Through the Pedagogy of Purity: Childhood Sexuality and the Purity Movement." *Journal of Historical Sociology* 20, no. 4 (2008), 441–461.

Einolf, Christopher J. "The Fall and Rise of Torture: A Comparative and Historical Analysis." *Sociological Theory* 25, no. 2 (2007), 161.

Eskridge, William N., Jr. *Dishonorable Passions: Sodomy Laws in America, 1861–2003*. New York: Penguin Group, 2008.

Finney, Peter. "Beyond the Postmodern Moment?" *Journal of Contemporary History* 40, no. 1 (January 2005), 149–165.

Foster, Travis M. "Matthiessen's Public Privates: Homosexual Expression and the Aesthetics of Sexual Inversion." *American Literature* 78, no. 2 (2006), 235–262.

Frankowski, B. L., and the American Academy of Pediatrics Committee on Adolescence. "Sexual Orientation and Adolescents." *Pediatrics* 113, no. 6 (June 2004), 1827–1832.

Garceau, Dee. "Nomads, Bunkies, Cross-Dressers, and Family Men: Cowboy Identity and the Gendering of Ranch Work." In *Across the Great Divide: Cultures of Manhood in the American West*, edited by Matthew Basso, Laura McCall, and Dee Garceau-Hagen, 149–168. New York: Routledge, 2001.

Ghobrial, John-Paul. "Seeing the World Like a Microhistorian." *Past & Present* 242, Supplement 14 (November 2019), 1–22.

Gibson, E. Lawrence. *Get Off My Ship: Ensign Berg vs. the U.S. Navy*. New York: Avon, 1978.

Gilmour-Bryson, Anne. "Sodomy and the Knights Templar." *Journal of the History of Sexuality* 7, no. 2 (1996), 151–183.

Ginzburg, Carlo. *The Cheese and the Worms: The Cosmos of a Sixteenth-Century Miller*. Translated by John and Anne Tedeschi. Baltimore, 1980.

Ginzburg, Carlo. "The Philosopher and the Witches: An Experiment in Cultural History." *Acta-Ethnographica-Academiae-Scientiarum-Hungaricae* 37 (1991–1992), 283–292.

Ginzburg, Carlo. "Just One Witness." In *Probing the Limits of Representation: Nazism and the "Final Solution,"* 153–165. Cambridge, MA: Harvard University Press, 1992.

Gordon, Linda. *Woman's Body, Woman's Right: A Social History of Birth Control in America*. New York: Viking, 1976.

Griffen, Clyde. "Reconstructing Masculinity From the Evangelical Revival to the Waning of Progressivism: A Speculative Synthesis." In *Meanings for Manhood: Constructions of Masculinity in Victorian America*, edited by Mark C. Carnes and Clyde Griffen, 191–203. New Haven: Yale University Press, 1989.

Grossman, Jay. "Sexuality." In *Walt Whitman in Context*, edited by Joanna Levin and Edward Whitley, 227–238. New York: Cambridge University Press, 2018.

Grossman, Jay. "Whitman in Your Pocket: The History of the Book and the History of Sexuality." In *The New Walt Whitman Studies*, edited by Matt Cohen, 95–120. New York: Cambridge University Press, 2020.

Haines, Aubrey L. *The Yellowstone Story*, Vol. 2. Boulder: Yellowstone Library and Colorado Associate University Press, 1977.

Halwani, Raja. "Essentialism, Social Constructionism, and the History of Homosexuality." *Journal of Homosexuality* 35, no. 1 (1998), 25–51.

Hampton, H. Duane. *How the U.S. Cavalry Saved Our National Parks*. Bloomington: Indiana University Press, 1971.

Hanson, Victor Davis. *The Western Way of War: Infantry Battle in Classical Greece*. Berkeley: University of California Press, 2009.

Harding, Rick. "Commanders Quietly Ignore Antigay Rule to Build Gulf Forces." *The Advocate*, February 26, 1991, p. 20.

Haynes, Jack Ellis. *Yellowstone Stage Holdups*. Denver, CO: Brand Books, 1952.

Higbie, Frank Tobias. *Indispensable Outcasts: Hobo Workers and Community in the American Midwest, 1880–1930*. Urbana: University of Illinois Press, 2003.

Hinojosa, Ramon. "Doing Hegemony: Military, Men, and Constructing a Military Hegemony." *Journal of Men's Studies* 18, no. 2 (2020), 179–194.

Hoganson, Kristin. *Fighting for American Manhood: How Gender Politics Provoked the Spanish-American and Philippine-American Wars*. New Haven: Yale University Press, 1998.

Hughes, C. H. "Erotopathia – Morbid Eroticism." *Alienist and Neurologist* 14 (1893), 531–578.

Humphrey, Mary. *My Country, My Right to Serve: Experience of Gay Men and Women in the Military, World War II to the Present*. New York: Harper Collins, 1990.

Hustvedt, Asti. *Medical Muses: Hysteria in Nineteenth-Century Paris*. New York: W.W. Norton & Company, 2011.
Iggers, Georg G. *Historiography in the Twentieth Century: From Scientific Objectivity to the Postmodern Challenge*. Hanover, NH, 1997.
Jabor, Anya. "Male Friendships and Masculinity in Early National South: William Wirt and His Friends." *Journal of the Early Republic* 20 (spring 2000), 83–111.
Jackson, Helen Hunt. *A Century of Dishonor: A Sketch of the United States Government's Dealings With Some of the Indian Tribes*. Boston: Roberts Brothers, 1881.
Jacobson, Peter D. "Sexual Orientation and the Military: Some Legal Considerations." In *Out in Force: Sexual Orientation and the Military*, edited by Gregory M. Herek, Jared B. Jobe, and Ralph M. Carney, 39–64. Chicago: University of Chicago Press, 1996.
Johnson, Susan Lee. "A Memory Sweet to Soldiers': The Significance of Gender in the History of the West." *The Western Historical Quarterly* 24, no. 4 (November 1993), 497–498.
Kaplan, Amy. *The Anarchy of Empire in the Making of U.S. Culture*. Boston: Harvard University Press, 2005.
Karnow, Stanely. *In Our Image: America's Empire in the Philippines*. New York: Random House, 1989.
Kaster, Gregory L. "Labor's True Man: Organized Workingmen and the Language of Manliness in the U.S.A., 1827–1877." *Gender & History* 13, no. 1 (April 2001), 24–64.
Katz, Jonathan Ned. *Gay/Lesbian Almanac: A New Documentary*, 82–84, 104–131. New York: Harper and Row, 1983.
Katz, Jonathan Ned. "The Invention of Heterosexuality." *Socialist Review* 20 (January–March 1990), 6–20.
Katz, Jonathan Ned. *Gay American History: Lesbians and Gay Men in the U.S.A*. New York: Penguin Group, 1992.
Katz, Jonathan Ned. *Love Stories: Sex Between Men Before Homosexuality*. Chicago: University of Chicago Press, 2001.
Katz, Jonathan Ned. *The Invention of Heterosexuality*. Chicago: University of Chicago Press, 2007.
Kennedy, Hubert. "Research and Commentaries on Richard von Krafft-Ebing and Karl Heinrich Ulrichs." *Journal of Homosexuality* 42, no. 1 (2001), 165–178.
Kimmel, Michael S. *Manhood in America: A Cultural History*. Oxford: Oxford University Press, 2006.
Kyle, Donald G. *Sport and Spectacle in the Ancient World*. Oxford: Blackwell, 2007.
Lamoreaux, Naomi R. "Rethinking Microhistory: A Comment." *Journal of the Early Republic* 26, no. 4 (Winter 2006), 555–561.
Laqueur, Thomas. *Making Sex: Body and Gender From the Greeks to Freud*. Cambridge, MA: Harvard University Press, 1990.
Lehring, Gary L. *Officially Gay: The Political Construction of Sexuality by the U.S. Military*. Philadelphia: Temple University Press, 2003.
Leitao, David. "The Legend of the Theban Band." In *The Sleep of Reason: Erotic Experience in Sexual Ethics in Ancient Greece and Rome*, edited by Martha C. Nussbaum and Juha Shivola, 200–221. Chicago: Chicago University Press, 2002.
Leitao, David. "Sexuality in Greek and Roman Military Contexts." In *A Companion to Greek and Roman Sexualities*, edited by Thomas K. Hubbard, 230–243. West Sussex: John Wiley & Sons, Ltd., 2013.
Leon, Philip W. *Bullies and Cowards: The West Point Hazing Scandal, 1898–1901*. Westport, CT: Greenwood Press, 2000.
Leonard, Elizabeth D. *Men of Color to Arms!: Soldiers, Indian Wars, and the Quest of Equality*. Lincoln, NE: Bison Books, 2012.
Lepore, Jill. "Historians Who Love Too Much: Reflections on Microhistory and Biography." *The Journal of American History* 88, no. 1 (2001), 129–144.
Lockhart, Paul. *The Drillmaster of Valley Forge*. Boston: Harper Perennial, 2008.

Lowry, Thomas. *The Story the Soldiers Wouldn't Tell: Sex in the Civil War*, 109–123. Mechanicsburg, PA: Stackpole Books, 2012.

Lundberg, Christin. *The Essential Guide to Rhetoric*. Boston: Bedford St. Martins, 2018.

Lyndston, G. Frank. "Sexual Perversion, Satyriasis and Nymphomania." *Medical and Surgical Reporter* 61 (1889), 253–258.

Magnusson, Sigurdur Gylfi. "The Singularization of History: Social History and Microhistory Within the Postmodern State of Knowledge." *Journal of Social History* 36 (Spring 2003), 701–735.

Malin, Marko. *Aristotle's Modal Syllogistic*. Cambridge: Harvard University Press, 2013.

Mankayi, Myameka. "Masculinity, Sexuality and the Body of Male Soldiers." *Psychology in Society* 36 (2008), 24–44.

McChristian, Douglas C. *Regular Army O!: Soldier on the Western Frontier, 1865–1891*. Norman, OK: University of Oklahoma Press, 2017.

McHale, Susan M., Ann C. Crouter, and Shawn D. Whiteman. "The Family Contexts of Gender Development in Childhood and Adolescence." *Social Development* 12, no. 1 (February 2003), 125–133.

McIntosh, Mary. "The Homosexual Role." *Social Problems* 16 (1968), 189–202.

McPherson, James M. *For Cause and Comrades: Why Men Fought in the Civil War*. New York: Oxford University Press, 1997.

Michael B. Donley, Norton A. Schwartz, and James A. Roy. *Memorandum for ALMAJCOM-FOA-DRU/CC: Subject: Repeal of Don't Ask, Don't Tell (DADT)*. September 20, 2011, https://web.archive.org/web/20120105175738/http://cdn.theatlantic.com/static/mt/assets/steve_clemons/Repeal%20of%20DADT.pdf.

Moore, Jacqueline. *Cow Boys and Cattle Men: Class and Masculinities on the Texas Frontier, 1865–1900*. New York: New York University Press, 2010.

Morgan, Daniel. "Theater of War: Combat, the Military, and Masculinities." In *Theorizing Masculinities,* edited by Harry Brod and Michael Kaufman, 165–182. London: Sage Publishers, 1994.

Morgan, Sue. "'Wild Oats or Acorns?' Social Purity, Sexual Politics and the Response of the Late-Victorian Church." *Journal of Religious History* 30, no. 2 (2007), 151–168.

Muir, Edward, and Guido Ruggiero, eds. *Microhistory and the Lost People of Europe*. Translated by Eren Branch. Baltimore, 1991.

Murphy, Lawrence R. "Cleaning Up Newport: The U.S. Navy's Persecution of Homosexuals After World War I." *Journal of American Culture* 7, no. 3 (1984), 57–64.

Murphy, Lawrence R. *Perverts by Official Order*. New York: Haworth, 1988.

Norton, Rictor. *The Myth of the Modern Homosexual: Queer History and the Search for Cultural Unity*. London: Bloomsbury, 1997.

Norton, Rictor. *The Homosexual Revival of Renaissance Style, 1850–1930*. London: Routledge, 2016.

Nye, Robert. "Western Masculinities in War and Peace." *The American Historical Review* 112, no. 2 (April 2007), 417–438.

Oaks, Robert F. "'Things Fearful to Name': Sodomy and Buggery in Seventeenth-Century New England." *Journal of Social History* 12 (1978), 268–281.

Oriard, Michael. *Reading Football: How the Popular Press Created an American Spectacle*. Chapel Hill: University of North Carolina Press, 1993.

Ortiz, Daniel R. "Creating Controversy: Essentialism and Constructivism and the Politics of Gay Identity." *Virginia Law Review* 79, no. 7 (October 1993), 1833–1857.

Pinker, Steven. *The Stuff of Thought: Language as a Window into Human Nature*. New York: Viking, 2007.

Pivar, David J. *Purity Crusade: Sexual Morality and Social Control, 1868–1900*. Westport, CT: Holtzbrink, 1973.

Powell, Collin L., with Joseph E. Persico. *My American Journey*. New York: Random House, 1995.

Putney, Clifford. *Muscular Christianity: Manhood and Sports in Protestant America, 1880–1920*. Cambridge, MA: Harvard University Press, 2001.

Rand Corporation. *Sexual Orientation and U.S. Military Personnel Policy: Options and Assessment*. Santa Monica, CA: Rand Corporation, 1993.

Reed Museum. *Reed Museum Gallery Guide, 2D Cavalry Regiment*. Vilsek, Germany: Reed Museum, 2019. Accessed February 22, 2022, https://history.army.mil/museums/fieldMuseums/reedMuseum/docs/2CRGalleryGuide2019.pdf.

Reis, Elizabeth. "Impossible Hermaphrodites: Intersex America, 1620–1960." *Journal of America History* 92, no. 2 (2005), 411–441.

Rotundo, Anthony. *American Manhood: Transformations in Masculinity From the Revolution to the Modern Era*. New York: Basic Books, 1993.

Rust, Thomas C. "'An Undesirable Station': U.S. Army Soldiers at Fort Yellowstone and the Creation of the National Park Service Ranger Program." *Montana: The Magazine of Western History* 67, no. 4 (2017), 17–38.

Sarbin, Theodore R., and Kenneth E. Karols. *Nonconforming Sexual Orientation in the Military and Society*. Washington, D.C.: Defense Personnel Security Research and Education Center, PERS-TR-89-002, December 1988. Accessed January 12, 2023.

Savage, William W. *Cowboy Life: Reconstructing the American Myth*. Norman: University of Oklahoma Press, 1975.

Savola, Paolo. "Sexual Science and Self-Narrative: Epistemology and Narrative Technologies of the Self Between Krafft-Ebing and Freud." *History of Human Sciences* 23, no. 5 (2010), 18–38.

Sayer, Andrew. "Essentialism, Social Constructionism, and Beyond." *The Sociological Review* 45, no. 3 (1997), 453–487.

Seidman, Steven. "Deconstructing Queer Theory or the Under-Theorization of the Social and the Ethical." In *Social Postmodernism: Beyond Identity Politics*, edited by Linda Nicholson and Steven Seidman, 116–141. New York: Cambridge University Press, 1995.

Shaw, J. C., and G. N. Ferris. "Perverted Sexual Instinct." *Journal of Nervous and Mental Disease* 10 (1883), 185–204.

Sheridan, Paul. *The Sacred Band: Three Hundred Theban Lovers Fighting to Save Greek Freedom*. London: Routledge, 2008.

Shilts, Randy. *Conduct Unbecoming: Lesbian and Gays in the U.S. Military, Vietnam to the Persian Gulf*. New York: St. Martin's Press, 1993.

Sinclair, G. Dean. "Homosexuality and the Military: A Review of the Literature." *Journal of Homosexuality* 56, no. 6 (July 31, 2009), 701–718.

Sullivan, Harry Stack. "Selective Service Psychiatry." *Psychiatry* 4 (1941), 442–451.

Terry, Jennifer. "Theorizing Deviant Historiography." *A Journal of Feminist Cultural Studies* 3, no. 2 (1991), 55–74.

Testi, Arnaldo. "Theodore Roosevelt and the Culture of Masculinity." *Journal of American History* (March 1995), 1509–1533.

Testimony of Colonel Frederick Peck, USMC. "Homosexuals in the Military, Part 1." May 11, 1993. Accessed November 24, 2021.

Testimony of U.S. Army General (ret.) Norman Schwarzkopf. U.S. Senate Armed Services Committee, May 11, 1993. "Homosexuals in the Military, Part 1." Accessed November 24, 2021.

Tucker, Spencer C. *The Encyclopedia of the Spanish-Americana and Philippine-American Wars: A Political, Social, and Military History*. Santa Barbara, CA: ABC-CLIO, 2009.

Ulrich, Laurel T. *A Midwife's Tale: The Life of Martha Ballard Based on Her Diary, 1785–1812*. New York: Knopf, 1990.

United States Army. *Manual for Courts-Martial: Court of Inquiry, and Retiring Boards, and of Other Procedure Under Military Law*. Washington, D.C.: Government Printing Office, 1908.

Vestal, Allan W. "The First Wartime Water Torture by Americans." *Maine Law Review* 69 (2017), 1–67.

von Krafft-Ebing, Richard. *Psychopathia Sexualis, with Especial Reference to Contrary Sexual Instinct: A Medico-Legal Study*. 7th ed. Translated by Charles Gilbert Chaddock. New York: F.A. Davis Co., 1894.

Wake, Naoko. "The Military, Psychiatry, and 'Unfit' Soldiers, 1939–1942." *Journal of the History of Medicine and Allied Sciences* 62, no. 4 (2007), 459–482.

Watry, Elizabeth A., and Lee H. Whittlesey. *Images of America: Fort Yellowstone*. Charleston, SC: Arcadia Publishing, 2012.

Weeks, Jeffrey. "'Sins and Diseases': Some Notes on Homosexuality in the Nineteenth Century." *History Workshop* 1 (Spring 1976), 207–221.

Weeks, Jeffrey. *The Language of Sexuality*. London: Routledge, 2006.

Whitely, Nora. "The Mysterious Mrs. Nash." *14th Annual Symposium Custer Battlefield Historical & Museum Association*, 29–31. Hardin, MT: Custer Battlefield Historical & Museum Association, 2000.

Whites, LeeAnne. *The Civil War as a Crisis in Gender: Augusta, Georgia, 1860–1890*. Athens, GA: University of Georgia Press, 1995.

Whitt, Jacqueline E. "Queering American Military History." *International Journal of Military History and Historiography* 42 (2022), 106–134.

Wilkerson, William S. *Ambiguity and Sexuality*. London: Palgrave Macmillan, 2007.

Williams, Colin J., and Martin S. Weinberg. *Homosexuals and the Military: A Study of Less Than Honorable Discharge*. New York: Harper and Row, 1971.

Wood, Leonard. *Manual for Physical Training in the United States Army*. Washington, D.C.: Government Printing Office, 1914.

Index

For Product Safety Concerns and Information please contact our EU representative GPSR@taylorandfrancis.com
Taylor & Francis Verlag GmbH, Kaufingerstraße 24, 80331 München, Germany

www.ingramcontent.com/pod-product-compliance
Lightning Source LLC
LaVergne TN
LVHW021130300926
849160LV00010B/946
* 9 7 8 1 0 3 2 8 7 0 6 4 9 *